Spirit Beings in European Folklore 1
Compendium 1: 292 descriptions – Ireland, England, Wales, Cornwall, Scotland, Isle of Man, Orkney's, Hebrides, Faeroe, Iceland, Norway, Sweden and Denmark
Author: © Benjamin Adamah
2022

Lay-out: Sylvia Carrilho
Editor: Orenda Bol

ISBN 978-94-92355-55-3

Publisher:

VAMzzz Publishing
P.O. Box 3340
1001 AC Amsterdam
The Netherlands
www.vamzzz.com
vamzzz@protonmail.com

– 292 DESCRIPTIONS –
Ireland, England, Wales, Cornwall,
Scotland, Isle of Man, Orkney's,
Hebrides, Faeroe, Iceland,
Norway, Sweden and Denmark

SPIRIT BEINGS
IN EUROPEAN FOLKLORE 1

COMPILED & EDITED BY

BENJAMIN ADAMAH

CONTENTS

INTRODUCTION — 8
CLASSIFICATION — 13

4

5

6

INTRODUCTION

Compendium 1 of this 4 volume-series *Spirit Beings of European Folklore*, focuses on Ireland, Great Britain, the Hebrides, Orkney's, Faeroe, Island and Scandinavia. Initially written as one encyclopedia of about thousand pages, we decided to divide the work into four separate compendia and use a cultural-geographical classification. Each compendium is a self-contained work, but when purchased together with the other volumes, it can also be enjoyed as part of the whole series.

These four volumes contain a comprehensive survey of Europe's mysterious hidden creatures – preserved in centuries, sometimes millennia – of folklore and now on the brink of extinction; although on the other hand a renewed interest in these creatures can also be observed. In compiling this series, I had to draw a line between "spirit beings" and "gods", but in some cases, this boundary is not watertight. This is especially true of various eastern European and Basque entities, which, under the influence of Christianity, were devalued to lower nature beings, while many gods were already so immanently intertwined with natural phenomena that in modern times they would classify as "daemon", rather than "god" or "goddess", because of their often explicit earthly manifestations. A god or deity is usually a supernatural entity worshiped by believers as a powerful, often immortal being and considered responsible for certain aspects of reality, or even for reality as a whole. Creatures at the daemon/demon, nature-spirit or phantom level are generally thought to exist more closely to our physical realm of existence. The terms "demon", "daemon" (minor god) and spirit are often interchangeable in this work and intermingle with local varieties on the theme, like the Spanish term *Duende*, the Basque *Irelu*, the *Fairy*, *Faery* and *Fee* of Celtic Britannia, Ireland, Scotland and France, the Baltic *Mātes*, etc. Unlike the devilish "demon" of the state religions, in folk beliefs "demon" does not necessarily stand for "evil". Although there are exceptions, in most cases demons are raw forces of nature, that – like many classified spirit beings in this book – can manifest both a benevolent and malevolent side, which is usually directly triggered in correlation to the behavior of humans in their presence, especially when they occupy the same accommodation, like *household demons* or *spirits* living in barns etc.

Many creatures mentioned in these four compendia unfairly owe their
negative image to centuries of Christian demonization-politics, and the
inherent dictate that equates "the divine" with "the transcendent". Within
this exclusively patriarchal state-religions-related doctrine there is hardly
any room for anything divine or supernatural that manifests itself as
immanent, or *earthly.* Overlapping the complexity of separating gods
from the lower classes of spirit beings is the fact that *nature demons*, all
kinds of nocturnal visitors and also household-spirits, often arise from
the spirits of deceased people (or even aborted fetuses). Usually men,
women, children, who were torn from their social tradition and security
by trauma, injustice, grief, or neglected baptismal or funeral rites. In cases
where one of the many European varieties of *Alp*-type creatures is in the
spotlight, it may even be the projected etheric double of a conscious living
person, that attacks the sleeping.

Postmodern technological, artificial and screen-dominated digital
lifestyles, and a correlated mindset, have infected society with a "tunnel-
vision rationality" that – with the exception of Netflix – leaves little room
for anything mysterious like a *Brook-horse*, *Elf* or *Hulder.* Especially in the
Slavic countries, which were once covered with dense, pristine forests, a
very clear correlation can be seen between the industrial felling of trees
and the decline of belief in nature-spirits, such as the *Leshy* and many
others. This is nevertheless a relatively new trend in human history. Even
at the beginning of the 20th century, quite a few of the entities described
in this book were still an important part of daily life in rural Europe – as
they had been for many centuries. Only a few decades ago one could still
observe some deliberately leftover ears in the cornfields, after harvest, as a
contract with the local field-spirit. And not long before that, people took
precautions against the nocturnal visit of the *Alps*, or kept specific rules
in Russian bathhouses so as not to annoy the *Bannik* who stayed there at
night. Until the 19th century, many farms in Eastern Europe considered
it vital for prosperity and protection of the farm, the animals, and the
harvest, to stay on friendly terms with the *barn-demon* and household-
spirits. As late as the 17th and 18th centuries, *vampiric Revenants* or
etheric Vampires were a serious concern in many parts of Iceland,
eastern Europe, parts of Germany, the Balkan countries and Greece. In
medieval times the household-spirit that lived behind the fireplace, was
as invaluable to the family as a smoothly functioning internet connection
is today. When people moved from one home to another, great care was

taken to ensure that the spirit moved along with the family to their new place and took up residence behind the stove. Because of the household-spirit that lived behind the stove, the hook that hung over the fireplace was the most important object in the house, as the beneficial spirit was attached to it.

Before the creation of a book-series on spirit beings, my lifelong interest in this particular aspect of European folklore had been catalyzed by reading the masterpieces of the 19th century German folklorist Wilhelm Mannhardt (1831-1880) and the very recent publications of Claude Lecouteux. Some years ago I started publishing articles on this subject on the blog associated with our publishing house, and in the fall of 2021 I decided to compile an encyclopedia, which we later divided into four volumes. Several works have already been written on the subject, but I could not so far find a work that covered the entire European continent. Mannhardt and Jacob Grimm for example, wrote mainly about spirits of the Germanic and Nordic regions, and there are quite a few works written by English, Irish, Welsh and Scottish writers about mainly the *Fairies* of the British Isles and the land of the *Banshee* and the *Leprechaun*. Ralston left us fine and valuable information about some well-known Russian spirits, but all these works concerned isolated areas. The most interesting thing about creating this encyclopedic series was the discovery that – although there are quite a few spirits that are typical of specific geographic locations – many spirits, known by different names, are essentially the same entities, with often the same folkloric rituals associated with them. Measures against *Alp*-attacks are more or less the same throughout Europe, as is, for example, the *changeling*-phenomenon and the method of determining whether or not a baby is a changeling by having it drink from an egg-shell. This tradition can be found from Spain to Eastern Europe.

This series is therefore the result of much translation work. In addition to the books added in the literature list, and apart from other online sources, I collected a substantial amount of useful wikicommons-licensed data fragments, which I edited into new, often more complete texts, after translating the fragments from German, Spanish, Portuguese, Basque, Polish, Russian, French, Czech, Lithuanian, Latvian, Estonian, Finnish, Swedish, Norwegian, Romanian, Hungarian and other sources. Especially my knowledge of German and Low Saxon (the language I grew up with and spoke as a child) proved to be very useful, and made it possible to make accessible many unique folklore records that have never before been presented in English. The question that inevitably arises between the lines in creating such an elaborate compilation of folkloric creatures is: *"Are these beings real and what exactly is "real" in these cases?"* To put it more bluntly: *"Is this series of compendia nothing more than a collection of primitive superstitions or is there more to it?"* As a pragmatic ritual magician who works every week with Venusian angels and daemons, and a Goetic demon called *Bune*, this is one of those questions that makes me scratch behind my ear. Personally, I am no longer in a position to doubt the existence of a considerable number of spirit beings. However, there is also a substantial gray area that extends through the dimensions of both magic and folklore – and anecdotal accounts of individuals.

People usually accept something as "real" when it fits into some adopted consensus, made up of some cognitive grid, or simply because it conforms to a certain tradition or official opinion. This grid, tradition, or official opinion, usually wins out over an unconditional acceptance of the naked truth, as the latter easily undermines things like mind-frames (that are often correlated to one's "identity" or "profile"). The observer's concept of reality determines the outcome of the observed, but "determines", here, often degenerates into "distorts", "blinds", or "denies" – under pressure from certain scientific, philosophical or public opinion, scientism, (social)media-consensus, or because of some religious dogma. Not even modern technology can change that. There is a wagon-load of genuine video footage showing paranormal phenomena such as ghosts, apparitions, poltergeist phenomena, moving orbs, etc. Yet the general opinion of Western civilization regards a person who believes in ghosts as someone who is deranged, irrational or forgot to take those pills, the doctor prescribed. I once read a scientific study that concluded that most people have at least one paranormal experience or encounter in their life; something they cannot explain by conventional means. But where the exception on the consensus – when "rationality" is respected in its true sense – should trigger a *revision* of that consensus, the "cognitive" is usually abused or politicized to protect a default truth, whose only function seems to be to indulge a false sense of security and social cohesion, or not violate the current trends of *scientism* – for whatever non-scientific, or even commercial, reason. Scientism is design-science shaped by a popular and academic accredited tunnel-vision, which currently replaces religion as the mental base for the postmodern "normal" and "rational" on a mega-scale.

The medieval *Incubus / Succubus* is a creature, defined by Australian metaphysician and OBE-expert Robert Bruce as a special kind of *astral wild life*. Many people, both women and men, still have experiences with this creature and the same goes for the Alp, which also sits on its victim at night, but usually causes nightmares instead of an extreme erotic experience, usually ending in a very intense orgasm. Children under the age of three often see nature spirits, Elementals, dwarf-like creatures etc. Seeing ghosts or some kind of phantom is a common experience, shared by many people all over the world. Personally, I am familiar with the Alp and its ability to materialize and dematerialize. My son, who had extreme clairvoyant abilities when he was between two and about ten years old – sometimes causing him a lot of anxiety – could see many creatures that were invisible to the average adult. The last person from whom you would expect anything unusual in this regard, might be an accountant. Nevertheless, I had an accountant whose life turned upside down after he encountered a *Kabouter* or *Kobold*-like entity in a shed, clearly visible, as if it were real, that started to take his energy. This experience opened his mind to other things than working with numbers and tax-filings all day. A door, he never knew existed, had opened and the last time we met, I gave him a book about Findhorn.

– Benjamin Adamah, Amsterdam, August 6, 2022

CLASSIFICATION

Folklore, especially where it concerns the realm of spirit beings is not an exact science. It is possible to draw up a grid of classes and species, but it was the great German folklorist Wilhelm Mannhardt, who already in the 19th century observed that many creatures undergo some sort of evolution, especially where they interact with the human world. He pointed out that certain *forest-spirits* can become *field-spirits* as well. Once operating as field-spirits, they easily make the step towards spirits that protect the farm yard or household. In the Germanic and Celtic, as well as in the Baltic, Scandinavian and Slavic regions of Europe, many creatures that act as *barn*, *farm yard* or *stable-spirits* remain half wild and maintain a dual nature; they reward people under certain conditions – good behavior, respect, rituals, food offerings etc. – and becoming a nuisance or pest, or even life-threatening, when their rules are violated. Although in many cases they simply leave, taking their gift of prosperity with them. There are more "fixed" versions of *household-spirits*, like the ones related to the hearth for example, with roots most likely going back to the *Lares* and *Penates* or Roman times.

Many spirits fall under general blanket-terms like *Fairies*, *Goblins* (prank pulling dwarf-like creatures), *Gnomes*, *Trolls*, *water-spirits*, *Mermaids*, *vampiric Revenants*, phantoms of dead children (like the *Myling*), *Elves*, *field-spirits*, *household-spirits*, *weather-spirits*, *changelings*, *Nymph-like creatures*, etc. Most of these spirits cannot be categorized into one single class, but fall in two or sometimes three or more different categories. Although an arbitrary indexation, one could state that roughly the following "classes" are the most notable:
• Alp or Mare-type spirits
• Aquatic Nymphs and Nymphs-like spirits
• Aufhocker-type spirits
• Banshee and Dames blanches type spirits
• Basque Ireluak
• Bogeys
• Changeling-type spirits
• Dangerous water-spirits
• Evil spirits of the dead
• Evil nocturnal spirits
• Female vampiric beings
• Field-spirits

- Forest-spirits
- Grim-like phantom dogs or creatures
- Hags or hideous Crone-type child luring spirits
- Household-spirits
- Icelandic spirits
- Incubus-Succubus type spirits
- Kobolds or dwarfish humanoid looking spirits
- Local spirits
- Midday women
- Mountain-spirits
- Neutral or friendly water-spirits
- Prankster spirits
- Sea-spirits
- Shapeshifters
- Spirits evolved out of spirits of dead children
- Spirits born from a rooster-egg
- Spirits rooted in Greek-Etruscan-Roman culture
- Spirits rooted in Turkish-Mongolian culture
- Spirits rooted in Jewish culture
- Spirits that are derivatives of ancient pagan gods
- Tree-spirits
- Vampiric beings or Revenants
- Weather and wind-spirits
- Were-animals, like Werewolves
- Wild Men and Wild Women
- Wilderness demons leading people astray
- Will-o'-the-wisps

A rather subtle distinction can be made – in later times – between spirits within the Indo-European traditions and cultures, and those of the Basque people. The Basques know a folklore of many kinds and types of *Iruliak* or *Genii* – who in most cases are all in the dual position of being both a unique or local entity and a manifestation of one of the gods or goddesses – and in most cases this concerns the goddess *Mari*, regardless of whether the *Irelu* is masculine, like a bull or billy goat. Also, within this context, Mari, or her spouse *Sugaar* for example, are not gods in the sense of the classic Indo-European supreme Celestials, but more a kind of major *Devas* or daemons, who represent and cause many kinds of weather phenomena and other manifestations of nature. They are immanent gods, strongly connected to the Earth and wild nature, and part of it; and so are their manifestations as the many different Ireluak. But not only the Basques knew these immanent gods. In fact, all of Europe, before Christianity, had these systems of nature gods, many of whom were gods or daemons that were more immanent nature forces than transcendent heavenly beings. Currently, there is a kind of renaissance going on in rediscovering the old pagan traditions and entities, especially in Eastern Europe and the Baltic states, which, like the Basques, were Christianized fairly recently in history.

Numerous spirits are also *Bogeys*, called upon in various tales to keep children away from dangerous places. The *Alp / Mare*-type spirit, which has many variations all over the continent, regularly merges with the *Incubus / Succubus* or the Hag. Most useful household-spirits also act like Goblins, pulling pranks or causing *poltergeist*-like phenomena (or even setting barns on fire). Many spirits of entirely different types can manifest as Will-o'-the-wisps and multiple Fairies are known to rob children and replace them with changelings. Several kinds of nature-spirits, even water-sprites, can act as Vampires, who in turn often fuse with the Werewolf. With the exception of the many *Vampire / Werewolf / Revenant* type creatures, which are always harmful, most spirits have a dual nature, and can act as a blessing or a curse for humans. More than is the case with humans, it is always all or nothing, heaven or hell, especially where spirits enter into a relationship with a human partner, which is for instance not uncommon with *Water-Nymphs*. Sexual relations with humans are described of several spirit beings, very rarely producing a special hybrid type of offspring called a *cambion*. Iron, the crowing of the rooster at dawn, modern technology and traffic, church bells (and other Christian expressions) are a nuisance to most spirits, and, just like rude human behavior, may chase them away for good.

Nature-spirits, Incubi, Alps, Fairies and especially the *vampiric Revenants* of Eastern Europe, the Balkan, Scandinavia and Iceland are not always of a diffuse spirit-substance or ethereal fabric, but can materialize and manifest in a very physical way. This is also the case with creatures like the German *Aufhocker* – which jumps on the back of a nocturnal wanderer and grows heavier and heavier – and with the Celtic Brook-horses of Britain, Ireland, Scotland and the islands between Scotland and Iceland. The ability to materialize in a more condensed and physical state and to dematerialize quickly, is a characteristic of many spirits described in this Compendia-series – see also *From the same series* at the end of this book.

A

Afturgöngur

In Icelandic folklore *Afturgöngur* (those who have returned to walking
in life) is used as a generic term for ghostly figures or returning dead of
different categories. Among them we can distinguish in the first place
those who already had an evil nature during their life (the so-called
Illhryssingar), then the *Titburdir* (foundlings), the *Fépukar* (misers) and
furthermore the *Heimselskendur* and *Hefnivargar*, who for some reason
always haunt one particular location, or a living person they want to take
revenge on.

Alfemoe

In Icelandic folklore the *Alfemoe* is a type of parasitic *Alp*; a creature that
visits people or animals at night to harass them by pressing their chest, or in
the case of animals, drive them mad with fear. The Alfemoe is mentioned
by Elard Hugo Meyer in his chapter on *Alps* in *Mythologie der Germaner*.

Alp-luachra

In Celtic mythology the *Alp-luachra*, also known as *Joint-eater*, *Just-halver*
or *Alp-loochra* (Ireland) is a type of parasitical spirit who invisibly sits at
the table and consumes half of their victim's food. When a person falls
asleep by the side of a spring or stream, the Alp-luachra appears in the
form of a newt and crawls down the person's mouth, feeding off the food
that they had eaten. In Robert Kirk's *Secret Commonwealth of Fairies*, this
creature feeds not on the food itself, but on the "pith or quintessence"
of the food. A person haunted by an Alp-luachra will never grow fat,
because he/she only digests food robbed of its nutritional value. People
who consume newts are thought to be plagued in this way. In Douglas
Hyde's collection of folk tales, *Beside the Fire*, a farmer, who was starving
from an Alp-luachra, was eventually rid of the spirit. He was instructed
to eat large amounts of salted meat and, when he could eat no more, lie
still with his mouth open just above the surface of a stream. After having
been driven to thirst by the salt, the offspring of the Alp-luachra, and
eventually the Alp-luachra mother herself, jumped into the water.

Apple-Tree Man

In Somerset the oldest apple-tree in the orchard is called the *Apple-Tree Man* and it seems that the fertility of the orchard is supposed to reside there as a spirit being. Tales about the Apple Tree Man were collected by the folklorist Ruth Tongue in the cider-producing county of Somerset. In one story a man offers his last mug of mulled cider to the trees in his orchard on Christmas Eve (a reflection of the custom of apple wassailing – a ritual offering of bread and toast to the trees, performed by young men). He is rewarded by the Apple Tree Man who reveals to him the location of buried gold, more than enough to pay his rent.

Arkan Sonney

Arkan Sonney (lucky urchin or plentiful little pig) is the Manx term for both a hedgehog and a Fairy creature. It is also called *Erkin sonna* or *Lucky Piggy* which is the name given to the *Fairy Pig of Man*. In Manx folklore it is a type of Fairy animal that takes the form of a white pig that brings good fortune to those who manage to catch it. If you caught one you would always find a silver coin in your pocket and it was even considered a favorable omen just to have seen the "lucky piggy".

Walter Gill in *A Manx Scrapbook* mentions a Fairy pig seen near Niarbyl by a girl, who told him about it some fifty years later as an old woman. It was a beautiful little white pig, and as the Fairy pigs are supposed to bring luck, she called to her uncle to come and help her catch it. But he called back to her to leave it alone, and then it soon disappeared. Dora Broome has a tale of a little Fairy pig in her *Fairy Tales from the Isle of Man* (1951). Her little pig is white, with red ears and eyes like most Celtic Fairy animals. Arkan Sonney can alter its size, but apparently not its shape.

Askafroan

Askafroan or *Askfrun* is an ash tree-spirit in southern Swedish folklore, a reminiscent of the *Dryads* and *Hamadryads*. Like the elder tree, the ash tree was in ancient times a common tree of care, to which the luck of the farm was believed to be linked. To this tree both food and drinks were sacrificed, according to several records. It is mainly in Skåne that the spirit of the ash tree was called Askafroan (Ash tree-woman). She was believed to live in the ash tree or under its roots.

Gunnar Olof Hyltén-Cavallius, in his book *Wärend och wirdarne*, 1863, writes about this spirit:

"Thus in the district of Ljunit the people still know of a wondrous creature, which dwells in the ash-tree, and is therefore called the Askafroan. It was the custom of the ancients to sacrifice to the Askafroan, on Ash-Wednesday-morning before the sun rose, by striking water over the roots of the tree. They used the words, "Now I sacrifice, and you do us no harm". If anyone broke the leaves or branches of the ash-tree, he was thought to get pain or sickness. Likewise, in Skåne (Gärds härad and others), there is talk of a twisted natural being in the pine or elder tree. This being is called the Hyllefroan. If anyone does damage to the pine tree or messes around with it, he gets a disease called Hylleskåll, which is cured by pouring milk over the roots of the tree."

Asrai

In English folklore the *Asrai* is a type of Water-Fairy, that lives in seas and lakes and is similar to the *Mermaid* and *Nixie*. They are sometimes described as timid and shy, standing 2-4 ft (0.61-1.22 m) tall, or may be depicted as tall and lithe. Ruth Tongue recollected Asrai-folklore in *Forgotten Folk-Tales of the English Counties*. There are two tales almost identical from Cheshire and Shropshire. In both tales a fisherman dredges up an Asrai and puts it in the bottom of his boat. The creature pleads to be set free, but its language is incomprehensible. In the Cheshire tale the fisherman bound it, and the touch of its cold, wet hands burned him so that he was marked for life. In both stories the Asrai is covered with wet weeds and it lays moaning in the bottom of the boat, but its moans grow fainter, and by the time the fisherman reaches the shore it has melted away leaving only a little water on the bottom of the boat. Ruth Tongue heard other references to Asrai from the Welsh Border, always in the same strain. The inability of Asrai to survive daylight is similar to that of *Trolls* from Scandinavian folklore.

Some folktales describe the creatures as having green hair and a fishtail instead of legs, or with webbed feet. Asrai are said to live for hundreds of years and will come up to the surface of the water once each century, to bathe in the moonlight which they use to help them grow.

If the Asrai (usually depicted as female) sees a man, she will attempt to lure him with promises of gold and jewels into the deepest part of the lake to drown or simply trick him. However, she cannot tolerate human coarseness and vulgarity, and this will be enough to frighten her away. The oldest known appearance of Asrai in print was with the poem *The Asrai* by Robert Williams Buchanan, first published in April 1872. Buchanan described them in this fragment as nature-loving spirits who could not tolerate sunlight:

...

Yet far away in the darkened places,
Deep in the mountains and under the meres,
A few fair Spirits with sunless faces
Lingered on with the rolling years,
And listened, listened, luminous-eyed,
While the generations arose and died,
And watch'd, watch'd, with sad surprise,
The gleaming glory of earth and skies,
Beyond their darkness. But ever, by night,
When the moon arose with her gentle light,
The Asrai, hidden from human seeing,
Drank the moonlight that was their being,

...

Awd Goggie

Awd Goggie is a *Bogey*-figure from English folklore who has to keep children from wandering alone into orchards. The Awd Goggie is said to inhabit fruit orchards, where it will attack children.

B

Bäckahäst or Bækhest

In the Scandinavian languages the *Bäckahäst* or *Bækhest* is a Brook-horse.
A creature of Scandinavian mythology, the Bäckahäst was a beautiful
white horse that would emerge from bodies of water such as lakes or
ponds, particularly during foggy weather. Anyone who climbed onto its
back would not be able to get off again. The horse would then jump into a
river, drowning the rider, whether adult or child. The brook horse could
also be harnessed and made to plough, either because it was trying to
trick a person or because the person had tricked the horse into it. It has a
close parallel in the *Nykur* of the Faeroe Islands, the Scottish *Kelpie*, and
the Welsh *Ceffyl Dŵr*. The following tale is classic for the Bäckahäst, or
any brook horse. Again – as in many tales about water-spirits – iron is
used as protection against the evil inclinations of the spirit:

*"A long time ago, there was a girl who was not only pretty but also big
and strong. She worked as a maid on a farm by Lake Hjärtasjön in
southern Nerike. She was ploughing with the farm's horse on one of the
fields by the lake. It was springtime and beautiful weather. The birds
chirped and wagtails flitted in the tracks of the girl and the horse in
order to find worms. All of a sudden a horse appeared out of the lake.
It was big and beautiful, bright in colour and with large spots on the
sides. The horse had a beautiful mane which fluttered in the wind and
a tail that trailed on the ground. The horse pranced for the girl to show
her how beautiful he was. The girl, however, knew that it was the brook
horse and ignored it. Then the brook horse came closer and closer and
finally he was so close that he could bite the farm horse in the mane.
The girl hit the brook horse with the bridle and cried: "Disappear you
scoundrel, or you'll have to plough so you'll never forget it." As soon as
she had said this, the brook horse had changed places with the farm
horse, and the brook horse started ploughing the field with such speed
that soil and stones whirled in its wake, and the girl hung like a mitten
from the plough. Faster than the cock crows seven times, the ploughing
was finished and the brook horse headed for the lake, dragging both the
plough and the girl. But the girl had a piece of steel in her pocket, and
she made the sign of the cross. Immediately she fell down on the ground,*

and she saw the brook horse disappear into the lake with the plough. She heard a frustrated neighing when the brook horse understood that his trick had failed. Until this day, a deep track can be seen in the field."

Banshee

A *Banshee*, *Banshie* or *Bean sí* is a supernatural female creature of Irish Celtic mythology, considered a magician or messenger of the Other World (Sidh). It is comparable to other mythological creatures in Europe (Welsh or Nordic mythology) like the French *Dames blanches* and *Witte wieven* in the Netherlands. Many Irish families have their family-Banshee, who heralds the death of a family member, usually by wailing, shrieking, or keening. The cry of the Banshee is clearly from a human or animal cry, and it is always only heard at night. It is heard in the late evening by those who are still awake, or it wakes people up during their sleep.

The apparition is known by different names. The most common current designation is of course the English term Banshee, which by the way, was first used in 1771, phonetically derived and borrowed from Irish Gaelic. In Ireland, the term *Bean sidhe*, *Bean sí*, formerly *Ben síd* or *Baintsíde* is used. In Scottish Gaelic she is called *Bean sith*, literally meaning "woman of the sidh", the sidh (or sí, síd, sith, sidhe) being the Other World i n the Gaelic mythology. Later this term took the meaning of a "hill, or mound" which gives access to the kingdom of the *Gods*, *Fairies* and death. This finally led to the translation of the Banshee as "Woman of the Fairy mound" or "Fairy woman". It is however difficult to determine the original meaning of Bean sí, because of the mixture of pagan and Christian concepts in medieval texts. In the past, *bean* could have meant a "mystical or magical quality" (sí) attached to a "woman" (bean). It would only be from the eighth century onward that *bean* would take on the meaning of "Woman of the Other World" in the texts.

Bean sídhe and Bean chaointe

According to tradition, the Banshee sometimes announces death by crying, moaning or lamentation; or more precisely: "funeral melodies". By this behaviour, she is thus called in Irish *Bean chaointe*, in Scottish *Caointeach* and *Keening woman* in English. These "keening" melodies refer directly to the ancient Gaelic practice of weeping women; women who improvised vocal lamentations during funeral processions and burials, in order to pay tribute to the dead and their families. This funeral practice, present in many parts of the world, was documented in Ireland and Scotland during the Middle Ages. It has gradually disappeared, following the prohibition of this practice by the Catholic Church in Ireland. These weeping women (sometimes paid) generally imitated the aspects of the legendary banshee, wearing, for example, their hair untied, a long dress, bare feet. According to folklorist Shane Broderick the keen or lament was a central component in the rituals concerning death and from almost all the accounts passed down we can see that it was primarily a female role. The lamentations are usually performed by women, and very rarely by men. The lamenting of the women had the function of a psychopomp, thus leading or pushing the soul of the deceased towards the Otherworld. In southeastern Ireland, the Banshee is also referred to by different dialectal forms of *badhbh*; this term derives from *Badh* (formerly *Bodhb*), the name of a protective (or warrior) goddess in Celtic or medieval mythology.

The appearances of the Banshee

The descriptions of Banshees sighted in Ireland vary. There are some features that are common to all Banshees. There is always only one Banshee, assigned to an autochthonous family. She is usually represented as a deadly pale woman dressed in white, with long whitish or black hair. Her eyes are often glowing red from constant crying. In most descriptions she is an old woman, rarely young and beautiful. Sometimes she has long streaming hair and wears a gray cloak over a green dress. She may be dressed in white with red hair and a ghastly complexion, according to a firsthand account by Ann, Lady Fanshawe in her Memoirs. Lady Wilde in Ancient Legends of Ireland provides another:

> *"The size of the Banshee is another physical feature that differs between regional accounts. Though some accounts of her standing unnaturally tall are recorded, the majority of tales that describe her height state the Banshee's stature as short, anywhere between one foot and four feet. Her exceptional shortness often goes alongside the description of her as an old woman, though it may also be intended to emphasize her state as a fairy creature."*

Sometimes the Banshee assumes the form of some sweet singing virgin of the family who died young, and has been given the mission by the invisible powers to become the harbinger of coming doom to her mortal kindred. Or she may be seen at night as a shrouded woman, crouched beneath the trees, lamenting with a veiled face, or flying past in the moonlight, crying bitterly. And the cry of this spirit is mournful beyond all other sounds on earth, and betokens certain death to some member of the family whenever it is heard in the silence of the night. The Banshee is heard more often than seen; she usually sits in front of the family window a few days before the death of a family member and cries (Banshee wail). The Banshee preferably appears at the ancestral home of the long-established Irish family to which it has joined, even if the family member to whom the lament is directed lives abroad. It is often seen or heard at the edge of paths or waters. The person whose death the Banshee announces does not hear her lamentation her/himself. Allegedly, every indigenous family in Ireland has its own Banshee and she would even follow the family if it moved to another country.

Scotland

In Scottish popular belief – especially in the western highlands – the *Bean-nighe* or *Nigheag na h-àth* (the Washerwoman at the ford) is the counterpart to the Irish Banshee; she does however not wail under a window, but is found in nature washing shrouds. The Bean-nighe is said to have sagging breasts, one single nostril and protruding teeth, which makes her look extremely ugly. A more feared female creature is the *Baobhan sith*. The Baobhan sith are female Vampires in the folklore of the Scottish Highlands, though they also share certain characteristics with the Banshee, the *Succubus/Incubus* and the Fairy.

Related female apparitions

The Banshee-folklore concerns all legends and popular beliefs of the British Isles (Ireland and Great Britain). These legends were passed down from generation to generation, usually by oral transmission (stories, tales, songs, rites). The Banshee remained an object of belief from the Middle Ages until the beginning of the 20th century, when legends and folk tales were starting to be collected by researchers. Banshee-like apparitions are however not restricted to Ireland and the British Isles. In Dutch folklore and legends, the *Witte wieven* (also known as *Witte Wijven*) are spirits of wise women or *Elfin* beings. The mythology dates back to at least the pre-Christian era (7th century) and was known in the present-day regions of the Netherlands, Belgium and parts of France. In some places they were

known as *Juffers* or *Joffers* (ladies), or as *Dames blanches* (White Ladies).
In France the folklore of the *Dames blanches* sometimes merges with
that of the Banshee. The Lady of the Bourbon Palace for example, who
appeared the day before the death of a member of this family, acted like
the traditional Irish Banshee.

Baobhan sith

The *Baobhan sith* is a seductive female *Vampire* in the folklore of the
Scottish Highlands, although she also shares certain characteristics
with both the Banshee, the *Succubus/Incubus* and *Fairy*. Baobhan-sith
preferably preys on pretty young boys. She appears mainly in forests or in
other wild areas. According to the Scottish folklorist Donald Alexander
Mackenzie, the Baobhan sith usually appears as a beautiful young
woman, wearing a long green dress that conceals the deer hooves she
has instead of feet. Like other Vampires she drinks the blood of human
victims and will vanish with the rising sun. She may also take the form
of a hooded crow or raven. The color of her dress indicates both her
connection with the forest and the nature-spirits roaming in it, and death
and seduction, since the color green in connection with beautiful women
has always been considered mysteriously fascinating and mischievous at
the same time.

One of the many legends surrounding the Baobhan-sith tells of four
hunters who spend the night in a forest clearing. Since it is cold, they try
to warm themselves up by singing and dancing. Soon, four enchantingly
beautiful girls with curly hair and green dresses emerge from the forest
to keep the hunters company. The hunters are delighted to meet them,
except for one of them, who feels uneasy about the whole thing. He
refrains from dancing with the girls and spends the night farther away,
taking refuge among their horses. When he returns the next morning, he
finds his comrades pale and dead. The Baobhan sith have drained them
down to the last drop of blood. The folklorist Katharine Briggs suggested
that the Baobhan sith was unable to catch the fourth man among the
horses because of the iron with which the horses were shod, iron being a
traditional Fairy vulnerability.

Just as there are many stories about Banshees, there are also numerous
stories about the Baobhan sith, with a general theme of hunters being

attacked in the wilderness at night. One recurring motif in these stories is that the Baobhan sith appears almost immediately after the hunters express their desire for female companionship. This is connected with a traditional Scottish belief that if one were to make a wish at night without also invoking God's protection, then that wish would be granted in some terrible manner.

Barghest

In Northern English folklore, the *Barghest* or *Barguest* is a mythical monstrous black dog with large teeth and claws, although in some cases the name can refer to a ghost or household *Elf*, especially in Northumberland and Durham, such as the Cauld Lad of Hylton. The origin of the name Barghest is interesting, as it could have a relation with German agricultural daemons in dog or wolf shape, like *Gerstenwolf* (barley-wolf), *Roggenhund* (rye-hound) or *Roggenwolf* (rye-wolf). "Ghost" in Northern England was pronounced "guest", which seems to originate from *burh-ghest* (town-ghost). Others explain it as cognate to German *Berg-geist* (mountain-spirit/ghost) or *Bär-geist* (bear-ghost). Another mooted derivation is *Bahr-geist*, German for the "spirit of the funeral bier".

In one notable case it is said to frequent a remote gorge named Troller's Gill in the Yorkshire Dales, Yorkshire, England. A ballad entitled *The Legend of the Troller's Gill* can be found in William Hone's *Everyday Book* (1830). It recounts the tale of a man who ventures forth "to the horrid gill of the limestone hill" in order to summon and confront the Barghest in an act of ritual magic. The man's lifeless body is discovered soon after, with inhuman marks upon his breast. There is also a story of a Barghest occasionally entering the city of York, where, according to legend, it preys on lone travelers in the city's narrow Snickelways (backstreets). Whitby in North Yorkshire is also said to be haunted by the specter.

In the 1870s a shape-shifting Barghest was said to live near Darlington and was said to take the form of a headless man (who would vanish in flames), a headless lady, a white cat, a rabbit, a dog or a black dog. Another was said to live in an "uncanny-looking" dale between Darlington and Houghton, near Throstlenest, and yet another haunted an area of wasteland between Wreghorn and Headingley Hill, near Leeds.

The Barghest often serves as an omen of death. At the passing of a notable person the Barghest may appear, followed by all the other dogs of the local area in a kind of funeral procession, heralding the person's death with howling and barking. If anyone were to get in the Barghest's way, it would strike out with its paw and leave a wound that never heals. Besides taking the form of a large black dog with fiery eyes, it may also become invisible and walk about with the sound of rattling chains. It may also foretell the death of an individual by laying across the threshold of his or her house, and like the *Vampire*, the Barghest is unable to cross rivers.

Beithir

In Scottish lore the *Beithir* is considered one of the *Fuath*; also referred to as *Bbeithir-nimh* (venomous serpent) and *Nathair* (serpent, or adder). It is reported that it can be observed when flashes of light are seen in the sky. The word *beithir* in Scottish Gaelic means "lightning, great serpent, wild beast, bear". In Irish and in older Scottish Gaelic it can also mean "bear," although the word "mathan" is more common for it today. Since "bear" in Celtic denotes strength, the term has also been applied to "warrior," which is why Beithir can also be a metaphor for "warrior." Scholar James MacKillop speculated that the word Beithir was derived from the Old Norse word for "bear" (bjǫrn) or "lightning."

In the 1908 *Celtic Review*, folklorist E. C. Watson wrote that the Beithir was an inhabitant of mountain caves and cauldrons, describing it as a "venomous and destructive creature." He believes that the folk belief is related to the fact that lightning looks like a snake. The creature possesses a long tail, but is not comparable to the fierce dragons in Germanic mythology. A mountain south of Glencoe is called "Ben Vair" or "Ben Vehir" and is said to commemorate a Beithir who sought refuge there. John Gregorson Campbell wrote that a snake's head must be removed from its torso to prevent the two parts from rejoining, which would bring it back to life as a Beithir. The Beithir is described as "the largest and most deadly kind of serpent", or as a "dragon" (but without the typical draconic features such as wings or fiery breath) and is equipped with a venomous sting. If people are stung by the Beithir, they must head for the nearest body of water such as a river or loch. If they can reach it before the Beithir does, they are cured, but if the monster reaches it first, his victims are doomed. Another cure for the sting is water in which the head of another snake has been placed.

Dwelling on the edge of cryptozoology, the big beast of Scanlastle in Islay was believed to be a Beithir. It devoured seven horses on its way to Loch-in-daal. A ship was lying at anchor in the loch at the time, and a line of barrels filled with deadly spikes, and with pieces of flesh laid upon them, was placed from the shore to the ship. Tempted by the flesh, the "loathly worm" made its way out onto the barrels and was killed by the spikes and a cannon.

Ben-Varrey

Ben-Varrey is the name for a Mermaid, of which many tales are told around the coasts of Man. She bears the same general character as Mermaids do everywhere, enchanting and alluring men to their death, but occasionally showing softer traits. In Isle of Man the Mermaid shows, on the whole, the softer side of her nature. Ben Varrey became famous for her love of apples – via a story told by Kathleen Killip (1911 - 1991).

Bendith Y Mamau

Bendith Y Mamau or *the Mother's Blessing'* is a Glamorganshire name for the local *Fairies*. They steal children, replace them with changelings, Alp-ride horses and enter houses. Bowls of milk were put out for them to keep them friendly.

Bergsrået

In Norse folklore, the *Bergsrået*, or *Mountain Troll* or *Mountain King*, was a supernatural being who lived in a mountain and ruled over its ore. The Bergsrået often distorts the view of those who have accidentally discovered ore deposits, so that they later cannot find them. In many stories, the Bergsrået is surrounded by his family and a court of Goblins. The Bergsrået could also be female. Intercourse between humans and the Bergsrået was long ago something that was seen as a reality: a human who had done this, was taken into the mountains, something called *mountain taking*, a well-known phenomenon in Bergsrået-mythology. In 1691, a farmhand, Sven Andersson, from the Vättle district in Västergötland, was sentenced to death for having had sexual intercourse with a female Bergsrået. The boy, a young man in his teens, had been noticed by the vicar of Lundsby during the harvest, looking sickly and exhausted.

Hobgoblin (1792) by Richard Newton (1777-1798) after George Moutard Woodward

The boy had explained that he had fallen asleep in the woods near a mountain while looking for a runaway goat, and had been taken into the mountain by a woman in white. The woman had given him food and drink and then had sexual intercourse with him. For this the boy was sentenced to death by the district court.

Berrey Dhone

In the folklore of the Isle of Man, *Berrey Dhone* or *Brown Berry* is a gigantic *Hag* of a particularly aggressive nature. She will stride across oceans and mountains to defeat her enemies. She lived either on top of North Barrule Mountain or inside it, and her rocky heel-print can still be seen on the mountainside.

Biasd Bheulach

Biasd Bheulach is a nocturnal shapeshifter that haunts the Odail Pass on the Isle of Skye, and one of the Highland demon spirits. It is also known as the *Biasd Bealach Odail* (Beast of Odal Pass). It was described by John Gregorson Campbell in *Witchcraft and Second Sight in the Scottish Highlands:*

> "*From Kyle-rhea (Caol-Redhinn), the narrowest part of the Sound of Skye, the Pass of Odal stretches westward and forms one of the most striking Pass-views in the Highlands. It was, that the first public road was made in Skye, about sixty years ago. At the time the Pass was haunted by "something awful" – its character was not distinctly known, but enjoyed an evil reputation far and wide as "The Beast of Odal Pass" (Biasd Bealach Odail). This thing, whatever it was, did not always appear in the same shape. Sometimes it bore the form of a man, sometimes of a man with only one leg; at other times it appeared like a greyhound, or beast, prowling about; and sometimes it was heard uttering frightful shrieks and outcries, which made the workmen leave their workplaces in horror. It was only during the night that it was seen or heard. People who travelled through the Pass at night were often thrown down and hurt by it, and with difficulty made their way to a place of safety. It ceased when a man was found dead at the roadside, pierced with two wounds, one on his side and one on his leg, with a hand pressed on each wound. It was considered impossible these wounds could have been inflicted by a human being.*"

Billy Blind

Billy Blind, also known as *Billy Blin, Billy Blynde, Billie Blin*, or *Belly Blin*
is an English and Lowland Scottish *household-spirit*, much like a *Brownie*.
He appears however only in ballads, where he frequently advises the
characters. It has been speculated that the character of Billy Blind is a folk
memory of the (one eyed) god *Wotan, Wodan* or *Odin* from Germanic
mythology, in his "more playful aspect". Others believe him to be the
same character as *Blind Harie*, the "blind man of the game" in Scotland.

Black Annis

Black Annis, also *Black Agnes*, is a terrifying specter of British folk tales
that can be traced back to Celtic origins. Black Annis is described as a
blue-faced old crone with claws as hard as iron and a taste for human
flesh, especially children's flesh. She is also said to have been seen as a cat.
She is said to be particularly evasive in Leicestershire, where she lives in a
cave in the Dane Hills, a region west of the city of Leicester. The entrance
to her cave, called Black Annis Bower, can be identified by an ancient
oak tree. She dug the cave herself with her iron claws. The legend of this
cave was first recorded in writing as early as the 18th century. She roams
around at night, looking for unsuspecting children and lambs, which
she shreds to pieces and eats with her claws, she hangs their skins in the
trees and later wears them on her belt. She is also said to enter houses to
prey on children. The figure of Black Annis is therefore used by parents
as a threatening specter to make disobedient children obey. There is a
similarity to the Welsh *Gwrach*, the Scottish *Gentle Annie* and the Irish
mythical figures of *Anu, Danu, Banshee* and *Cailleach*. A linguistic
connection with *Annea*, an ancient Gaulish mother deity, is also possible.
However, historian Ronald Hutton suspects a real person behind the
legend, namely Agnes Scott, a medieval hermit and Dominican nun from
the Dane Hills, who was reinterpreted as a witch during the Glorious
Revolution.

Black dog

Black dog is often used as a synonym for ghost dog, though some
phantom dogs are white instead of black. Black dogs have been reported
from almost all the counties of England, the exceptions being Middlesex
and Rutland. Phantom dogs, included the ones with big eyes that glow

like fire in the dark, are also seen on the European mainland and in many other places in the world. Often they play a role in local legends and folklore.

Black Dog of Aylesbury

A man who lived in a village near Aylesbury in Buckinghamshire would go each morning and night to milk his cows in a distant field. One night on his way there he encountered a sinister black dog, and every night thereafter, until the man brought a friend along with him. When the dog appeared again, the man attacked it, using the yoke of his milk pails as a weapon, but when he did so the dog vanished and the man fell senseless to the ground. He was carried home alive, but remained speechless and paralyzed for the rest of his life.

Black Dog of Lyme Regis

Near the town of Lyme Regis, in Dorset, stood a farmhouse that was haunted by a black dog. This dog never caused any harm, but one night the master of the house in a drunken rage tried to attack it with an iron poker. The dog fled to the attic where it leaped out through the ceiling, and when the master struck the spot where the dog had vanished, he discovered a hidden cache of gold and silver. The dog was never again seen indoors, but to this day it continues to haunt at midnight a lane which leads to the house called Haye Lane (or Dog Lane). Dogs who are allowed to stray late at night in this area often mysteriously disappeared. A bed and breakfast in Lyme Regis is named The Old Black Dog, and part of the legend states that the man who discovered the treasure, used it to build an inn that originally stood on the site.

Black Dog of Newgate

The *Black Dog of Newgate* has been said to haunt the Newgate Prison for over 400 years, appearing especially before an executions takes place. It appears as a giant black phantom dog, wearing chains. The former Newgate Prison of London was located next to the Old Bailey (the Central Criminal Court), close to St. Paul's Cathedral, in London, England. Although believed to have long existed in folklore previously, the earliest recorded account of the *Black Dog of Newgate*-legend dates

from 1596, and is credited to a prison inmate called Luke Hutton.
A notable copy of the book and its woodcut frontpiece is held at the
Guildhall Library, London. This sinister Black Dog apparently was often
seen gliding up and down the streets adjacent to the ivy-covered wall at
the end of Amen Court, and sometimes crawling along the top of the wall
itself, dragging a heavy chain, just before an execution was due to take
place at the original Newgate Prison nearby (the new Newgate Prison
was built there in 1783). This creature is supposed to have pursued the
escapees to wherever they went or tried to hide, until it had avenged itself
upon all of them.

13th Century legend

The story goes that during a famine in the reign of King Henry III of
England (1207-1272), a scholar was incarcerated in Newgate prison who
had the reputation of being a sorcerer, or warlock, who had "done much
hurt to the Kings' subjects with his Charms and Devilish Witchcraft".
The famine was so severe and the conditions so bad during this terrible
period that the prisoners had already resorted to cannibalism, and soon
after his arrival they consumed this scholar, who was unable to physically
defend himself. Shortly after this crime was committed, the inmates
guilty of his death reportedly began seeing the specter of a monstrous
Black Dog walking up and down the prison, which they were convinced
was the sorcerers spirit, returning to avenge himself upon his murderers.
This Black Dog reportedly killed and consumed those responsible one by
one, until the last survivors, driven mad by fear, broke out of the prison
and escaped.

Relation to the Grim

Grim (or *Fairy Grim*) is the name of a shape-shifting *Fairy* that sometimes
took the form of a black dog according to a 17th-century pamphlet entitled
The Mad Pranks and Merry Jests of Robin Goodfellow. The Grim was also
referred to as the "Black Dog of Newgate", but although this phantom dog
also enjoyed frightening people, it never did any serious harm.

Black Dog of Northorpe

In the village of Northorpe in the West Lindsey district of Lincolnshire
(not to be confused with Northorpe in the South Kesteven district) the
churchyard was said to be haunted by a *Bargest*. Some black dogs are

said to be human beings with the power of shape-shifting. In another nearby village there lived an old man who was reputed to be a wizard. It was claimed that he would transform into a black dog and attack his neighbors' cattle. It is uncertain if there was any connection between the Barghest and the wizard.

Black Dog of Tring

In the parish of Tring, Hertfordshire, a chimney sweeper named Thomas Colley was in 1751 executed by hanging for the drowning murder of Ruth Osborne, whom he accused of being a witch. Colley's spirit now haunts the site of the gibbet in the form of a black dog, and the clanking of his chains can also be heard. In one tale a couple of men who encountered the dog saw a burst of flame before it appeared in front of them, big as a Newfoundland, with the usual burning eyes and long sharp teeth. After a few minutes it disappeared, either vanishing like a shadow or sinking into the earth.

Black Shuck

Black Shuck, Old Shuck, Old Shock or simply *Shuck* is the name given to a ghostly black dog which is said to roam the coastline and countryside of East Anglia, one of many ghostly black dogs recorded in folklore across the British Isles. Accounts of Black Shuck form part of the folklore of Norfolk, Suffolk, the Cambridgeshire fens and Essex, and descriptions of the creature's appearance and nature vary considerably; it is sometimes recorded as an omen of death, but in other instances is described as companionable. The creature was first described in 1127. According to the *Oxford English Dictionary*, the name Shuck derives from the Old English word *scucca* – "devil, fiend", from the root word *skuh* – to terrify. The first mention in print of "Black Shuck" is by Reverend E.S. Taylor in an 1850 edition of the journal *Notes and Queries* which describes "Shuck the Dog-fiend":

> *"This phantom I have heard many persons in East Norfolk, and even Cambridgeshire, describe as having seen as a black shaggy dog, with fiery eyes and of immense size, and who visits churchyards at midnight."*

Abraham Fleming's account of the appearance of a strange, and terrible black dog in 1577 at Bungay, Suffolk is a famous account of the beast. Images of black sinister dogs have become part of the iconography of the area and have appeared in popular culture. Writing in 1877, Walter Rye stated that Shuck was "the most curious of our local apparitions, as they are no doubt varieties of the same animal." Descriptions of Black Shuck vary in both shape and size, from that of a large dog to being the size of a calf or horse. W. A. Dutt, in his 1901 *Highways & Byways* in East Anglia describes the creature thus:

"He takes the form of a huge black dog, and prowls along dark lanes and lonesome field footpaths, where, although his howling makes the hearer's blood run cold, his footfalls make no sound. You may know him at once, should you see him, by his fiery eye; he has but one, and that, like the Cyclops', is in the middle of his head. But such an encounter might bring you the worst of luck: it is even said that to meet him is to be warned that your death will occur before the end of the year. So you will do well to shut your eyes if you hear him howling; shut them even if you are uncertain whether it is the dog fiend or the voice of the wind you hear. Should you never set eyes on our Norfolk Snarleyow you may perhaps doubt his existence, and, like other learned folks, tell us that his story is nothing but the old Scandinavian myth of the black hound of Odin, brought to us by the Vikings who long ago settled down on the Norfolk coast."

Bloody Mary

Bloody Mary, apart from a world famous cocktail, is a phantom, or spirit, conjured to reveal the future. She is also known by the names *Mary Worth, Mary Whales, Hell Mary* and *Mary Jane*. Swedish folklore tells of a *Svarta Madame* who is said to correspond to Bloody Mary. She appears in a mirror when her name is chanted repeatedly. The Bloody Mary apparition may be benign or malevolent, depending on historic variations of the legend. Bloody Mary appearances are mostly "witnessed" in group participation play, or by a man who is about to die. Historically, the divination ritual encouraged young women to walk up a flight of stairs backwards, holding a candle and a hand-mirror, in a darkened house. As they gazed into the mirror, they were supposed to be able to catch a view of their future husband's face. There was, however, a chance that they would see a skull (or the face of the Grim Reaper) instead, indicating that they were going to die before they would have the chance to marry.

In the ritual of today – popular in the UK and USA among young people – Bloody Mary allegedly appears to individuals or groups who ritualistically invoke her name in an act of catoptromancy. This is done by repeatedly chanting her name into a mirror placed in a dimly-lit or candle-lit room. The name must be uttered thirteen times (or some other specified number of times). The Bloody Mary apparition allegedly appears as a corpse, witch, or ghost, that can be friendly or evil, and is sometimes seen covered in blood (hence the name). The lore surrounding the ritual states that participants may endure the apparition screaming at them, cursing them, strangling them, stealing their soul, drinking their blood, or scratching their eyes out. Bloody Mary is said to appear only in mirrors (mainly bathroom mirrors), usually as a girl or young woman with long hair and pale skin. Blood is said to run down from her forehead from a long gash. Alternatively, her spirit is said not to appear herself, but instead the summoner sees a bleeding version of his/her own reflection.

Blue-cap

Blue-cap is an industrious mine spirit which appeared as a light-blue flame and who for a long time haunted Shilbottle Colliery near Alnwick, Northumberland. The Blue-cap was said to have enormous strength, being able to toil for long hours. He assisted miners and expected to be compensated for his help. Every fortnight his wages were left in a corner of the mine. If they were a farthing below his due, the indignant Blue-cap rejected the money, but if it was a farthing above his due, he would leave the surplus where he found it. Most of the above information comes from an account of him that appeared in the *Colliery Guardian* in May 1863.

Blue Men

In the North Hebrides it was said that fallen angels were driven out of Paradise in three divisions. One group became the *Fairies* of the land, one the *Blue Men* of the sea, and the third the *Nimble Men* or *Fir Chlis* or *Merry Dancers* of the sky. As to these fallen angels, their sin was not so great as those who were cast into the bottomless pit. The Blue Men were found in the strait between Long Island and Shiant Isles, which is called *Sruth nam Fear Gorm* (Stream of the Blue Men). They were, as the name

suggests, blue in color, with a long grey face, and floated from the waist
out of the water. People had nothing to fear from them if they allowed
them to have the last word, and rhymes confused them. They had the
power of conjuring up storms but when they were asleep the weather
would be calm. In Argyll the Blue Men are unknown.
See also under *Na fir ghorma.*

Boakie

Boakie is in Moray, Aberdeen, Banff and on the Shetland Isles a term for
a *Sprite*, a *Hobgoblin*. Boakie is related to the Norwegian *Bokje*, Islandic
Bocke, *Bokki* and the Teutonic *Bokene* (phantasma, specter). In Sanskrit
Buka is the name of an evil spirit.

Bòcan

Bòcan is the Scottish Gaelic term for ghost, apparition, specter, spirit, and
Goblin. They are seen about fords, or bridges, and near the public roads in
lonely places, and are held responsible for every unusual sight and sound
in their locality. Most of these *Bòcain* (pl.), however, are dependent not so
much on the imagination of the individual spectator as on accumulated
rumors, which often become greatly exaggerated over time, yet contribute
strongly to form a thought-form or servitor version aka prolongation
of the apparition, which can thereby even grow stronger and produce
poltergeist-like effects. This is the case with almost every well-known
haunting entity or haunted place.

Bocanách

In Irish folklore, the *Bocanách* is a huge menacing ghostly goat or goat-
like specter that haunted travelers on lonely roads at night.

Bòchdan

The term *Bòchdan* (pron. Baucan) is a general name for terrifying objects
seen at night, and taken to be supernatural, *Bugbears*, ghosts, apparitions,
Goblins, etc., in all their variety. John Gregorson Campbell presents an
excellent description of the term in *Witchcraft & Second Sight in the
Highlands & Islands of Scotland (1902):*

"The term "Bòchdan" (pron. Baucan) is a general name for terrifying objects seen at night, and taken to be supernatural, bugbears, ghosts, apparitions, goblins, etc., in all their variety. The word conveys as much the idea of fright in the observer as of anything hurtful or violent in the object itself. It is derived from "bòchd", to come in a swelling and resistless flood, not an unapt description of the manner in which fear takes possession of its victims. Any object, indistinctly seen, may prove a hobgoblin of this kind. It may be merely a neighbour playing pranks by going about in a white sheet, a stray dog, a bush waving and sighing in the night wind, or even a peat-stack looming large in the imperfect light. There is a story of a man on Loch Rannoch-side who fought a bush, in mistake for a ghost, in a hollow, which had an evil name for being haunted. The conflict continued till dawn, when he was found exhausted, scratched, and bleeding.

Sometimes the Baucan, or terrifying object, causes fright by its mere appearance, sometimes by the noises it makes, and sometimes by its silence. In appearance it is commonly a man or woman moving silently past, and not speaking till spoken to, if even then; but it has also been encountered as a black dog, that accompanies the traveller part of his way, as a headless body (a particularly dangerous form of ghost), as a he-goat, or simply a dark moving object. At other times it is terrific from having a chain clanking after it, from its whistling with unearthly loudness, by horrible and blood-freezing cries and sounds of throttling, and sometimes it makes its presence known only by faint and hardly audible sounds. In fact, the number and variety of things by which superstitious terror may be awakened at night are countless.

In most cases the Baucan is deemed the precursor of a sudden or violent death to occur at the place where it is seen or heard. It is remembered after the event that an unaccountable light was seen there at night, or a horse had become uneasy and could not be induced by its rider to pass, or something extraordinary had been observed, which the popular imagination connects with the subsequent event. At other times the Baucan is the spirit of the dead revisiting the earth, that it may be spoken to, and unburden itself of some secret that disturbs its rest. Sometimes it is an evil spirit on some message of darkness and sometimes merely a sound or indistinct object by which the wayfarer is frightened, but of which he is unable to give any lucid description. Fright is destructive of curiosity, and a person ready to faint with terror cannot be expected to be critical in his observations, nor afterwards coherent in his statements. Besides, vagueness or indistinctness as to the cause—an element to which the obscurity of night lends a ready aid—tends to render fear more frantic. If the observer had a distinct view of the object of his alarm, and knew exactly what it was, even though it were a spirit of darkness, his terror would be less. "Omne ignotum pro magnifico" is an axiom that holds especially true in such cases, and it is ignorance of its own cause that gives terror its wildest forms. A ghost or apparition seen in the day time, if that were possible, would not be at all so dreadful.

It may be said, that every Highland village has near it a locality where a ghost or baucan is, or was, to be seen. A favourite haunt for these unearthly visitants is by the fords of rivers (beul àth na h-aimhne), where generally bridges have been built in modern times, near churchyards, on dark moors, and in hollows, or rather at the top of the ascent from hollows, traversed by the public road. Not unfrequently there is a projecting rock (sròin creige) near the spot, and this may have its own share in producing that sense of loneliness and awe, which makes the belated peasant prone to convert stray animals and unusual appearances into ghosts and spirits. It is a noticeable feature in ghost stories, that it is principally to those travelling alone, and not accustomed to walk the night, that ghosts are visible. They have been seen in houses, and even in towns, but ordinarily they affect lonely places, where naturally men are more apt to be timorous."

Bockie

In the Shetland Islands and the Orkney Islands, a *Hobgoblin*, probably derived from Norwegian dialect *Bokke*. One of the many *Bogle* varieties.

Bockle

In Cornwall, a Bockle is a supernatural appearance, a cross between ghost and Goblin.

Bodach

The Bodach is a type of nursery *Bogie* or *Bugbear* that comes down the chimney to fetch naughty children. In other areas it is a term for *Imp* or *Fairy*. John Gregorson Campbell devotes a paragraph to the creature in his *Witchcraft & Second Sight in the Highlands & Islands of Scotland* (1902):

"The Bodach (a carle, an old man) is perhaps the commonest form of "Bòchdan" (Baucan – a general term for terrifying objects or creatures seen at night), so common that in some districts – e.g. the Lord Reay country (Dùthaich Mhic Aoi), as the seven parishes nearest to Cape Wrath are called – that they have no other name for apparitions or terrifying objects seen at night. It is the figure of a man, who is no "living wight," seen at night, and as may readily be imagined, this kind of apparition is frequently seen when children are obstreperous, querulous, or crying without cause, as their manner is. The "Beckoning Old Man" (Bodach an Sméididh) appears about the corners of houses, making signs with his hand for people to come to him. The "Corra-lòigein", whatever his name may mean, stands in places which it is desirable to keep children from wandering to after dark, and will ill-treat any of whom it gets a hold. The principal of these Lemures is "The Son of Platter-pool," whose full title is: "The Son of Platter-pool from grey spike, silken spike, great caterpillar." This, as his name indicates, is really a frightful "Bugbear"; he looks in at windows, flattens his face against the panes, sharpens his teeth with much noise, and takes away children in a twinkling, unless they keep quiet. Neither he, however, nor any of his brother Bugbears, enter a house unless called in. The threat of doing so is generally quite sufficient to silence the most ill-grained child."

Bodachan sabhaill

Described by J.G. Campbell (in *Superstitions of the Highlands and Islands of Scotland*, 1900) the Bodachan sabhaill (Little old man of the barn), is a Scottish *Household-spirit*. In the Highlands of Perthshire, each farm or village had its own Bodachan sabhaill, who helped to thresh the corn, made up the straw into bundles, and saw that everything was kept in order. They worked all night, and were never mischievous, but very useful. The Bodachain had the appearance of old men and were very wise.

The Blacke Dogge of Newgate:
both pithie and profitable
for all Readers.

Vide, Lege, Caue.

Time shall trie the trueth.

by Luke Hutton

Bogey

When children try to scare each other, they often hide themselves, to appear quite suddenly and shout "Buh!" ("Boe!" in my country, the Netherlands). This "Buh" seems to be something Pan-European, as many cultures have Bogey's with the root "pu", "bu", "bo", "ba", "pa" or a combination of these: *Bogeyman*, *Puck* (English), *Bogle* (Scottish), *Bòcan*, *Púca*, *Pooka* or *Pookha* (Irish), *Pixie* or *Piskie* (Cornish), *Pwca*, *Bwga* or *Bwgan* (Welsh), *Boeman* (Dutch), *Butzemann*, *Bögge*, *Böggelmann* (German), *Busemann* (Norwegian), *Bøhmand / Bussemand* (Danish), *Puki* (Old Norse), *Bubulis* (Latvian), *Baubas* (Lithuanian), *Mumus* (Hungarian), *Bogu* (Slavic), *Buka* (Russian, бука), *Babau* (Ukrainian, бабай), *Bauk* (Serbo-Croatian), *Bobo* (Polish), *Abubakar* (Czech and Slovak) *Torbalan* (Bulgarian, торбалан) *Bebok* (Silesian) *Pampoulas* (Greek, Μπαμπούλας) *Bua* (Georgian, ბუა) *Babau* (Italian) *Baubau* (Romanian), *Papão* (Portuguese), *Babau* (French).

Blanket term

The *Bogey* is a blanket-term for an imaginary folkloric creature that had the function of keeping children away from dangerous places; most often to prevent them from drowning, getting lost in a corn field etc. Sometimes the Bogey is rooted in witch-like figures or some historical figure, who lived many centuries ago. Many Bogeys are a hybrid product of some nature demon or field or water-spirit, whose original role and being has been lost, or got eroded over time and became a "tulpa" or "thought form" created by endlessly repeating certain stories and imaginings in the process. Many nature and field-spirits who "remained intact" over the years have the Bogeyman-phenomenon as a side effect. The question whether or not a local Bogey is just a fantasy or has some form of (astral/etheric) existence and reality, is not so easy to answer. From a modern chaos-magical technical point of view all Bogeys who have been kept fresh in memory and use, have some degree of real existence.

Boggart

A *Boggart* is a *Bogey*-like creature in English folklore, either a household-spirit or a malevolent Genius Loci (a geographically-defined spirit) inhabiting fields, marshes, or places with other topographical features. In some areas, such as Northumberland, it was believed that helpful household sprites, *Silkies* or *Brownies*, could turn into malevolent Boggart if offended or ill-treated. The Scots variant is the *Bogle* (or *Boggle*) or a river-Boggart, called a *Shellycoat*. Other names of this group include *bug, bugbear, Bogey* and *bogun.* Presumably these names are all derived from (or related to) Old English *pūcel,* and related to the Irish *púca* and the *pwca* or *bwga* of Welsh mythology. The household form causes mischief and things to disappear, milk to sour, and dogs to go lame. The Boggarts inhabiting marshes or holes in the ground are often attributed with more serious evildoing, such as the abduction of children.

Many Boggards are described as relatively human-like in form, though usually uncouth, very ugly and often with bestial attributes. T. Sternberg's 1851 book *Dialect and Folk-lore of Northhamptonshire* describes a certain Boggart as *"a squat hairy man, strong as a six year old horse, and with arms almost as long as tacklepoles".* Other accounts describe Boggarts as having more completely beast-like forms. The *Boggart of Longar Hede* from Yorkshire was said to be a fearsome creature the size of a calf, with long shaggy hair and eyes like saucers. It trailed a long chain after itself, which made a noise like the baying of hounds. The *Boggart of Hackensall Hall* in Lancashire had the appearance of a huge horse. At least one Lancashire Boggart was said to sometimes take the forms of various animals, or indeed more fearful creatures. The Boggarts of Lancashire were said to have a leader, or master, called *Owd Hob*, who had the form of a Satyr or archetypal devil: horns, cloven hooves and a tail.

Being a malevolent creature, the household Boggart will follow its family wherever they flee. It is said that the Boggart crawls into people's beds at night and puts a clammy hand on their faces. Sometimes he strips the bedsheets off them. Sometimes a boggart will also pull on a person's ears. Hanging a horseshoe on the door of a house and leaving a pile of salt outside your bedroom are said to keep a Boggart away. In Northern England, at least, there was the belief that the Boggart should never be named, for when the Boggart was given a name, it would not be reasoned with nor persuaded, but would become uncontrollable and destructive. Within the folklore of North-West England, Boggart can cause mischief in homes, but tend to live outdoors, in marshland, holes in the ground, under bridges and on dangerous sharp bends on roads. The book *Lancashire Folklore* of 1867, makes a distinction between *"House boggarts"* and other types. In Lancashire, a skittish or runaway horse was said to have *"took Boggart"* – that is, been frightened by a, usually invisible, Boggart. When a person got lost in a marsh and was never seen again, people were sure that a Boggart had caught the poor unfortunate and devoured him. The name of at least one Lancashire Boggart was recorded, *"Nut-Nan"*, who flitted with a shrill scream among hazel bushes in Moston near Manchester. In Yorkshire, Boggarts also inhabit outdoor locations; one is said to haunt Cave Ha, a limestone cavern at Giggleswick, near Settle.

Boggle or Bogill

A *Boggle* or *Bogill* is a Scots and Northumbrian term for a ghostly, usually Boggart-like (but less malicious) being or specter. Boggle is synonymous with *Doolie, Cow, Bogill-bo, Bugin, Beagle, Bugaboo*, etc. It is used for a variety of related folkloric creatures including *Shellycoats, Barghests, Brags*, the *Hedley Kow* and even *Giants* such as those associated with Cobb's Causeway (also known as *Ettins, Yetuns* or *Yotuns* in Northumberland and *Etenes, Yttins* or *Ytenes* in the South and South West). They are reputed to live for the simple purpose of perplexing mankind, rather than seriously harming or serving them.

The name Boggle is derived from the Middle-English *Bugge* – of which the term *Bogey* is also derived – which is in turn a cognate of the German word *bögge*, of which *Böggelmann* is derived and possibly the Norwegian dialect word *bugge*, meaning *important man*. The Welsh *bwg* could also be connected, and was thought in the past to be the origin of the English term; however, it has been suggested that it is itself a borrowing from Middle English. The Irish Gaelic word *bagairt* meaning "threat" could also be related.

Boobrie

The *Boobrie* is a mythological shape-shifting entity inhabiting the lochs of the west coast of Scotland. It commonly adopts the appearance of a gigantic waterbird resembling a cormorant or great northern diver, but it can also materialize in the form of various other mythological creatures, such as a Water-bull. Being a generally malevolent entity, the Boobrie typically preys on livestock being transported on ships, but it is also fond of otters, of which it consumes a considerable number. In its manifestation as a Water-horse the creature is able to gallop across the surface of lochs as if galloping over solid ground. During the summer months it is seen infrequently as a large insect, sucking the blood of horses.

Boobrie may derive from *boibhre*, meaning *cow giver* or *cow bestowing*. Edward Dwelly, a Scottish lexicographer, lists *Tarbh-boidhre* as "Monster, demon" and "God capable of changing himself into many forms"; *Tarbh-aoidhre* is given as a northern counties variation. The simpler component of *tarbh* as a single word is defined by E. Dwelly as "bull." Transcribers of the tale have used several differing spellings of the second component, some even adopting inconsistent variations throughout their own renditions. George Henderson for instance, a folklorist and Celtic scholar, used five alternatives: *Bo'eithre*; *Boidhre*; *Bo-oibhre*; *Eithre*; and *Fhaire*. Spelling variations employed by other writers include *Aoidhre*; *Baoighre*; *Baoidhre*; *Eighre*; and *Oire*.

In its favored bird manifestation the Boobrie resembles a gigantic great northern diver or cormorant, but with white markings. According to folklorist Campbell of Islay, a detailed account of its dimensions provided by an authoritative source claims that it is "larger than seventeen of the biggest eagles put together". It has a strong black beak about 11 inches (28 cm) wide and 17 inches (43 cm) in length, of which the final 5 inches (13 cm) taper like that of an eagle. The creature's neck is almost 3 feet (91 cm) long with a girth of a little under 2 feet (61 cm). Short black powerful legs lead to webbed feet with gigantic claws. An imprint of a Boobrie's foot, left in some lakeside mud, equalled "the span of a large wide-spreading pair of red deer's horns". It bellows noisily with displeasure, sounding more like a bull than a bird. The design of its wings is more conducive to swimming rather than for flight. Its evil powers when in the form of a bird were said by Campbell of Islay to have "terrified a minister out of his propriety". The Boobrie's insatiable appetite for livestock posed a threat to local farmers, as they relied on their animals as a means of providing income and food.

Boodie

In Aberdeen and surroundings, *Boodie* or *Boodie-bo* was the name for a ghost or Hobgoblin. *Boodie fear* is used as a synonym for a fear of ghosts.

Bortbyting

Bortbyting is the Swedish term for *changeling,* a child that is not human, but was swapped for a human child by such supernatural beings as *Goblins, Fairies, Midday women,* etc. In Scandinavia however the Bortbyting was often a child of a *Troll.*

Brag

A *Brag* or *Braag* is a mischievous shape-shifting *Goblin* in the folklore of Northumberland and Durham and often takes the form of a horse or donkey. It is fond of letting unsuspecting humans ride on its back before bucking them off into a pond or bush and running away laughing. One notable example is the *Picktree Brag,* an apparition that used to haunt the village of Picktree, near Chester-le-Street. The Brag was said to appear like a calf, also like a galloway; once it appeared like four men holding up a white sheet, and once like a naked headless man; but more often like a coach-horse or a male ass. One who mounted the brag was thrown off into a pond at the 'Four 'lonin ends', while the brag ran off laughing. It was also said to appear at the time of death, or to herald some misfortune. A Brag at Humbleknowe was never seen but made hideous noises in the night.

Bran

Bran was a legendary dog owned by Fionn mac Cumhaill, which reputedly was of *Elfin*-breed. It had a venomous shoe (*bròg nimhe*), with which it killed whatever living creature it struck, and when at full speed, and like its father *(dol ri athair)*, was seen as three dogs, intercepting the deer at three passes. The Bran was also multi-colored, according to popular tradition:

> "*Bran had yellow feet,*
> *Its two sides black and belly white;*
> *Green was the back of the hunting hound,*
> *Its two pointed ears blood-red.*"

Brigidi

In Shetlandic folklore, *Brigidi* was a kind of whale or large fish. Its backfin was about the size and shape of a boat's sail. Whenever it noticed a boat, it rushed at it and cut it in half with its large and sharp fin. Other times it would hit the boat with the fin sideways, thus crushing it or flattening it down on the water. Formerly, offerings seem to have been made, possibly of coins and pieces of iron thrown to it in the water. There was another creature with exactly the same habits, called a *Sjafer*.

Brollachan

The *Brollachan* (Scottish Gaelic: *Brollachan* (something entwined, entangled, interwoven) is a very dangerous demonic being in the Scottish highlands. The Brollachan is shapeless and takes on the appearance of the person or object on which it sits or which it touches. Nobody knows his true form. The only things you can see of him are the eyes and the mouth. Furthermore, he can only say "I" or "you" (Scottish Gaelic: *mi-fhèin –* I myself or *thu-fhèin –* you yourself), which makes it extremely difficult to communicate to the creature. The Brollachan has no shape of its own, because it is still so young and has not yet learned how to maintain a fixed form. It appears as a dark, nebulous unit with two bright eyes and a mouth in the middle. It is believed that one should be able to evoke a Brollachen in this form through magical rituals. Its size varies from sixty centimeters to two meters. It is not a very brave creature and loves to hide in the shadows. However, it prefers the bare hills to the dense forests. Because of his descent from the *Fuath*, whose son he is said to be, he often spends time near water.

Persons possessed with a Brollachan have a dark complexion and glowing, red eyes. Most of the time these people stand out for their wild and uncontrolled behavior, as if they were trying to shake off the intruder. The Brollachan is believed to be especially dangerous for children. Due to the intensity of a Brollachan-possession, people usually die within a few days and the demon has to find a new host. With the help of the dying, he attracts other living beings nearby. Exorcising a Brollachan is very difficult. This can only be done through traditional herbs. The expulsion is supported by ritualized chants. However, it is difficult to get the herbs you need and as soon as the Brollachan is aware of the fact that one tries to drive him out of its host, he becomes very dangerous and will try to enter the exorcist and if he fails at that, the Brollachan will curse him. Bright light seems to be the most successful way to drive it off. He also fears fire, since, despite his shapelessness, he can be burned. If possible

the Brollachan should not be harmed, as this can draw the rampant anger
of his family on people.

Brown Man of the Muirs

In the folklore of the English-Scottish border, the *Brown Man of the Muirs*
is a ferocious and very strong *dwarf* or *Duergar* who serves as a guardian-
spirit of wild animals. The Brown Man appears as a solitary creature, but
in fairytale literature he is described as a member of a class of similar
beings, known as the *Brown Men of the Moors and Mountains*. By day
they are said to mine the mountains for gold and diamonds, and by night
they feast in their underground hall, or dance on the moors. They were
believed to kidnap human children and kill any man they catched alone
in the wilderness. However, they could be made subservient by repeating
the incantation: *Munko tiggle snobart tolwol dixy crambo!* William
Henderson provides an account of the Brown Man and a pair of hunters
in the year 1744 (in *Folklore of the Northern Counties*, 1879), taken from
a letter sent by the historian Robert Smith Surtees (1805 – 1864) to Sir
Walter Scott (1771 – 1832):

> *"In the year before the Great Rebellion two young men from Newcastle*
> *were sporting on the high moors above Elsdon, and at last sat down*
> *to refresh themselves in a green glen near a mountain stream. The*
> *younger lad went to drink at the brook, and raising his head again*
> *saw the "Brown man of the Muirs", a dwarf very strong and stoutly*
> *built, his dress brown like withered bracken, his head covered with*
> *frizzled red hair, his countenance ferocious, and his eyes glowing*
> *like those of a bull. After some parley, in which the stranger reproved*
> *the hunter for trespassing on his demesnes and slaying the creatures*
> *who were his subjects, and informed him how he himself lived only*
> *on whortleberries, nuts, and apples, he invited him home. The youth*
> *was on the point of accepting the invitation and springing across*
> *the brook, when he was arrested by the voice of his companion, who*
> *thought he had tarried long, and looking round again "the wee brown*
> *man was fled." It was thought that had the young man crossed the*
> *water the dwarf would have torn him to pieces. As it was he died*
> *within the year, in consequence, it was supposed, of his slighting the*
> *dwarf's admonition, and continuing his sport on the way home."*

Browney

The *Browney* (not to be confused with the Brownie) is mentioned by folklorist Katharine Mary Briggs (1898 – 1980) as the Cornish *Guardian of the bees*. When the bees swarm, the housewife beats a can and calls 'Browney! Browney!' and the Browney is supposed to come invisibly to round up the swarm. It is possible, however, that 'Browney' is the name of the bees themselves, like 'Burnie, Burnie Bee' in the Scots folk rhyme.

Brownie

A *Brownie*, also *Brounie* or *Urisk* in Scots, Scottish Gaelic *Brùnaidh*, *Ùruisg* or *Gruagach*, is originally a figure in the household in English and Scottish folklore. There is also a lot of folkloric material which describes the Brùnaidh, Gruagach and Ùruisg as different spirits with unique features. In some parts of Scotland the Brownie was called *Shellycoat*, of which the origin is unclear. Regional Brownie-variants in England and Scotland include *Hobs* and *Silkies*. Variants outside England and Scotland are the Welsh *Bwbach* and the Manx *Fenodyree*. Brownies are especially popular in the north, where they refer to a type of little *Fairy*. They can be compared to the German *Heinzelmännchen* and the *Tomte* in Scandinavia. Brownies originated as domestic tutelary spirits, very similar to the *Lares* of ancient Roman tradition. They live in harmony with people. Whoever offends the house spirits, who bear their name because of their brown clothes, is punished: the little ones take bitter revenge on their tormentors.

Appearance and behavior

The Brownie resembles a *Leprechaun*. It is often described as a person of small stature with a wrinkled face. Brownies are virtually always male, but female Brownies, such as *Meg Mullach* (or "*Hairy Meg*"), have occasionally been described as well. They are usually envisioned as ugly and their appearances are sometimes described as frightening or unsettling to members of the homes in which they reside. They received their name from the fact that they are usually described as brown-skinned and completely covered in hair. In the earliest traditions, brownies are either the same size as humans or sometimes even larger, but, in later accounts, they are described as "small, wizened, and shaggy". They are often capable of turning invisible and they sometimes appear in the shapes of animals. They are always either naked or dressed in rags.

If a person attempts to present a Brownie with clothing or if a person attempts to baptize him, he will leave forever.

Brownies live in houses and help with chores. They only work at night, performing necessary housework and farm tasks while the human residents of the home are asleep. The presence of the brownie is believed to ensure household prosperity and the human residents of the home are expected to leave offerings for the brownie, such as a bowl of cream or porridge, milk, sweets or a small cake. These are usually left on the hearth. The Brownie will punish household servants who are lazy or slovenly by pinching them while they sleep, breaking or upsetting objects around them, or causing other mischief. Sometimes they are said to create noise at night or leave a mess, simply for their own amusement. In some early stories, Brownies are described as guarding treasure, a non-domestic task outside of their usual repertoire. They leave the house when you call the gifts to them payments or when the house owners deliberately try to take advantage of them. Brownies are almost always described as solitary creatures who work alone and avoid being seen. There is rarely said to be more than one Brownie living in the same house. They live in the unused parts of the residence, usually in attics or holes in the walls of the house. Brownies rarely talk to people, but despite their solitary way of life, they are believed to hold conversations with each other. They are also believed to hold regular gatherings, usually in remote areas and on rocky shores. In some districts in the Scottish Highlands, these gatherings were called *Peallaidh an Spùit* (Peallaidh and the gushing out), *Stochdail a' Chùirt* and "*Brùnaidh an Easain*" (Brownie from the little waterfall).

Brownie or Ùruisg
Once every house in Scotland was believed to have its Ùruisg, which is why in the kitchen, near the fire, there was an unoccupied chair for the Brownie. One house on the banks of the River Tay was even claimed to be haunted by such a spirit until the early 20th century, and one room of the house was called "*Seòmar Bhrùnaidh*" (*Brownie's room*) for centuries. In 1703, John Brand, a minister of the Church of Scotland, wrote in his description of Shetland:

> *"As late as 40 or 50 years ago, every family had a Brownie or "evil spirit" (Ùruisg), so called because he served them and they had to make an offering to him for his service. When they made butter, they*

*gave him his share and wet every corner of the house with the milk;
they did the same when they brewed. They had a stone which they
called "Brownie's stane" (Brownie's stone). In it was a hole where
they poured some beer wort as a gift. They also had some bundles of
grain, which they called Brownie's bundles, that were never blown
away by a storm, no matter how strong, although they were not
tied together with straw ropes or fastened in any other way."*

Researcher William J. Watson noted that every stream in Breadalbane
(Scottish province) had a Ùruisg (the Scottish Gaelic *ùrruisg* means
flooding), whose king was *Peallaidh*. Peallaidh's name is still preserved in
Obair Pheallaidh, in English *Aberfeldy*. It may therefore be that the *ùruisg*
merged with a *water-spirit*, or that the Ùruisg was originally a water-spirit
that merged with the Brownie. The Ùruisg or Scots Urisk is described as a
poor lonely water-spirit who seeks the proximity of people. However, his
strange appearance frightens anyone who approaches him.

Brugh or Bru

A *Brugh*, or *Bru* (pronounced: broo) was mentioned by Katharine Mary
Briggs. According to J. G. Campbell (in his *Superstitions of the Scottish
Highlands*) a Brugh or Bru is the interior of a *Fairy-mound* or *knowe*
and the same word as *borough*. It generally means a place where quite a
number of Fairies live together, and not just the home for a family. The
outside of the Brugh is the *sithien*.

Brùnaidh

The *Brùnaidh*, a *Brownie*-like being with household-spirit features, was
a relatively harmless being, but he made mischief unless every place
was left open at night. He was fed with warm milk by the dairy-maid.
The Brùnaidhean (pl.) might work about the barn, and at night ground
with the hand-mill one or two bags of grain. If rewarded for their work,
they leave with their gifts and never come back. According to the author
Thomas Pennant, the creature was "*...stout and blooming, had fine flowing
hair, and went about with a wand in his hand.*" (*A tour in Scotland, and
voyage to the Hebrides* - 1772). On the islet of Càra, west of Kintyre, a
Brùnaidh haunted an old house that once belonged to the Macdonalds.
It drank milk, and made a terrific outcry when hurt. Although he was

heard, no one ever saw more than just a glimpse of the creature. It disliked anything dirty being left in the house for the night, and before the arrival of strangers he put the house in order. Dogs had to be put out for the night, as he often killed those left in the house. Persons who soiled the house in the dark would often receive a slap from him.

Bucca

Bucca is the name of a spirit that in Cornwall was once thought necessary to propitiate. The Bucca was mainly regarded as a male sea-spirit, a *Merman*, that inhabited mines and coastal communities as a *Hobgoblin* during storms. Newlyn fishermen left a fish on the sands for *Bucca-boo*, and during the harvest a piece of bread was thrown over the left shoulder at lunch-time, and a few drops of beer spilled on the ground for him, to ensure good luck. He is also known as *Bwcïod*. The mythological creature is a type of water-spirit, likely related to the *Púca* from Irish, the *Pwca* from Welsh folklore, and the female *Mari-morgans*, a type of *Mermaid* from Welsh and Breton mythology. Rev W. S. Lach-Szyrma, a 19th-century writer on Cornish antiquities, suggested the Bucca had originally been an ancient pagan deity of the sea, such as Irish *Nechtan* or British *Nodens*. In the west of England there was the belief in the *Bucca gwidden*, the white or good spirit, and in a *Bucca dhu*, the black, malevolent one. Bucca, or Bucca-boo, was also the terror of children, who, when crying, were often told "that if they did not stop he would come and carry them off." Finally, it was also the name of a ghost who had nothing to do with the Merman-Bucca. In the late 19th century, to call a person a "great Bucca" simply implied "fool" or "idiot".

Buggane

In Manx folklore a *Buggane* or *Boagane* is a huge *Ogre*-like mischievous shapeshifter, with poltergeist behavior, that chases and frightens people. It has black hair, eyes like torches, glittering sharp tusks, and lives in caves. One Buggane haunted the church of St. Trinion, tossing the roof to the ground as soon as it was nearly finished. Some have considered them akin to the Scandinavian Troll. As magical creatures, Bugganes were unable to cross water or stand on hallowed ground. According to legend, Bugganes were occasionally called upon by the benevolent Fairies to punish people that had offended them. The Buggane of Glen

Maye would have pitched a lazy housewife into a waterfall for putting off baking until after sunset, had she not cut loose the strings of her apron to escape. The Buggane from Gob-na-Scuit was known for tearing the thatch off the haystacks, puffing smoke down chimneys, and pushing sheep over the edge of the brooghs (a steep bank or grassy cliff). The *Buggan ny Hushtey* lived in a large cave near the sea and was known for disliking lazy people. However, it should not be confused with the *Cabyll-ushtey*, the Manx Water-horse.

Burach-Bhaoi

In the western Highlands of Scotland the *Burach-Bhaoi* (also: *Burach, Burach Bhadi, Wizard's Shackle*) is a kind of vampiric Fairy that resembles a huge eel with nine eyes. It preferably hides in water near roadways, and there have been sightings of it in Badenoch, Loch Tummel, and some streams in Argyll. The Burach-bhaoi lies in wait for a horse, with or without a rider, to pass by near enough so that it can attack, wrapping itself around the horse's feet. Then it pulls tight, dragging the horse, rider and all, into the water, where it will drown its prey before draining it dry of blood.

The Burach-Bhaoi is almost certainly a mystification (or "whiskeyfication") of the lamprey (nicknamed *Vampire-eel*), who almost exactly matches the description, including the "nine eyes" and the sucking of blood (which it does). The sea lamprey for example is native in Northern Europe. It has an eel-like body without paired fins. Its mouth is jawless, round and sucker-like, and as wide – or may be wider – as the head; sharp teeth are arranged in many consecutive circular rows. Adult lampreys can reach a length of up to 120 cm (47 inch) and a body weight up to 2.3 kg (5.1 lb). The Dutch call a lamprey *negenoog* (nine-eye) due to the row of holes near the head, seven of which are for breathing, the eighth is a real eye, and the ninth is the nose-opening.

Bwbach

The *Bwbach*, or *Boobach*, is a good natured *Goblin* that does good turns for the tidy Welsh maid who wins its favor by a certain course of behavior recommended by long tradition. The maid having swept the kitchen, makes a good fire the last thing at night, and having put the churn, filled with cream, on the whitened hearth, with a basin of fresh cream for the Bwbach on the hob, goes to bed to await the event. In the morning she finds (if she is in luck) that the Bwbach has emptied the basin of cream, and plied the churn-dasher so well that the maid has but to give a thump or two to bring the butter in a great lump. Like the *Ellyll* which it so much resembles, the Bwbach does not approve of dissenters and their ways, and especially strong is its aversion to total abstainers.

As reported by Wirt Sikes (in *British Goblins: Welsh Folk-Lore, Fairy Mythology, Legends and Traditions*) there was a Bwbach belonging to a certain estate in Cardiganshire, which took great umbrage at a Baptist preacher who was a guest in the house, and who was much fonder of prayers than of good ale. Now the Bwbach had a weakness in favor of people who sat around the hearth with their mugs of *'cwrw da'* and their pipes, and it took to pestering the preacher. One night it jerked the stool from under the good man's elbows, as he knelt pouring forth prayer, so that he fell down on his face. Another time it interrupted the devotions by jangling the fire-irons on the hearth and it was continually making the dogs fall a-howling during prayers, or frightening the farm boy by grinning at him through the window, or throwing the maid into fits. At last it had the audacity to attack the preacher as he was crossing a field. The minister told the story in this way:

> *"I was reading busily in my hymn-book as I walked on, when a sudden fear came over me and my legs began to tremble. A shadow crept upon me from behind, and when I turned round – it was myself! My person, my dress, and even my hymn-book. I looked at its face for a moment, and then fell insensible to the ground."*

And there, insensible still, they found him. This encounter proved too much for the good man, who considered it a warning to him to leave those parts. He accordingly mounted his horse the next day and rode away. A boy from the neighborhood, whose veracity was, like that of all boys, unimpeachable, afterwards said that he saw the Bwbach jump up behind the preacher, on the horse's back. The horse ran like lightning, with eyes like balls of fire, and the preacher looking back over his shoulder at the Bwbach, saw that it grinned from ear to ear.

The same confusion in outlines which exists regarding the Bogie and Hobgoblin, gives the Bwbach a double character, as a *Household-Fairy* and as a terrifying phantom. In both aspects it is ludicrous, but in the latter it has dangerous practices. To get into its clutches under certain circumstances is no trifling matter, for it has the power of whisking people off through the air. Its services are brought into requisition for this purpose by troubled ghosts who cannot sleep on account of hidden treasure they want removed; and if they succeed in getting a mortal to help them with removing the treasure, they employ the Bwbach to transport the mortal through the air.

According to Sikes, the Bwbach is in France represented by the *Gobelin*. Mothers threaten children with him. *Le gobelin vous mangera, le gobelin vous emportera* (Père l'Abbé, *Etymologie*). In the English *Hobgoblin* we have a word apparently derived from the Welsh *hob*, *to hop*, and *Coblyn*, a *Goblin*, which represents a hopping Goblin, and suggests the *Pwca* (with which the Bwbach is also confused), but should in English simply mean the "Goblin of the hob", or Household-Fairy.

Bwca

The *Bwca* is a *Brownie* that will perform housework in return for bread and milk, but if disrespected he may become angry and violent before abandoning the home. Tricking him into revealing his name will also cause him to leave. They are not normally mischievous, but in one tale the Bwca had a human friend who was sent off to war and was killed. The Bwca became distraught after his human friend died and started playing disruptive pranks until a cunning-man (magician) was brought in to banish him from the house.

Bwgan

Bwgan is a Welsh supernatural creature of fearful implications; a kind of *poltergeist*-like *Goblin* or *Bogey*. Probably from *bwg* (ghost, hobgoblin) + an.

Bwgwl

A spirit in Welsh folklore that inspired terror. The Welsh *bwgwl* (pronounced: *bugul*) means "*terror, terrifying*".

Bygel and Bygel-nos

The *Bygel* (from *bygylu*; "to terrify") or *Bugail*, is a *Hobgoblin* of the night in Welsh folklore. In Britanny there is the "Shepherd or Lad of the night" called *Byguel-nos*. Whereas for the Welsh *Bygel-nos* means "phantom", it is sometimes mistaken for *Bugail nos*. The latter means a "Hobgoblin of the night" and the word *bwg* (bug) means "ghost". Another form in northern English dialect is *Boggle*, found from Lincolnshire across the country towards Cumberland.

Bysen

In Gotlandic folklore, the *Bysen* (pl.: *Bysar*) is a small forest-creature that lures people to get lost, or causes trouble for the forest workers. He is the guardian of the forest and nature, and regarded by some as the equivalent of the *Lyktgubbe* and the *Skogsrået* on the mainland. Anyone seen by the spirit in the forest has his/her vision distorted, so that one cannot find one's way home again. By turning a garment inside out, the victim can regain normal vision. The Bysen also delays transports and overturns timber loads. He often appears as a tree-stump or a small gray, inconspicuous old man, and is accused of all sorts of mischief. He is also dressed in gray, sometimes with a red cap, and carries an ax, as his job is to cut down Gotland's forests. However, this is done slowly; sometimes even as slow as one tree per century.

Bysar also correspond to the *Feurige Männer* of Bavaria in the sense that, to some sources, they are believed to be deceased people, who stole someone else's land by moving the rough marks that marked the boundary between two properties – just like the moved boundary stones of the Feurige Männer. As a punishment, they are not allowed to rest in their graves, but are condemned to walk along the wrong land border and move the pegs that are on the wrong land. It is also said that they can be heard walking and muttering, *"Here is right, here is wrong"* as they move the sticks marking the boundary. If a human follows Bysen and moves the wrong border markers back to the right place, then the Bysen will be at peace. On the Swedish mainland, the equivalent is called *Skälvrängare* (*skäl* can mean "border" or "rough mark" or "unclean surveyor").

C

Cabyll-ushtey

In Manx folklore the *Cabyll-ushtey* appears in only a few Manx legends.
It is a dangerous Water-spirit, pale-grayish in color, and similar to the
Gaelic *Each uisge*. Cabyll-ushtey literally means "Water-horse" in Manx
(*cabyll* = "horse" and *ushtey* = "water"). Like all *Water-horses*, the Cabyll-
ushtey lives in a lake or deep river and lures humans to follow it into the
water. When a human follows it into the water, the beast pulls its victim
under the surface and tears it to pieces. The Cabyll-ushtey attracts both
humans and animals. Furthermore, the Water-horse brings unrest to
groups of people and herds of animals, causing potential victims to run
away or stampede (in case of cattle), and scatter the people or animals
widely. The Cabyll-ushtey then catches the slowest person or animal and
kills the unlucky one. The creature may occasionally steal children.

Cailleach

Cailleach, (Irish pl. *Cailleacha* Scottish Gaelic pl. *Cailleachan*) in Celtic
mythology refers to a group of Gaelic legendary figures from Scotland,
Ireland, and the Isle of Man. The Cailleacha are witch-like giantesses and
are mostly associated with the weather. The term Cailleach means "nun",
"the veiled one", "witch" or "old woman" and derives from the Latin word
pallium, a "veil" or ecclesiastical garment worn by women. In Old Irish,
the noun *caillech* (the veiled one) is found for *caille* (veil). Differentiated
terms in modern Gaelic are *Cailleach dhubh* (nun), *Cailleach Oidhche*
(owl – literally: night-woman), *Cailleach Feasa* (soothsayer), and
Cailleach Phiseogach (*sorceress*). Related to cailleach are the modern
Scottish Gaelic *lexemes caileag* (young woman, girl) and Scots *carline/
carlin* (old woman, witch).

Most Cailleachan are considered to be the embodiment of winter, others
are seen as the cause of storms, protectors of animals or creators of
certain lakes, rivers, mountains or islands. Traits of older Celtic local and
earth goddesses have been transferred to the Cailleach figures. Related
figures are the *Black Annis* or *Gentle Annie, Gwrach y Rhibyn, Banshee,
Bronach* and *Mal*. According to Max Dashu, Irish oral tradition links

the Cailleach with Neolithic monuments. Some passage-tombs bear her name, others she is said to have erected. Examples include Calliagh Birra's House at Slieve Gullion in County Armagh, Leabhadh Chailligh and the "Crone's Bed" in County Cork, but in particular she is associated with Loughcrew.

There is another folklore which links her more to a classic field demon. Cailleach, the old woman or old wife, was a spirit of whom people were afraid during harvest time. The person last done with the shearing had to feed her till next harvest. In spring, Cailleach was engaged with a hammer in keeping the grass under.

Cailleach Bera

According to Katharine Mary Briggs the Irish *Cailleach Bera*, or *Beara* is almost identical with the *Cailleach Bheur* of the Scottish Highlands, except that she is not so closely connected with winter nor with the wild beasts. She is a great mountain builder, and, like many other gigantic Hags, she carried loads of stones in her apron and dropped them when the string broke.

Cailleach Bheur

The *Cailleach Bheur* of the Scottish Highlands, is a the blue-faced lean *Hag* who personified winter and summer. For Katharine Mary Briggs she is one of the clearest cases of a supernatural creature who was once a primitive goddess, possibly among the ancient Britons before the Celts, that eroded in time to the level of nature-spirit. The Cailleach Bheur also is the guardian spirit of a number of animals. The deer have the first claim on her. They are her cattle; she herds and milks them and often gives them protection against the hunter. Swine, wild goats, wild cattle and wolves were also her creatures. In another aspect she was a fishing goddess. The Cailleach Bheur was also the guardian of wells and streams.

Cally Berry

Cally Berry is an Ulster version of the Scottish weather-spirit *Cailleach Bheur*, the personification of winter and guardian of the wild deer. Except here she is more likely a malignant, supernatural *Hag*, than a nature-spirit.

Cambion

In late European folklore and literature, and since at least the 19th century, the *Cambion, Campion* or *Campsorus* is the half-human half-demon offspring of an *Incubus, Succubus* or other demon, and a human. In its earliest known uses, it was related to the word for "change" and was probably cognate with *changeling*. The word Cambion appeared on an early first century AD inscription in Gaul (Roman France). Linguist Benjamin W. Forston IV opines that: ...*cambion* is from the Celtic root *-kamb* "crooked", also referring to a back and forth motion and to exchange. It is the source for English change via late Latin *cambiare*, a borrowing from Celtic (*Indo-European Language and Culture: An Introduction*, Benjamin W. Forston IV, p. 17). William of Auvergne, in his 13th century work *De Universo*, wrote of *cambiones* as the *"sons of incubi demons"* that were substituted for human babies. These infants constantly wail for milk and cannot be satisfied – not even by four nurses. (Richard Firth Green notes that this "was to become the standard scholastic explanation for changelings throughout the Middle Ages.")

Typically, a child born with a physical defect was suspected of being a demonic half breed, especially twins. A common test that was performed to see if a child was a Cambion or not was to have a holy man simply touch it. Being demonic, a Cambion would cry out in pain. Incredibly dense and weighing more than its looks would suggest, a Cambion would grow into a tall and well-muscled individual who may have an apparent physical defect of some description. Its nature was described as bold and wicked, and it would develop some sort of supernatural ability; most develop a talent for using magic spells and go on to become sorcerers. Merlin was believed to be a Cambion, his mother being a nun and his father an *Incubus*. Romulus and Remus were also supposed to be Cambions, as was Alexander the Great, Caesar Augustus, Martin Luther, Plato, Scipio Africanus, and the father of William the Conqueror. In 1275, a woman by the name of Angela de Labarthe of Toulouse was burned at the stake for giving birth to a child who allegedly had the head of a wolf and a tail that resembled a snake. It was deduced that only an Incubus could have fathered such a child as hers, and therefore had visited her from Hell.

Jacques Collin de Plancy in his *Dictionnaire Infernal* (1818) proposes the Cambion as the child of an Incubus and Succubus. The 1825 edition of that book has the following entry:

*"CAMBION,—Enfants des Demons. Delancre et Bodin pensent que
les démons incubes peuvent s'unir aux démones succubes, et qu'il nait
de leur commerce des enfants hideux qu'on nomme cambions..."*
(CAMBION,—Children of Demons. Delancre and Bodin believe that
incubus demons can unite with succubus demons, and that born of
their exchange are hideous children which are called cambions....").

In 1874, Victor Hugo's *Toilers of the Sea* defined a Cambion as the son of a
woman and the devil.

Malleus Maleficarum

The concept of offspring born to humans and demons was a subject
of debate in the Middle Ages. The influential *Malleus Maleficarum,*
which has been described as the major compendium of literature in
demonology of the fifteenth century, states that demons, including the
Incubus and the *Succubus*, are incapable of reproduction:

*"Moreover, to beget a child is the act of a living body, but devils
cannot bestow life upon the bodies they assume; because life formally
proceeds only from the soul, and the act of generation is the act
of the physical organs which have bodily life. Therefore bodies
which are assumed in this way cannot either beget or bear.
Because of this inability to create or nurture life, the method of the
creation of a cambion is necessarily protracted. A succubus will
have sexual relations with a human male and so acquire a sample
of his sperm. This she will then pass on to an incubus, who then
corrupts and strengthens the seed. The incubus will, in his turn,
transfer this sperm to a human female and thus impregnate her.
Yet it may be said that these devils assume a body not in order that they
may bestow life upon it, but that they may by the means of this body
to preserve human semen, and pass the semen on to another body."*

However, the *Malleus Maleficarum* never uses the word cambion,
referring to the children of incubi as *Campsores* or *Wechselkinder*.

Caoineag

The *Caoineag* or "Weeper" is a variant of the *Ban-sìthe* or *Bean-sith*, found
in the northern Highlands of Scotland and in the Hebrides (see under

Banshee). Other local names for her include *Caointeag, Caoineachag, Caointeachag* and *Caoidheag.* She is normally invisible and foretells death in her clan by lamenting in the night at a waterfall, stream or Loch, or in a glen or on a mountainside. Unlike the related death portent known as the *Bean nighe*, the Caoineag cannot be approached or questioned or be made to grant wishes. The Caoineag can be classified as a *Fuath*, a generic term for evil or feared spectral beings in Highland Gaelic folklore. The *Caointeach* is another version of this death spirit attached to various clans in Islay, Argyllshire, Skye and some of the neighboring islands, like the Macmillans, Mathisons, Kellys, Mackays, Macfarlanes, Shaws and Curries. When a death from illness was about to occur she would appear outside the sick person's house wearing a green shawl and begin lamenting at the door. In one account she is said to have been banished from the premises after having been pitied and given a gift of clothing to cover herself. She is sometimes conflated with the Bean nighe who haunts desolate streams and washes the clothing of those about to die, but in this context the Caointeach is more formidable. If she is interrupted she will strike at a person's legs with her wet linen and the victim will lose the use of them.

Capelthwaite

In Westmorland and adjacent parts of Yorkshire there was a belief in *Capelthwaite*, who could take the form of any quadruped but usually appeared as a large black dog. He took his name from the barn in which he lived called Capelthwaite Barn, near Milnthorpe. He performed helpful services for the people on the farm such as rounding up the sheep, but toward outsiders he was very spiteful and mischievous until one day he was banished by a vicar. As both a helper and a trickster the Capelthwaite behaved more like a domestic *Hobgoblin* than a typical black dog.

Cat-sìth or Cait-shith

Cat-sìth (Scottish Gaelic, pl. *Cait-shìth*), in Irish *Cat sí*, is a Fairy creature from Celtic mythology, said to be as large as a dog, black, with a white spot on its breast, with an arched back and erect bristles. Legend has it that the spectral cat haunts the Scottish Highlands. The legends surrounding this creature are more common in Scottish folklore, but a few occur in Irish. Some common folklore suggested that the cat-sìth was not a Fairy, but a witch that could transform into a cat nine times. Because of its presumed connection with the so-called *Kellas cat*, which was first sighted in 1984, it is also assigned to cryptozoology.

Cat-sìth is known as the Highland Fairy-cat. Many Highlanders believed that these cats were transformed witches, not Fairies. The people of the Scottish Highlands did not trust the Cat-sìth. They believed that it could steal a person's soul, before it was claimed by the gods, by passing over a corpse before burial. Therefore, watches called the *Fèill Fhadalach* (Late Wake) were performed night and day to keep the Cat-sìth away from a corpse before burial. Methods of "distraction" such as games of leaping and wrestling, catnip, riddles and music would be employed to keep the Cat-sìth away from the room in which the corpse lay. In addition, there were no fires where the body lay, as it was said that the Cat-sìth was attracted to the warmth. On Samhain, it was believed that a Cat-sìth would bless any house that left a saucer of milk out for it to drink and those houses that did not put out a saucer of milk would be cursed into having all of their cows' udders go dry.

An even larger and more ferocious "cat", the demonic god of the cats, appeared in answer to an inhuman ceremony called the *Taghairm*. *This ceremony* consisted in roasting successive cats alive on spits for four days and nights until *Big Ears* appeared and granted the wishes of the cowards who tortured these animals. The last ceremony of Taghairm was said to have been performed in Mull and was described in detail in the *London Literary Gazette* (March 1824). The account is quoted by D.A. Mackenzie in *Scottish Folk-Lore and Folk Life* (p. 245). But Big Ears was a monstrous demon cat who had only a slight connection with the Cat-sìth. Gustav Meyrink (1868 - 1932) refers to this horrifying burning of cats-ritual in his novel *Der Engel vom westlichen Fenster* (1927).

Cearb

Cearb means "Killing one". It is a malevolent spirit in Scottish Gaelic folklore, which attacks human beings and cattle. Even though it is widely cited, little is known about this spirit. Another one of these is *Cear* (Blood one).

Ceasg

The *Ceasg* is a *Mermaid* in Scottish folklore, with the upper body of a beautiful woman merging with the tail of a grilse (a young salmon). The Scottish folklorist Donald MacKenzie suggested that the Ceasg may originally have been a sea goddess to whom human beings were sacrificed. In Scottish Gaelic the Ceasg is also known as *Mmaighdean na tuinne* (Maid of the wave) or *Maighdean mhara* (Maid of the sea). The Ceasg habitat is the sea, but she can also be found in rivers and streams, and can be made to grant three wishes to anyone who captures her. Marriages sometimes occur between Ceasg and humans, and famous maritime pilots are often reputed to be descended from such unions. Even when these marriages end and the Ceasg returns to the sea, they will always take an interest in their human descendants, protecting them in storms or guiding them to the best fishing grounds. The Ceasg is sometimes imagined as something more monstrous. In some tales she swallows a man, who then remains alive inside her stomach.

Ceffyl dŵr

Ceffyl Dŵr literally means "Water-horse" from Welsh (*ceffyl* - horse and *dŵr* - water). It is related to the other widespread Water-horses in Celtic mythology, cf. Scottish Gaelic *Each uisge*, Irish Gaelic *Each uisce*, Anglicized Irish *Aughisky*, but not as vicious as these. In Welsh folklore, the Ceffyl dŵr often appears as a beautiful little horse to the weary or short-sighted traveler. When the latter, exhausted, mounts the animal, it escapes into the air, where it dissipates as a misty haze, throwing off its rider in the process, and usually harming the rider. It is usually spotted under waterfalls or on the shores of mountain lakes, where it grazes peacefully. The Ceffyl Dŵr has a grayish shimmering coat and is surrounded by a misty haze; its tail is also made of water haze. It is also described as a horse with a dark complexion, glowing eyes and fire breath. As a shapeshifter, it can also take other forms, such as a squirrel or a goat, to scare people.

According to North Welsh beliefs, the beast may also kill its victims from ambush by emerging from the water and strangling the unsuspecting humans with its four legs. If it fails to do so, the horse cruelly tramples its victims. Some people, realizing the vicious nature of the animal, tried to slay it. But no matter how many times it is slain, its body simply

disappears, leaving behind only a shapeless gelatinous mass. This more
brutal conception may go back to the Scottish Each uisge, which exhibits
similarly cruel traits. In contrast, the South Welsh tales tend to describe
Ceffyl Dŵr as a bright, friendly and playful animal that teases people or
causes them minor harm by shape-shifting. In North Wales, people claim
that the Ceffyl dŵr interbred with native horses, giving rise to the small-
bodied ponies or "merlyns".

Changeling

In folk beliefs of the European Middle Ages, the changeling (or in German
Wechselbalg) was usually an infant (obsolete "brat") foisted on a woman
in childbirth by a demonic being in exchange for her own child, with the
intention of harassing and harming people. The changeling cannot be
defined as one specific kind of spirit or demon, but more as a product
many kinds of spirits were capable off. *Elves, field-spirits, midday-spirits,
forest-spirits, household-spirits* and other creatures – including the *Mare*
and *Incubus/Succubus* types – could all act as an entity that conceived
or delivered a changeling-baby. In non-Christian beliefs, the changeling
could be conceived and foisted by some spirit or daemon, or simply
put into the cradle of a human child whereby the creature abducted the
human child for reasons that vary according to the type of creature. The
oldest German literary evidence for the term "changeling" is found in a
translation of the *Psalms* by the Benedictine monk Notker III (950-1022),
where he paraphrases *fremediu chint* with Old High German *wihselinc*.
From *filii alieni* Notker makes *uuihselinga iudei* and this obviously means
foisted children. Consequently, this was a familiar idea in his time. In
the St. Paul fragments Notker uses the word *Wehselkint*. The common
German term *Wechselbalg* "exchange baby" comes from *wechseln* (to
exchange) + *Balg* (baby, brat) cognate to Dutch *Wisselbalg* or *Wisselkind*
(exchange child). The changeling is often characterized in contradictory
ways. He appears in the form of a child, but with the face of an old man.
Compared to human children of the same age, the changeling is usually
much smaller, but sometimes much larger, because he has a fat body with
clumsy limbs. He is retarded in his development or so malformed that he
hardly resembles a human being. It could also have a beard, or long teeth.
Predominantly boys are exchanged, tales of girls are rare. Even though he
looks small and weak, he has an excessive appetite and devours as much
food and drink as several adults combined. According to some tales, he

eats anything he can find, even frogs, mice, raw fish, and pig food. The changeling spends most of his time in bed, occasionally crawling around the room and crouching in a corner. He is lazy, stupid, mischievous, dirty, screams and makes incomprehensible noises. On the other hand, he is clever and fakes his stupidity only to annoy people, because in reality he is smart and clever. Although he learns to speak very late, or never, he is not deaf and dumb. In most cases he does not live long (up to the age of 18 or 19), but sometimes (as a court or house spirit) he can live as long as several human lives.

Baby swapping spirits could also take adult humans, especially newly wed and young mothers; young adults were taken to marry *Fairies*, while new mothers were often taken to nurse Fairy babies. Often, when an adult was taken instead of a child, an enchanted object such as a log was left in place of the stolen human, to make it look like the person was still there. This object left behind in place of the human would seem to sicken and die, only to be buried by the human family, while the living human was among the Fairies. *Bridget Cleary* is one of the most well-known cases of an adult thought to be a changeling by her family; her husband killed her, in an attempt to force the Fairies to return his 'real' wife. Bridget Cleary (Bríd Uí Chléirigh 1869 – 15 March 1895) was an Irish woman killed by her husband in 1895. Her death is notable for several peculiarities: the stated motive for the crime was her husband's belief that she had been abducted by Fairies with a changeling left in her place; he claimed to have slain only the changeling. The gruesome nature of the case – she was either burnt to death or set on fire immediately following her death – prompted extensive press coverage. The trial was closely followed by newspapers in both Ireland and Britain. As one reviewer commented, nobody, with the possible exception of the presiding judge, thought it was an ordinary murder case.

The term changeling, or its many local synonyms in the European continent, is sometimes confusing in the sense that the baby abducting spirit was sometimes called a changeling as well, just as the creature that was put in a human baby's place. In Christian popular belief changelings were associated with the devil and witches. In general, children with some kind of mental or physiological defect were suspected of being a changeling, often with horrible consequences. The German term for changeling, *Wechselbalg*, associated with "evil and sinister", first appeared in the early 11th century. This practice, according to which the handicapped or malformed children were often mistreated or killed, reached its peak at the same time as the persecution of witches from the 15th to the 17th centuries and continued to have an impact far into the 19th century. Probably the earliest conceptions of exchanged children in Europe are found among the haunting, but not always malevolent spirit beings of Celtic and Germanic mythology.

In the Nordic saga-world *Elves* occasionally steal a child from a woman and in return submit a *Cuckoo child*. Such mythical creatures, which also include *Dwarves* and, in Scandinavia, *Trolls*, do this primarily because their own children are so ugly that they would like to exchange them for beautiful human children. In Celtic mythology, *Tylwyth Teg* are *Goblins* who occasionally deposit changelings. Known in the mountains of northern Spain in the region of Asturias, *Xanas* appear as beautiful women who reside at springs and occasionally exchange human children for their own. In Eastern European myths, *Water-spirits* (there are many different types) exchange children; in Baltic mythology these *Fairy*-like beings sometimes called *Lucky* or *Earth women*, are also called *Laumes*; in Slavic mythology, *Vilen*; and in Lapland, *Uldas*. The *Midday woman* (Polish *Południca*, Czech *Polednice*) appears in Slavic mythology on hot days at noon in the fields, driving people mad or paralyzing their limbs. Since she also steals children and leaves changelings behind, among the Sorbs and Czechs women in childbed are not supposed to leave the house around noon as a precautionary measure. The Brothers Grimm also report something similar about the *Roggemuhme*, a corn demon of German legend.

In the 16th century, the Latin terms for *Wechselbälge* were *Cambiones*, *Campsiones*, *Campsores*, and *Cambiti* (from *cambare*, "to change, to exchange"), paraphrased as *infantes suppositi* (supposed children). *Wechselbutte* or *Butte* was common in Upper German; *Wechselbür*, *Wechselburt* and *Wechselbalggebürde* were rare in Low German. M. Gottfried Voigt in his *In Disputationem physicam de infantibus supposititiis*, Wittenberg, 1667, uses the term *Freßbutten*. In Scandinavian languages, a changeling was called a *Bortbyting, Bytesbarn, Bytisungar, Forbyttet barn,* and *Umbetbarn,* all of which go back to the verb *bytta* (to exchange, change). The English terms *changeling* and *changeling child* are equivalent to the French *Enfant changé*. *Auf* and *Oaf* in Middle English

are derived from *Elf*. The Polish *Podciep*, also *Podjeb* is composed of *pod* (down) and *ciepnać* (to throw, to toss) accordingly, a changeling in Silesia is called a *Underchisel*. Names that involve the process of swapping also occur in other Slavic languages. Sometimes the local name of the creature reveals its source, like the German *Zwergwechselbalg*, *Wichtelbalg* and *Wichtelkind*. In the Palatinate dialect, *Elbentrötsch*, *Nixkind*, *Wasserbalg* and *Wasserbutte* occur, in Bavaria *Hexenbutte*, in Tyrol *Nörglein* and *Nörggl*. Other names of origin are *Trollbyting* and *Viterby* (from *vitre*, *vätte*, "underground") in Scandinavia, in English *Elf-child* and *Fairy-changeling*, and in French *Enfant des fées* (child of the Fées). In Saxony and in the Palatinate the perpetrators were named *Wechselbutte*, in Austria *Wechsler* (son of the *Klagemütterl*) and in East Germany *Wechselfrau*. *La bête Havette* in Normandy, *Margot la Fée* and *Korrigan* in Brittany. The *Witten Wiwer* in northern Germany were also accused of child-swapping. A Gothic court book of 1690 further mentions *Underbyggarna*, the Poles know *Mamuny* and *Boginki* or *Biegonki*. The demonic or magical properties are referred to with the term *Koblickskind* (Goblin child) and especially in Northern Germany *Kielkropf*, which goes back to Old High German *Chelckropf*, *Chelchropf* and *Kielkopf*.

To detect whether a child was indeed a changeling *"by forcing him to reveal his true nature"*, many rituals – which according to folklore acted as a "truth serum" or "lie detector" – could be applied:
- Placing as many eggshells as possible on the stove, on the floor, in front of the child, or elsewhere. Occasionally, more detailed instructions about the type and exact number of eggshells are added. They must be previously stored for a certain period of time, laid out on a certain day, or piled high.
- Brewing beer in an eggshell is a variant in northern Germany and Scandinavia, with occasional occurrences in the British Isles and the Netherlands.
- A large spoon in a small vessel also astonishes the changelings and makes them talk. In Hungary, people talk about a large wooden spoon in a small pot; in Scandinavia, people stir food in an eggshell with a large spoon. In Iceland, the stirring utensil has a handle so long that it reaches up into the kitchen chimney.
- One infallible (and insane) check was to lay the supposed changeling on a fire with this formula, *"Burn, burn, burn—if of the devil, burn; but if of God and the saints, be safe from harm"*. Then if it be a changeling

it would rush up the chimney with a cry – in one case after it changed itself into a black kitten.

- Luckily, in another case the creature is got rid of in a more gentle way. It is on record that once when a mother was leaning over a wizened changeling the latch lifted and a *Fairy* came in, carrying home again the wholesome stolen baby. *"It was the others,"* she said, *"who stole it."* As for her, she wanted her own child.
- The housewife can prepare an unusual sausage from a pig, a dog, a cat or a sparrow. In a Danish saga, the mother cooks blood sausage in a cat skin. In the other Scandinavian countries, the motif is also attested. In a saga from Oldenburg, this leads the changeling to ask: *"Wurst mit Haut und Wurst mit Haar? Wurst mit Augen und Wurst mit Knochen darin?"* (Sausage with skin and sausage with hair? Sausage with eyes and sausage with bones in it?) The Sami prefer a dog, and in England a whole pig is boiled down to pudding. In the Bohuslän region of western Sweden, a changeling confronted with dog-pudding reveals his age: *"Now I am so old that I have been suckled by 18 mothers, but never have I seen dog pudding."*
- Putting shoe soles in front of it is a method used in northern Germany and sporadically in the Netherlands. Among the Kashubs, other inedible things such as small stones, pieces of wood and leather are also put on the plate. A meager meal may further supplement it. The motif of putting porridge or gruel in front of it, is about a tiny amount of gruel that is cooked in a large pot.

In order to make the changeling disappear, or to get ones real child back, drastic methods of torture were used. He was held over a fire, immersed in cold or hot water, beaten, pricked with needles, or boiling water was poured over its head. This is intended to lure his true parents, who might feel pity for their child. On the other hand, the changeling is also susceptible to subtlety; if one succeeds in eliciting a laugh from it by astonishing it, it disappears. In other stories the creature is simply killed.

Changelings or Fairy children who are taken back by their own kind are happy, according to some accounts, having plenty of good living and music and mirth. Others say, however, that they are continually longing for their earthly friends. According to W.B. Yeats in *Fairy and Folk Tales of the Irish Peasantry,* author Lady Wilde (1821-1896) gives a gloomy interpretation of the tradition that there are two kinds of Fairies – one kind merry and gentle, the other evil, and sacrificing every year a life to Satan, for which purpose they steal mortals. But Yeats also concludes that no other Irish writer gives this tradition: *"If such Fairies there be, they must be among the solitary spirits like "Pookas", "Fir Darrigs", and the like"*. In medieval Scandinavia it was believed that Trolls considered it more respectable to be raised by humans than by their own kind, and would consequently seize any opportunity to give their own children a human upbringing. Beauty in human children and young women, particularly traits which evoke brightness or reflectivity, such as blonde hair and blue or silver eyes, are said to attract changelings, as they perhaps find preciousness in these perceived traits. According to common Scottish myths, a child born with a caul (part of the amniotic membrane) across their face is a changeling, will soon die, and is "of Fey (Fairy) birth".

Other folklore says that human milk is necessary for Fairy children to survive. In these cases either the newborn human child would be switched with a changeling baby to be suckled by the human mother, or the human mother would be taken back to the Fairy world to breastfeed the Fairy babies. It is also thought that human midwives were necessary to bring Fairy babies into the world. Some stories tell of changelings who forget they are not human and proceed to live a human life. Changelings who do not forget, however, in some stories return to their Fairy family, possibly leaving the human family without warning. The human child that was taken may often stay with the Fairy family forever. Feeling connected to the fate of a changeling, there are families who merely turn their changeling loose into the wilderness. Such a drama was the inspiration for the tale *A daughter of Pan* in *The Secrets of Dr. Taverner* (1922/1926) by Dion Fortune.

At Byerholm near Newcastleton in Liddesdale sometime during the early 19th century, a dwarf called Robert Elliot or Little Hobbie o' The Castleton as he was known, was reputed to be a changeling. When taunted by other boys he would not hesitate to draw his *gully* (a large knife) and dispatch them, however being that he was woefully short in the legs, they usually out-ran him and escaped. He was courageous, however, and when he heard that his neighbor, the six-foot three-inch (191 cm) William Scott of Kirndean, a sturdy and strong borderer, had slandered his name, he invited the man to his house, took him up the stairs and challenged him to a duel. Scott beat a hasty retreat.

Church Grim

The *Church Grim* is a guardian spirit in English and Scandinavian folklore that oversees the welfare of a particular Christian church and protects the churchyard from those profane who could commit sacrilege against it, including thieves, vandals, witches, warlocks, and the Devil himself. It often appears as a black dog but is known to take the form of other animals. Many folklorists have concluded that it had once been the custom to bury a dog alive under the cornerstone of a church as a foundation sacrifice so that its ghost might serve as a guardian. When a new churchyard was opened it was believed that the first person buried there had to guard it against the Devil. In order to prevent a human soul from having to perform such a duty a black dog was buried in the north part of the churchyard as a substitute. According to a related belief in Scotland, the spirit of the person most recently buried in a churchyard had to protect it until the next funeral provided a new guardian to replace him or her. This churchyard vigil was known as the *Faire chlaidh* or "Graveyard watch". A folktale of the Devil's Bridge type is also an example of the motif of a dog (in this case a dog also named Grim) being sacrificed in place of a human being. In the North Riding of Yorkshire attempts were made to build a bridge that could withstand the fury of the floods, but none were successful. The Devil promised to build one, on condition that the first living creature that crossed it should serve as a sacrifice. When the bridge was complete the people gave long consideration as to who would be the victim. A shepherd who owned a dog named Grim swam across the river, then whistled for Grim to follow. The dog ran over the bridge and became the Devil's sacrifice. The bridge then became known as Kilgrim Bridge and was later renamed Kilgram Bridge, which today crosses the River Ure in North Yorkshire. According to Yorkshire tradition, the Grim, like many spectral black dogs, is also an ominous portent and is known to toll the church bell at midnight before a death takes place. During funerals the presiding clergyman may see the Grim looking out from the church tower and determine from its aspect whether the soul of the deceased is destined for Heaven or Hell. The Grim inhabits the churchyard day and night and is also associated with dark stormy weather.

Kyrkogrim

The Scandinavian Church Grim is known as the *Kyrkogrim* (Swedish) and *Kirkegrim* (Danish) and likewise defined as the protective *Revenant* of an animal buried alive in the church foundation. It dwells in the church tower or some other place of concealment, or wanders the grounds at night, and is tasked with protecting the sacred building. It keeps order in the church and punishes those who break church rules. It is said that the first founders of Christian churches would bury a lamb (church-lamb) under the altar. A person entering the church when services are not being held may see the lamb, and if it appears in the graveyard (especially to the gravedigger) then it portends the death of a child. The lamb is meant to represent Christ (the Lamb of God) as the sacred cornerstone of the church, imparting security and longevity to the physical edifice and congregation. Other animals, apart from a dog or a lamb, that used to create the Scandinavian Church Grim included a boar, a pig and a horse. A grave-sow (or graysow), the ghost of a sow that was buried alive, was often seen in the streets of Kroskjoberg where it was regarded as an omen of death. There are tales of the Danish Kirkegrim and its battles with the *Strand-varsler* that tried to enter the churchyard. *Strand-varsler* are the spirits of those who die at sea, are washed up on the shore, and remain unburied.

Churnmilk Peg

In West Yorkshire folklore *Churnmilk Peg* is an Orchard-spirit that guards unripe hazelnut thickets. She spends her free time by smoking a pipe. In the North Country, generally, *Melsh Dick* performs the same function. A third nut protector was *Nut Nan*. *Churnmilk Peg, Melch Dick* and *Nut Nan,* guarded the hazels from theft with threats of burning naughty children with heated pokers. Churnmilk Peg looked like an old and very ugly Hag. She sat in the groves around Malham in North Yorkshire. Her name derives from the hazels in their green state, when they're called *churn-milk*. All she says, is: *"Smoke! Smoke a wooden pipe! – Getting nuts before they're ripe!"* and if this didn't work, she would abduct the disobedient youths. *Melsh Dick* apparently derives his name from the same unripe, *mushy* or *mulchy* nuts; he too will punish disobedient children. These Orchard-spirits were often assisted by *Clap-Cans*, a ghost or hobgoblin which makes a clanking noise, as if beating on empty tin cans. It is a being with no form or substance, whose sole purpose is to scare away youngsters by beating on tin cans with sticks. English folklore knows more Orchard-spirits. Some of the more famous are Owd Goggie, Lazy Laurence, the Coltpexy and the Gooseberry Wife of the south of England.

Cìrein cròin

Cìrein cròin (Grey crest) is a sea-monster in Scottish Gaelic tradition, reputed to be the largest of all creatures and even capable of devouring seven whales. Other names given to the creature are *Mial mhòr a' chuain* (Great beast of the ocean), *Cuartag mhòr a' chuain* (Great whirlpool of the ocean) and *Uile bhéisd a' chuain* (Monster of the ocean).

Clurichaun

The *Clurichaun* or *Clúrachán, Cluracan, Cluracaun, Cluricaun,* or *Cluricaune* (from Irish: *Clobhair-ceann*) is a mischievous *Fairy* in Irish folklore, known for his great love of drinking and a tendency to haunt breweries, pubs and wine cellars. He is related to the *Leprechaun* and has sometimes been conflated with him as a shoemaker and a guardian of hidden treasure. This has led some folklorists to suppose that the Clurichaun is merely a Leprechaun on a drinking spree, while others regard them as regional variations of the same being. Like the Leprechaun, the Clurichaun is a solitary Fairy, encountered alone rather than in groups, as distinct from the trooping Fairies. Folklorist Nicholas O'Kearney described the Clurichaun in 1855 as follows:

> *"The Clobhair-ceann was another being of the same class:*
> *he was a jolly, red-faced, drunken little fellow, and was ever*
> *found in the cellars of the debauchee, Bacchus-like, astride of*
> *the wine-butt with a brimful tankard in hand, drinking and*
> *singing away merrily. Any wine cellar known to be haunted by*
> *this sprite was doomed to bring its owner to speedy ruin."*

Katharine Briggs stated that he was a kind of buttery spirit, feasting himself in the cellars of drunkards or scaring dishonest servants who steal the wine. The Clurichaun is also described as a trickster and practical joker, and a disturber of order and quietness in a household, making noise day and night. But despite his often troublesome nature, the Clurichaun takes special care of the family to whom he has attached himself, endeavoring to protect their property and lives, provided he is not interfered with. This dual nature makes him similar to the domestic *Hobgoblin*. Besides his love of drinking, the Clurichaun also enjoys pipe smoking, and the small disposable clay pipes known as "Fairy pipes" that are often found while digging or plowing are said to belong to him.

He also knows the secret of making beer from heather. Though generally regarded as separate beings, certain characteristics of the Leprechaun have sometimes been merged with those of the Clurichaun, particularly as a shoemaker and treasure guardian. The Clurichaun also shares many attributes with the *Biersal*, a type of *Kobold* stemming from Germanic folklore.

Co-Walker

A *Co-Walker* is a phantom, or astral body, deemed to be separable from the physical body and capable of acting independently. In the North of Britain it is called a *Waff* and said to be a death token. The Germans call it a *Doppelgänger*. In many cultures and religions Co-Walker or Doppelgänger-like beings play an important role as shadows. In the form of a protective deity, it is considered to be the image of a man in plant or animal form. Man and god are strongly connected here. Robert Kirk, M.A. in his *The Secret Commonwealth* (1691) regards the *Doubleman* or Co-Walker as one of the subterranean Inhabitants (i.e. Fairies):

"They are clearly seen by these Men of the Second Sight to eat at Funeralls (and) Banquets; hence many of the Scottish-Irish will not teast Meat at these Meittings, lest they have Communion with, or be poysoned by, them. So are they seen to carrie the Beer or Coffin with the Corps among the middle-earth Men to the Grave. Some men of that exalted Sight (whither by Art or Nature) have told me they have seen at these Meittings a Doubleman, or the Shape of some Man in two places; that is, a superterranean and a subterranean Inhabitant, perfectly resembling one another in all Points, whom he notwithstanding could easily distinguish one from another, by some secret Tockens and Operations, and so go speak to the Man his Neighbour and Familiar, passing by the Apparition or Resemblance of him. They call this Reflex-man a Co-walker, every way like the Man, as a Twin-brother and Companion, haunting him as his shadow, as is oft seen and known among Men (resembling the Originall), both before and after the Originall is dead ; and wes also often seen of old to enter a Hous, by which the People knew that the Person of that Liknes wes to Visite them within a few days. This Copy, Echo, or living Picture, goes att last to his own Herd."

Coblynau

The *Fairies* which haunt the mines, quarries and underground regions of Wales – corresponding to the *Gnomes* – are called the *Coblynau*. The word *coblyn* has the double meaning of "knocker" or "thumper" and "sprite" or "fiend". It is applied by Welsh miners to *Pigmy-Fairies* which dwell in the mines, and point out, by a peculiar knocking or rapping, rich veins of ore. The faith is extended in some parts, so as to cover the indication of subterranean treasures generally, in caves and secret places of the mountains. The Coblynau are described as being about half a yard in height and very ugly to look upon, but extremely good-natured, and warm friends of the miner. Their dress is a grotesque imitation of the miner's garb, and they carry tiny hammers, picks and lamps. They work busily, loading ore in buckets, flitting about the shafts, turning tiny windlasses, and pounding away like madmen, but really accomplishing nothing whatsoever. They have been known to throw stones at the miners, when enraged at being lightly spoken of; but the stones are harmless. Nevertheless, all miners of a proper spirit refrain from provoking them, because their presence brings good luck. In his *British Goblins-Welsh Folk-Lore, Fairy Mythology, Legends and Traditions*, Wirt Sikes recorded some interesting data about this creature:

"The Coblynau are always given the form of dwarfs, in the popular fancy; wherever seen or heard, they are believed to have escaped from the mines or the secret regions of the mountains. Their homes are hidden from mortal vision. When encountered, either in the mines or on the mountains, they have strayed from their special abodes, which are as spectral as themselves. There is at least one account extant of their secret territory having been revealed to mortal eyes. I find it in a quaint volume (of which I shall have more to say), printed at Newport, Monmouthshire, in 1813 (A Relation of Apparitions of Spirits in the County of Monmouth and the Principality of Wales by Rev. Edmund Jones of the Tranch, Newport, 1813). It relates that one William Evans, of Hafodafel, while crossing the Beacon Mountain very early in the morning, passed a fairy coal mine where Fairies were busily at work. Some were cutting the coal, some carrying it to fill the sacks, some raising the loads upon the horses' backs, and so on; but all in the completest silence. He thought this 'a wonderful extra natural thing,' and was considerably impressed by it, for well he knew that there really was no coal mine at that place. He was a person of undoubted veracity,' and

what is more, 'a great man in the world and above telling an untruth.'

'That the Coblynau sometimes wandered far from home', the same chronicler testifies; "but on these occasions they were taking a holiday. Egbert Williams, 'a pious young gentleman of Denbighshire, then at school,' was one day playing in a field called Cae Caled, in the parish of Bodfari, with three girls, one of whom was his sister. Near the stile beyond Lanelwyd House they saw a company of fifteen or sixteen Coblynau engaged in dancing madly. They were in the middle of the field, about seventy yards from the spectators, and they danced something after the manner of Morris-dancers, but with a wildness and swiftness in their motions. They were clothed in red, like British soldiers, and wore red handkerchiefs spotted with yellow wound round their heads. And a strange circumstance about them was that although they were almost as tall as ordinary men, yet they unmistakably had the appearance of dwarfs, and one could call them nothing but dwarfs. Presently one of them left the company and ran towards the group near the stile, who were direfully scared thereby, and scrambled in great fright to go over the stile. Barbara Jones got over first, then her sister, and as Egbert Williams was helping his sister over they saw the Coblynau close upon them, and barely got over when his hairy hand was laid on the stile. He stood leaning on it, gazing after them as they ran, with a grim copper-colored countenance and a fierce look. The young people ran to Lanelwyd House and called the elders out, but though they hurried quickly back to the field, the dwarfs had already disappeared."

Cofgod

Cofgod (pl.: *Cofgodas* "cove-gods") was an Old English term for a household god in Anglo-Saxon paganism. The Classicist Ken Dowden opined that the *Cofgodas* were the equivalent of the *Penates* found in Ancient Rome. Dowden also compared them to the *Kobolds* of later German folklore, arguing that they had both originated from the *Kofewalt*, a spirit that had power over a room. Beings such as the English *Hob* and Anglo-Celtic *Brownie* could be the more modern versions of the *Cofgod*. However, the only instance of the word Cofgodas in Old English is as a gloss to the Latin word *Penates*.

Cù-sìth

The *Cù-sìth* or *Cù-sìthe* (pl.: *Coin-sìth(e)*; Irish - *Cú sídhe*), is a *Grim*-like hound found in Scottish and Irish folklore. It bears a resemblance to the Welsh *Cŵn Annwn*. The Cù-sìth inhabits the clefts of rocks, and roams the moors of the Highlands. It is usually described as having a shaggy, dark green coat and being as large as a small cow. The hound would occasionally let out three terrifying barks that could be heard for miles. Legend has it that those who hear the barking of the Cù-Sìth had to find a safe haven at the third bark or else they would be overwhelmed by a panic fear, which could become so intense that it killed them.

Cŵn Annwn

In Welsh mythology and folklore, *Cŵn Annwn* (hounds of Annwn) were the spectral hounds of *Annwn*, the otherworld of Welsh mythology. The Cŵn Annwn is associated with death, as it has red ears. The Celts associated the color red with death. They were also associated with a *Wild Hunt*, presided over by either *Arawn*, king of Annwn in the First Branch of the Mabinogi and alluded to in the Fourth, or by *Gwyn ap Nudd*, as the underworld king and king of the fair(y) folk is named in later medieval lore. In Wales, they were associated with migrating geese, supposedly because their honking in the night is reminiscent of barking dogs. Hunting grounds for the Cŵn Annwn are said to include the mountain of Cadair Idris, where it is believed *"the howling of these huge dogs foretold death to anyone who heard them"*. According to Welsh folklore, their growling is loudest when they are at a distance, and as they draw nearer, it grows softer and softer. Their coming is generally seen as a death portent. Arawn is believed to set the Cŵn Annwn loose to hunt mundane creatures. The hounds are sometimes accompanied by a fearsome *Hag* called *Mallt-y-Nos*, "Matilda of the Night". St Donat's Castle especially is said to be haunted by a phantom dog accompanied by a Hag.

An alternative name in Welsh folklore is *Cŵn Mamau* (Hounds of the Mothers). *Da Derga* is also known to have a pack of nine white hounds, perhaps Cŵn Annwn. *Culhwch* rode to King Arthur's court with two "Otherworld" dogs accompanying him, possibly Cŵn Annwn. The Cŵn Annwn are supposed to hunt on specific nights (the eves of St. John, St. Martin, Saint Michael the Archangel, All Saints, Christmas, New Year, Saint Agnes, Saint David, and Good Friday), or just in the autumn and winter. Some say Arawn only hunts from Christmas to Twelfth Night. The Cŵn Annwn also came to be regarded as the escorts of souls on their journey to the Otherworld. A Cŵn Annwn's goal in the Wild Hunt is to hunt wrongdoers into the ground until they can run no longer, just as the criminals did to their victims. Christians came to dub these mythical creatures as "The Hounds of Hell" or "Dogs of Hell" and theorized they were therefore owned by Satan. However, the Annwn of medieval Welsh tradition is an otherworldly place of plenty and eternal youth and not a place of punishment like the Christian concept of Hell.

Cyhyraeth

The *Cyhyraeth* (also *Cyoeraeth* or *Cyheuraeth*), probably derived from the noun: *cyhyr* "muscle, *sinew*, flesh" plus the suffix *-aeth*, meaning "skeleton, a thing of flesh and bone", "spirit", "death-bearer" and "wreath", all spirits of Welsh folklore, with a disembodied moaning voice that sounds before a person's death. The Cyhyraeth is known as the *Hag* of the mist, an awful being who is supposed to reside in the mountain fog, through which her supernatural shriek is heard. She is believed to be the very personification of ugliness, with torn and disheveled hair, long black teeth, lank and withered arms and claws, and a most cadaverous appearance; to this, some add wings of a leathery and bat-like substance. She is believed to form the torrent beds which seam the mountain side; for she gathers great stones in her cloak to make her ballast, when she flies upon the storm; and when about to retire to her mountain cave, she lets them drop progressively as she moves onwards, when they fall with such an unearthly weight that they lay open the rocky sides of the mountain. Legends associate the Cyhyraeth with the area around the River Tywi in East Dyfed as well as Glamorganshire. The sound is described as "painful and unpleasant", like the groans and moans of a terminally ill person. It is said to be heard three times, becoming fainter and quieter each time. It serves as a triple warning before the person passes away. Along the Glamorganshire coast, the Cyhyraeth is said to be heard before a ship sinks, accompanied by a somber "Corpse light." Like the Irish *Banshee* and the Scottish *Cailleach*, to which the Cyhyraeth (and the *Gwrach y Rhibyn*) are closely related, the Cyhyraeth sounds are also an announcement for Welsh natives dying far from home.

D

Dando's Dogs

The area around St Germans is haunted by a pack of hunting dogs known as *Dando's Dogs*. Dando was an unrepentantly sinful priest and an avid huntsman, who was carried off to Hell by the Devil for his wickedness. Since then, Dando and his hounds are sometimes heard in wild chase across the countryside, especially on Sunday mornings. The Devil's Dandy Dogs are another Cornish version of the Wild Hunt. They are often conflated with Dando's Dogs but are much more dangerous. The huntsman is the Devil himself and his dogs are not just ghosts but true hell-hounds, black in color with horns and fiery breath. One night a herdsman was journeying home across the moors and would have been overtaken by the Dandy Dogs, but when he knelt and began praying they went off in another direction in pursuit of other prey.

Dearg-Due

Dearg-Due is a female *Vampire* in Irish folklore. Possibly also known as *Dearg-Dul* – meaning: "drinker of human blood" – *Deamhain Fhola*, *Dearg-Dililat*, and *Dearg-Diulai*. According to Montague Summers, the Dearg-Dul is an Irish Vampire that can be held at bay by piling large amount of stones on its grave – but no Irish mythologist can find any reference to it. Dearg-Due means "red bloodsucker". The demon seduces men and then drains them of their blood. According to Celtic legend, an Irish woman who was known throughout the country for her beauty fell in love with a local peasant, which was unacceptable to her father. Her father forced her into an arranged marriage with a rich man who treated her terribly, and eventually, she committed suicide. She was buried near Strongbow's Tree in Waterford, and one night, she rose from her grave to seek revenge on her father and husband, sucking their blood until they dropped dead.

Derricks

A *Derrick* is a specific type of uncommon Fairy in Devonshire, England. The name Derrick seems to come from the Old English *dweorg* (dwarf). The creature is considered malignant and to enjoy leading travelers astray.

Imps depicted in Matthew Hopkins' (1620-1647) book *The Discovery of Witches* (1647)

Dinny Mara

The Manx *Dinny Mara* or *Dooinney Marrey* (Man of the Sea) is similar in appearance to *Mermaids*, but with the upper half of the body of a man and the lower half the tail of a fish. However, the Dinny Mara is quit ugly! He is believed to a have a pig snout for a nose that is red from drinking the brandy from shipwrecks and he has a wrinkled forehead. Folklore has it that a Dinny Mara can be recognized by his red cap. Alhough Dinny Mara's are ugly creatures, they are wonderful fathers and quite helpful and friendly to sailors, warning them of impending storms or bringing them fish to eat when the sailor's food supply runs low. The creature hates it however when someone whistles. So the fastest way to get on the bad side of a Dinny Mara is to whistle. The whistling will awaken and anger the Dinny Mara, which will cause him to seek revenge upon the sailor who disturbed his rest.

Dísir

Dísir (singular: *Dís*) or *Disen* are female mythical beings in Norse mythology, whose character cannot be precisely determined. Modern science assumes them to be lower vegetation deities. Sometimes a connection with the ancient Germanic matron cult and the Anglo-Saxon festival *Modraniht* "Mothers' Night", which was celebrated in winter, is suspected. Old Norse sources describe the Disen as midwives, personal guardian spirits of individuals or whole clans, and battle helpers as well as heralds of approaching death, even as death-bringing women. This brings the Disen close to the *Norns*, *Fylgjen* and *Valkyries*. In addition, *dís* can also simply mean "woman." In late medieval Iceland, it was customary to see in the Disen the souls of deceased women, one of the foundations of Icelandic folk belief. The *Idisi* mentioned in the *First Merseburg Spell*, who intervene in warlike actions, are often associated with the Norse Dísir. The battlefield *idistaviso* mentioned by Tacitus was interpreted by Jacob Grimm as *idisiaviso* (women's meadow) and also associated with the Idises and the Norse Valkyries. The etymology of the word is not explained. Added is *skt. dhiśanā* – "woman of the gods" and to the root *dhaya* – "to suckle". Since the word *dís* also means "woman", a possible connection with the Old High German *itis* is suspected, though the vowel sounding as *it* remains unexplained.

The Disen enjoyed cultic veneration in Scandinavia. Many Norwegian and Swedish place names derive from the Disen belief, such as *Disin* (Disen meadow), *Diseberg* (Disen Mountain), *Disevid* (Disen forest).

Dísablót (Disen sacrifice) was a nightly sacrificial festival in autumn or at the beginning of winter, with a banquet and a beer binge, celebrated in Norway. In Uppsala, Sweden, a center of the Ynglingen, there was a temple of Disen.

Another festival was the *Disting* (Old Swedish: *Disaþing*) held in Uppsala, Sweden, at the beginning of February, or more precisely at the full moon whose preceding new moon rose after the *Twelfth Night* or *Epiphany Eve* (25 December - 6 January). The exact dating rule is: *När trettondags nyt i fylle gå, då disating i Uppsala står*, which in translation means something like: "When the thirteenth day's new moon becomes a full moon, then Disting is in Uppsala." The festival may have been comparable in essence to the Fastnacht or Carnival.

Dobie or Dobby

A *Dobie* or *Dobby* is a kind of *Brownie*, although some were ghosts rather than Fairies. In Yorkshire folklore they are attached to particular homes and farms, and were said to be kind to children and servants. They were able to appear in different forms, but as humanoids they are described as looking rather shaggy and thin. Though naturally lazy, they were said to make incredible exertions for the family in case of trouble or difficulty. Dobies are attached to people instead of places, and will follow their family when moving to a new domicile, although those who haunted houses could be sent away by offering them gifts. In Lancashire any sort of outside ghost is called a Dobby, and in Morecambe Bay they live along the shoreline. In Durham County the *Shonton Dobby* appears at the birth and death of prominent people in the form of a cow, dog, donkey, goose, or horse. There is a type of wild Dobie that controls deer, inhabits bridges, old towers and the like, and frightens travelers by jumping behind them on horseback, and squeezing them so as to impede their breathing. In Sussex they are called *Dobbs* or *Master Dobbs*. It has been suggested Dobby is a nickname for the name Robin, and that the supernatural Dobby could be a reference to *Robin Goodfellow*.

Dökkálfar

Dökkálfar (Dark Elves) are ancestral guardians who protect people, though they can also be menacing, especially when treated rudely. They usually try to avoid the light, although they are not necessarily subterranean. In Norse mythology, Dökkálfar and *Ljósálfar* (Light Elves) are two contrasting types of *Elves*; the Dökkálfar dwell within the earth and have a dark complexion, while the *Ljósálfar* live in *Álfheimr* (Old Norse "Elf Home" or "Elf World"), and are "fairer than the sun to look at". The Ljósálfar and the Dökkálfar are attested in the *Prose Edda*, written in the 13th century by Snorri Sturluson, and in the late Old Norse poem *Hrafnagaldr Óðins*. As the concept of light and dark Elves is only recorded in the *Prose Edda* and *Hrafnagaldr Óðins*, it is unclear whether the distinction between the two types of Elves originated with Snorri, or if he was merely recounting a concept already developed. The sub-classification of Elves may have resulted from Christian influence, by way of importation of the concept of good and evil and angels of light and darkness. Jacob Grimm surmised that the "proto-Elf" was probably a "light-colored, white, good spirit" while the *dwarfs* may have been conceived as "black spirits" by relative comparison. But the "two classes of creatures were getting confounded", and there arose a need to coin the term "Light-Elf" (*Ljósálfar* or *Hvítálfar* – "White Elves") to refer to the "Elves proper". This was counterpart to the "Dark-Elf" (*Dökkálfar* or *Svartálfar* – "Black Elves"). Preferring it over duality, Grimm postulated three kinds of Elves (Ljósálfar, Dökkálfar, Svartálfar) present in Norse mythology.

Dooinney-Oie

In Manx foklore the *Dooinney-Oie* or the *Night-Man* is a kindly spirit or *Fairy*, who looks like an old man and lives in sea side caves. He warns away those who approach his cave by causing them to sprain their ankle or hurt themselves in some other way. Despite his desire to be alone he can be useful and warns of coming storms. He sometimes warns of an impending storm by shouting, sometimes by a misty appearance of a man figure who speaks and gives the warning, and sometimes by the blowing of a horn, which sounds a bit like a Swiss alpen-horn. Another creature called *Howlaa* seems almost indistinguishable from Dooinney-Oie, except that he never speaks, but only howls before storms.

Draugr or Draug

The *Draugr* or *Draug* (Old Norse: *Draugr*, pl. *Draugar*; modern Icelandic: *Draugur*, Faroese: *Dreygur* and Danish, Swedish, and Norwegian: *Draug*) is an undead creature from the Scandinavian saga literature and folktale. Draug means *spöke* (ghost) in Old Norse and Icelandic and is also referred to as a corpse ghost, as they are material Revenants rather than spirits. The Draugr is usually dangerous and hideous. It has superhuman strength, can change its body size (along with its weight), and is followed by an odor of decay. It retains traces of its intelligence and enjoys the suffering it causes. It emerges from its tomb in the form of smoke and changes shape. Draugar, at least in some cases, remain in their burial mound and attack grave robbers who try to seize the treasures buried with the deceased. Often, out of jealousy, the Draug would climb into a rich man's grave and guard the treasures as if they were his own.

In folk tales, Draugar could murder their victims in many ways, such as driving their victims mad, crushing them with their enormous weight, or eating their flesh and drinking their blood. As with Vampires and zombies, the Draugr's victims could become Draugar themselves. Draugar are driven by jealousy and greed, and often attack the living out of envy for possessing what they themselves now lack in death. They are also said to have an insatiable hunger.

A common way to avoid Revenants was to drive a stake through the body of the dead, just like with Vampires. That way, the corpse was nailed in place and prevented from haunting. Complete destruction of the body could also be achieved by burning the dead person at the stake and scattering the ashes into the sea.

Famous Draugar in Norse mythology are perhaps most notably the *Dreaded Glam* of *Grette's Tale*. In the tale there is both a brief description of it as alive, and a detailed account of its existence as a Draugr, until Grette beats it back to health. Another, somewhat unusual example of a Draugr, is the hero Gunnar in Njáls's tale, who becomes a Draugr after his death. *Draugadrotten* (Icelandic: *Draugadróttinn* "Lord of the Revenants") was one of Odin's nicknames.

Dreag or death-light

In Scotland the *Dreag* was a light seen in the sky, leaving a tail *(dreallsach)* behind it, and, according to some, stopping above the house where a death was soon to occur; according to others, proceeding from above the house to the churchyard, along the line the funeral procession was to take. The Dreag was seen only when a person of consequence was about to die. It was also a belief that if the death-light went along the road a funeral procession was to take.

Duergar

In the folklore of northern England, the *Duergars*, also known as *Simonside dwarfs*, *Brownmen* or *Bogles* are a very unpleasant local dwarf-species, particularly associated with the Simonside Hills of Northumberland. The word Duergar is most likely derived from the Old Norse word for dwarfs *(Dvergar)*, but may also come from the dialectal words for dwarf on the Anglo-Scottish border, which include *Dorch, Dwerch, Duerch, Duergh* and *Duerwe*, among others, often with the added Norse -ar (pl.). In F. Grice's telling of the traditional story *The Duergar in Folk Tales of the North Country* (1944), one of them is described as being short, wearing a lambskin coat, moleskin trousers and shoes, and a hat made of moss decorated with a feather. They do not tend to attack humans directly, but instead cause a great nuisance themselves by removing and reversing directional sign-posts, blocking paths and even trying to guide humans over the edges of cliffs and crags. The Simonside dwarfs were mentioned in the local newspaper, the *Morpeth Gazette*, in 1889, and in Margaret Tyndale's *Legends and Folklore of Northumbria*, 1930. These dwarfs delighted in leading travelers astray, especially after dark, often carrying lighted torches to lead them into bogs, rather like a *Will-o'-the-wisp*. The menacing creatures would often disappear at dawn. Duergars are strictly nocturnal and are almost always encountered in isolation, yet on rare occasions they have been said to congregate in packs in the vicinity of the Simonside Hills, near Rothbury. Their leader was said to be known as *Heslop*.

Duergar mythology

The book *Fairy Mythology* of Thomas Keightley gives us a more mythological picture of the Duerga; as Earth-spirits and extraordinary skilled dwarfish workmen in metals:

"These diminutive beings, dwelling in rocks and hills, and distinguished for their skill in metallurgy, seem to particularly belong to the Gotho-German mythology. Perhaps the most credible account of them is, that they are personifications of the subterraneous powers of nature; for it may be again observed that all parts of every ancient mythology are but personified powers, attributes, and moral qualities. The Edda thus describes their origin: 'Then the gods sat on their seats, and held a council, and called to mind how the Duergar had become animated in the clay below in the earth, like maggots in flesh. The Duergar had been first created, and had taken life in Ymir's flesh, and were maggots in it, and by the will of the gods 'they became partakers of human knowledge, and had the likeness of men, and yet they abode in the ground and in stones. "Modsogner" was the first of them, and then "Dyrin".' The Duergar are described as being of low stature, with short legs and long arms, reaching almost down to the ground when they stand erect. They are skillful and expert workmen in gold, silver, iron, and the other metals. They make many wonderful and extraordinary things for the "Aeser", and for mortal heroes, and the arms and armor that come from their forges are not to be paralleled. Yet the gift must be spontaneously bestowed, for misfortune attends those extorted from them by violence."

Dullahan and Cóiste-bodhar

In Ireland a *Dullahan* is a headless phantom. An omen that sometimes accompanied the *Banshee* is the coach-a-bower (*Cóiste-bodhar*), an immense black coach, mounted by a coffin, and drawn by headless horses driven by a Dullahan. It would go rumbling to someone's door, and if the person opened it, a basin of blood was thrown in the persons face. These headless phantoms are also found elsewhere than in Ireland. In 1807 two of the sentries stationed outside St. James's Park died of fright. A headless woman, the upper part of her body naked, used to pass by at midnight and scale the railings. After a time the sentries were stationed no longer at the haunted spot. In Norway the heads of corpses were cut off, to make their ghosts feeble. This – according to one folkloristic theory – brought the Dullahans into existence.

Dunters

Dunters, also called *Powries*, are sprites that inhabit forts, old castles, peel-towers, or dungeons of the border country between Scotland and England, as a less malevolent form of the more sinister *Redcaps*. They constantly make a noise there, as of beating flax, or bruising barley in the hollow of a stone. The folklorist William Henderson reports in his book *Notes on the Folk-Lore of the Northern Counties* (1879) that any increase in the volume of the noise is an omen of death or misfortune. According to tradition, the foundations of such towers and castles, supposedly built by the Picts, were sprinkled with the blood of a human or animal sacrifice, and the Dunters, like the Redcaps, are the spirits of those victims.

E

Each-uisge

The *Each-uisge* (also: *Each-uisgee, Each-uisce* – anglicized as *Aughisky* or *Ech-ushkya* in Ireland and *Cabyll-ushtey* on the Isle of Man) literally means "Water-horse". It is an aquatic, shape-shifting creature of the Fairy realm or the Otherworld in Scottish folklore, usually taking the form of a horse, similar to the *Kelpie*, although a Kelpie inhabits streams, pools and rivers, while the Each-uisge lives in the sea, sea lochs, and fresh water lochs. The Each-uisge is a shapeshifter, disguising itself as a fine horse, a pony, a handsome man or an enormous bird, such as a *Boobrie*. *In Fairy and Folk Tales of the Irish Peasantry* (1888), W. B. Yeats mentions the *Augh-ishka* or *Each-uisgé* as one of the many manifestations of the *Pooka* and describes it as a November-spirit:

> *"The Pooka, rectè Púca, seems essentially an animal spirit. Some derive his name from poc, a he-goat; and speculative persons consider him the forefather of Shakespeare's "Puck". On solitary mountains and among old ruins he lives, "grown monstrous with much solitude," and is of the race of the nightmare. 'In the MS. story, called Mac-na-Michomhairle, of uncertain authorship,' writes me Mr. Douglas Hyde, 'we read that 'out of a certain hill in Leinster, there used to emerge as far as his middle, a plump, sleek, terrible steed, and speak in human voice to each person about November-day, and he was accustomed to give intelligent and proper*

90
E

answers to such as consulted him concerning all that would befall them until the November of next year. And the people used to leave gifts and presents at the hill until the coming of Patrick and the holy clergy.' This tradition appears to be a cognate one with that of the Púca. Yes! Unless it were merely an augh-ishka [each-uisgé], or Water-horse. For these, we are told, were common once, and used to come out of the water to gallop on the sands and in the fields, and people would often go between them and the marge and bridle them, and they would make the finest of horses if only you could keep them away from the sight of the water; but if once they saw a glimpse of the water, they would plunge in with their rider, and tear him to pieces at the bottom. It being a November spirit, however, tells in favour of the Pooka, for November-day is sacred to the Pooka. It is hard to realise that wild, staring phantom grown sleek and civil. He has many shapes—is now a horse, now an ass, now a bull, now a goat, now an eagle. Like all spirits, he is only half in the world of form."

The Each-uisge can be encountered mainly in the form of a beautiful strapping stallion, noble horse or pony. It waits near the shore or the beach for people who – deceived by the magnificent figure – are lured to mount the horse. When a human is mounted, the Each-uisge immediately pushes off in the direction of the sea or lake. Due to a sticky substance that the Water-horse secretes on its back, the victim is no longer able to dismount from the animal's back or let himself fall off. After the creature reaches its wet element, it swims far out to sea or to the deepest part of the hole, drowns its rider, and almost completely consumes its human prey. Only the liver is not eaten. The human organ is driven to shore after an attack, which serves as an indication to the locals that the Water-horse has once again claimed a human life. As long as the horse is ridden on land, it is harmless, but the smell of water or the slightest accumulation of water means the fatal end of its unsuspecting rider. The Scottish Each-uisge is considered the most vicious and dangerous of all Water Horses.

When the creature assumes the human form it is usually to attract women. It can be recognized only by the water plants in its hair. Therefore, people in the Scottish Highlands approached by strangers and stray animals react suspiciously and extremely hesitantly. John Gregorson Campbell states that *"any woman upon whom it set its mark was certain at last to become its victim."* A young woman herding cattle encountered a Water-horse

in the form of a handsome young man who laid his head in her lap and
fell asleep. When he stretched himself she discovered that he had horse's
hooves and quietly made her escape (in variations of the tale she finds the
presence of water weeds or sand in his hair). In another account a Water-
horse in human shape came to a woman's house where she was alone,
and attempted to court her, but all he got for his unwanted advances was
boiling water hurled between his legs. He ran from the house roaring in
pain. In a third tale a father and his three sons conspired to kill a Water-
horse in the guise of a handsome young man, that came to the house to see
the daughter. When they grabbed the young man he reverted to his equine
form and would have carried them into the loch, but in the struggle they
managed to slay him with their dirks (long bladed thrusting daggers).
Despite its amorous tendencies, however, the Each-uisge is just as likely to
simply devour women in the same manner as its male victims.

Ellefolk

The *Ellefolk* are the *Elves* of Danish folklore. They live in the moors.
People are advised to keep their cattle away from the places where the
Ellefolk have been, or the animals may be stricken by some grievous
disease, which can only be cured by giving them a handful of St. John's
Wort, that has to be picked at twelve o'clock on St. John's night. It is also
possible that the cattle may sustain some injury by mixing with those of
the Elves, which are very large and blue and live on dew. To prevent this
from happening, a farmer has to go to the *Elle-hill* when he is turning
out his cattle, and say: *"Thou little Troll! May I graze my cows on thy
hill?"* If it is not prohibited, no harm will come to his animals. In Danish
folklore, the female members of the Ellefolk are young and fair with an
attractive countenance, but they are hollow at the back side. Young men
find it difficult to resist her, and with a stringed instrument she ravishes
their hearts. She is the Danish representative of the *Huldra* or *Skogsrå* of
Sweden and Norway. She is most frequently seen dancing in high grass
in the moonlight. The male members of the Ellefolk are the opposite of
the youthful females. According to Irish folklorist Thomas Keightley (*The
Fairy Mythology: Illustrative of the Romance and Superstition*, 1892) he
appears as an old man wearing a flat hat. He is often seen on the moors,
bathing himself in the sunbeams. If someone comes too close to him,
he will open his mouth and breathes upon that person, and his breath
produces sickness and pestilence.

Ellyl Idan

The *Ellyl Idan* is an *Elf*-like species, according to Wirt Sikes, corresponding to the English *Will-o'-the-wisp* or *Ignis fatuus*, the Scandinavian *Lyktgubbe*, the Breton *Sand Yan y Tad*, etc. The Welsh word *dan* means both "fire" and "a lure", thus the compound word suggests a "luring fire". Like all Goblins of this class, the Ellyl Idan was seen dancing about on marshy grounds, into which it led the belated wanderer. The Breton *Sand Yan y Tad* (St. John and Dad) – mentioned in Thomas Keightley's *Fairy Mythology* – is a double *Ignis fatuus-fairy*, carrying at its fingertips five lights, that are spinning around like a wheel. It moved with the French colonists to the southern states of the US, were the black population renamed it *Jack Muh Lantern*. They describe it as a hideous creature, five feet in height, with goggling eyes and a huge mouth, its body covered with long hair, and leaping and bounding through the air like a gigantic grasshopper. This frightful apparition is stronger than any man, and swifter than any horse, and compels its victims to follow it into the swamp, where it leaves them to die.

Ellyll

The *Ellyll* (pl.: *Ellyllon*) is descibed as a tiny, diaphanous creature, usually classified as a solitary *Fairy* or pigmy *Elf*, from Welsh folklore. The Ellyllon haunt the groves and valleys and are smaller than the *Tylwyth teg*, the better-known Welsh Fairies. Their food is specified in Welsh folk-lore as Fairy butter and Fairy food, *ymenyn tylwyth teg* and *bwyd ellyllon*; the latter is a kind of poisonous mushroom, the former a butter-resembling substance found at great depths in the crevices of limestone rocks, created by digging for lead ore. *Queen Mab* was believed to be the ruler of the Ellyllon. According to some folkloric tales the Ellyllon are the wandering souls of ancient druids, too good for hell and not good enough for heaven. The bells of the *Digitalis purpurea*, or fox-glove, are called *Menyg Ellylon*, "Elves' Gloves".

F

Faery People

The first detailed account of the *Faery People* of the Gaelic race was
made by the Reverend Robert Kirk in 1691. Faery or Faery People are
the same creatures as *Fairies*, but this paragraph is included because it
contains interesting data from the 17th century, when people first started
to write about them. Robert Kirk's book remained in manuscript till
it was discovered by Sir Walter Scott in 1815. It was called *The Secret
Commonwealth, an essay 'of the nature of the subterranean (and for the
most part invisible people) heretofore going under the names of Elves, fays,
and faeries'*. Kirk, a seventh son, said to have been gifted with second
sight, was a Gaelic scholar, a translator into Gaelic of the Psalms. Kirk
died a year after he had finished his manuscript or, as the people of his
parish said, was taken by the Faeries. The Reverend William Taylor,
a pastor of Abberfoyle, Kirk's old hometown, told folklorist Walter
Evans-Wentz (1878 - 1965) it was generally believed that at the time of
Kirk's death, the faeries had carried him off because he had looked too
deeply into their secrets. He seems to have fainted while walking upon
a Faery knoll (mount), a little way from his own door, and to have died
immediately.

Kirk describes "the subterranean people" or "the abstruse people," as he
sometimes calls them, much as they are described today in Galway or
in Mayo. He is clear that they are not demons and like Father Sinistrari,
a Catholic theologian of Padua, quotes the Scriptures in support of this
opinion. In his *Notes*, W.B. Yeats included several quotes from Robert
Kirk about the Faery People, which contrast strongly with the current
image of Fairies:

*"The "abstruse people" are not indeed without sin, though mid-way
between men and angels, but being in no way "drenched into so gross
and dredgy bodies as we are especially given to the more spiritual and
haughty sins." "Whatever their own laws, be sure according to ours and
equity natural civil and revealed" tThey do wrong by "their stealing of
nurses to their children and that other sort of Plaginism in catching
our children away (may seem to heir some estate in those invisible*

dominions) which never return. For the inconvenience of their succubi who tryst with men it is abominable, but for swearing and intemperance they are not observed so subject to this irregularity as to envy, spite, hypocrisy, lying, and simulation." Some have thought the spirit controls of our best mediums no better. "They are not subject to sore sickness, but dwindle and decay at a certain period all about ane age" and "they pass after a long healthy life into one orb and receptacle fitted to their degree till they come under the general cognism at the last day. "They are the "Sleagh Math or the good people" being called so by the "Irish" [. . .] "to prevent the dint of their ill-attempts" and being "of a middle nature betwixt man and angel" have "intelligent, studious spirits, and light changeable bodies (like those called astral) somewhat of the nature of a condensed cloud and best seen in twilight. Their bodies are so pliable through the subtlety of the spirits that agitate them that they can make them appear or disappear at pleasure. Some have bodies or vehicles so spongeous, thin, and desiccate, that they are fed by only sucking into some fine spirituous liquors that pierce like pure air and oil; others feed more gross on the foisone or substance of corns and liquors or corn itself that grows upon the surface of the earth which these faeries steal away, partly invisible, partly preying on the grain as do crows and mice."

Fairies

A *Fairy* (also *fay, fae, fey, fair folk,* or *faerie, faery*) is a generic English term for nature-spirits and other spirit-beings found in the folklore of multiple European cultures (including Celtic, Slavic, Germanic, English, and French folklore), often related to the Otherworld and sometimes to deceased humans, who appear in new forms as members of a unique class of entities. Fairies are usually reduced to the popular cliche picture of small creatures, hovering in the air like Peter Pan's Tinkerbell and being the size of a thumb or flower. Originally the Fairy as such does not exist in one fixed form, but is a blanket-term for a very divers family tree of supernatural creatures and a very varied folkloric history. The Fairy can be found in some form or other in almost every nation. From the Indian to the Iranian and Chinese lore, there are quite similar magical creatures to be found everywhere, with either evil or good intentions, that occupy a higher or at least a separate part of existence from man, but that have not yet reached the divine sphere. Their place in European folklore and the way they are portrayed varies from period to period, but they are

Puck and the Fairy by John Moyr Smith (1854-1912)

at least similar, if not identical, from one people to another. The reason for this is primarily historical, due to the infiltration of Greek culture into Roman culture, the expansion of the Roman Empire, and then the unifying efforts of the Christian Church in the Middle Ages, as well as the Renaissance's reverence for antiquity.

The label "Fairy" has at times applied only to specific magical creatures with a human appearance, magical powers, and a penchant for trickery. Fairy is sometimes used to describe any magical creature, including Goblins and Gnomes, while at other times, the term describes only a specific type of ethereal creature or *Sprite*. Fairy has at times been used as an adjective, with a meaning equivalent to "enchanted" or "magical". A recurring motif of legends about Fairies is the need to ward off Fairies by using protective charms. Common examples of such charms include church bells, wearing ones clothing inside out, a four-leaf clover, and food. Fairies were also sometimes thought to haunt specific locations, and to lead travelers astray using *Will-o'-the-wisps*. Before the advent of modern medicine, Fairies were often blamed for sickness, particularly tuberculosis and birth deformities. In addition to their folkloric origins, Fairies were a common feature of Renaissance literature and Romantic art, and were especially popular in the United Kingdom during the Victorian and Edwardian eras. The Celtic Revival also saw Fairies established as a canonical part of Celtic cultural heritage.

Etymology and origins of Fairy evolution
The English *Fairy* derives from the Early Modern English *faerie*, meaning "realm of the fays". Faerie, in turn, derives from the Old French form *faierie*, a derivation from *faie* (Latin: *fata*) with the abstract noun suffix *-erie*. In Old French romance, a *faie* or *fee* was a woman skilled in magic, who knew the power and virtue of words, stones, and herbs. Latinate *fay* is not related the Germanic *fey* (from Old English *fǣġe*), meaning "fated to die". Yet, this unrelated Germanic word "*fey*" may have been influenced by Old French *Fae* (*Fay* or *Fairy*) as the meaning had shifted slightly to "fated" from the earlier "doomed" or "accursed". The goddesses of *fatum*, *fate*, the *Parcae*, were transmitted to the Romans from Greek mythology, and were originally the *Moiras*, weavers of human fate. They were mostly imagined as figures independent of the gods, or even above them. However, some types of Fairy themselves show a very strong connection with the Greek Nymphs. In particular, there are many similarities

with the various forms of *Nymphs*: *Naiads*, *Nereids*, *Dryads*, which are represented as lake or Water-Fairies or Forest-Fairies; these forms were also shaped by the role and form of the hunting deities *Artemis/Diana*. They may also have been influenced by the Roman *Genii*, the spirits of goodness. Various folklore traditions refer to Fairies euphemistically as: *Wee folk*, *Good folk*, *People of peace*, *Fair folk* (Welsh: *Tylwyth Teg*), etc.

As each people populated its own world with many mythical, magical creatures, it was inevitable that the figures would blend when different cultures met. This was also the case with the Fairy, since the peoples of Europe – Celts, Germanic peoples, Slavs – also had other wondrous figures similar to, but somewhat different from, the Greek *Nymphs*, *Moirs*, Roman *Lares* and *Genii*, the Germanic *Norns*, *Valkyries*, Scandinavian *Trolls* and the *Fairies* of the Balkans: the South Slavic *Vila* and *Samodiva*, *Samovila*, the Albanian, Romanian *Zinâ*. After all these years, it is practically impossible to say which people can claim the most varied – and periodically changing – Fairy representations in the history of universal culture.

The Fairies of Celtic lore

The English/Irish Fairies were primarily shaped by the lore of Celtic mythology. The very word Fairy in the Anglo-Saxon language today means a tiny ethereal being with wings, living in a world of its own, who only interacts with humans on rare occasions, very similar to the much-loved treasure-hunting, mischievous Elf of Irish fairytales. But the world of the Irish Celtic Fairies is not so simple. There are many different kinds: *Banshee* (death messenger), *Finn* (mischievous spirit), *Gnoll*, *Gnome*, *Goblin*, *Miner*, *Brownie* or *Bwca*, and many other spirits, dwarves, *Water-Fairies*, *Mermaids* and other strange *half-Elves* that are difficult to distinguish from Fairies. Irish history and mythology present a varied picture of these creatures. The struggles and memories of the magical people who inhabited the island before the Irish Gaelic settlers are preserved in mythology. The magical creatures of the time, who after the Irish conquest were living in underground caves and caverns, play a major role in this. The ruler of these peoples (formerly known as *Tuatha Dé Danan*), the Dagda, and his descendants, continued to be central to Irish life and fables. The Irish often associate the concept of the afterlife with their realms. There are many such realms in the Irish tradition, some of the most notable being *Tír na nÓg* (Land of Youth), *Tír Tairngire* (Land of Promise), *Tír na mBan* (Land of Women). Another saga also deals with the realm of *Avalon*, which is likewise invisible to humans through the magic of Fairies and difficult to reach.

In English, there is another word for Fairy: *Elf*. Its meaning is complex and multifaceted; it can mean a tiny, evil little creature living underground, even dangerous to humans, it can mean the 'heroic' Fairy, but also other wondrous creatures. It does not only cover one or more specific creatures, but also includes the impersonators of the forces of nature themselves, working quietly in the background. The name is derived from Germanic mythology, and is also found in German, in the form of *Elf* or *elbe*, but also in similar forms and meanings among the Scandinavian peoples.

The Fairy-cult of the Balkans

The Balkan peoples have a specific Fairy-cult. It is mostly reminiscent of the Greek *Nymphs*, but it also has its own characteristics. The main characteristic of the Slavic Fairy, the *Vili*, is that most of its features have become witch-like, especially in Hungary, and its meaning has been merged with the meaning of the Fairy and witch in many places, such as Beauteous Woman, White Woman, Little Woman. But there are also other specific features: not only did the Slavic peoples have female Fairies with potentially harmful intentions, they also had Fairies in the form of thunderstorms and animals. The appearance of the *Vilik* often takes the form of a storm or whirlwind, also known as the dance of the Vilik. An interesting example of zoomorphic Fairies is the *Horse-Fairy*, the so-called *Todor-horse*. Another peculiarity of Slavic Fairies is their periodic appearance, linked to a calendar date or a special occasion. One more difference between the Slavic and medieval and Renaissance western folklore is the degree of danger of the Fairies; Slavic Fairies are more harmful than their western brothers and sisters.

Fear Gortagh

In Irish folklore *Fear Gortagh* (Hungry Grass"; also: *Féar Gortac*) is a distorted *Genius Loci*, that came into existence because one or more people died on that spot of starvation. The hunger, impregnated in the field, is said to cause a feeling of weakness, accompanied by a terrible longing for food, which comes over one even though it may be but a short time since eating. Some have suggested that Fear Gortagh is a Fairy curse.

It is said that someone who was eating bread walked by on this spot and let no crumbs fall, which caused the Fairies to curse the spot, because they were hungry and had he let any crumbs fall they would have eaten them and thus satisfied their hunger. One bite of oat-bread is sufficient to banish the hunger and someone having a picnic does well to spill some bread, as this act wards off the Fairy curse. Yet this Fairy-theory is less standard than the famine-theory of the Hungry Grass origin.

In general, and not restricted to Ireland, extreme human emotions can leave such a haunted location. Especially battle fields, sites where a serious accident took place and suicide locations can do the job. A feature of these distorted and negative genii loci is that the echo of the event can contaminate passersby, especially sensitive people, and affect them in a minor or sometimes even extreme way, thus causing a new traumatic event which enforces the spot or the negative Genius Loci. Today "Loaded Locations" are sometimes created deliberately by chaos magicians, usually with positive intentions and vibes, called *Chao-mines*.

Fír Gorta, the Man of Hunger
The term *Fír Gorta* or *Fear Gorta* seems often interchangeable with Fear Gortagh and Fear Gortac. The Fear Gortach I have just described, while *Fear Gorta* is more often used to denote a kind of famine-spirit, an anthropomorphic offspring of the Hungry Grass. He is a skeletal looking man that knocks on the doors and acts as a blessing when he is offered some food, but as a curse when food is refused. He is also depicted as a bad omen in general, announcing that a famine will soon strike the region or country. According to Yeats' *Fairy and Folk Tales of the Irish Peasantry* the *Fir Gorta* walks the Earth during times of famine, seeking alms from passers-by. In this version, the Fir Gorta can be a potential source of good luck for generous individuals. Steenie Harvey (in *Twilight places: Ireland's enduring Fairy Lore,* 1998) relates a myth that the Fir Gorta was a harbinger of famine during the Great Irish Famine of the 1840s, and that the spirit originally arose from a patch of Hungry Grass (Féar Gortach). In the region of Kiltubbrid, however, the term is also used to refer to a sudden hunger that can seize people traveling in the mountains, that will become fatal if not quickly satisfied.
I came across the following fragment preserved in the Irish *National Folklore Collection* (published at *duchas.ie* by the *University College Dublin*):

*"On the east side of Thanney Crag is a little múchán or heap of stones
marking the place where a man was found dead of féar gortach.
Close to Ballinaboy and on the Belderrig-Belmullet road there are
two muacháns within a hundred yards of each other where people
were found dead on different occasions of féar gortach it was believed.
On the road from Glenamoy to Rossport at Muingnabo is another
muachán where another man was found dead from féar gortach."*

Fenodyree

In the folklore of the Isle of Man a *Fenodyree* (also *Phynodderee,
Phynnodderee, Fynnoderee* or *Fenoderee*), is a supernatural creature, a
sort of *Sprite, Fairy* or *household-spirit* (Manx: *Ferrishyn*) covered with
copious amounts of body hair, and normally conducting itself in a naked
state without wearing any clothing. William Ralph Hall Caine (in *Isle
of Man*, 1909) suggests *"it was a giant, big and shaggy, with fiery eyes,
and stronger than any man"*, and I. H. Leney explains it measured only
two feet in height, still making it a "giant" among the "Good People"
(Fairies). The Fenodyree carries out chores to help humans, just like
the *Brownies* of the larger areas of Scotland and England, performing
arduous tasks like transporting large, heavy stones or clipping meadow
grass with stupendous speed. For his talent in the grass-cutting skill, he
has earned the nickname *Yn Foldyr* Gastey or *the Nimble Mower*. He also
helped herding cattle and repaired the nets of fishermen. A bit of leftover
food was all he asked for a reward. A gift of clothing would drive the
Fenodyree away, as attested in several tales.

The etymology of the word Fenodyree is very inconclusive, because of
several options. Fenodyree consists of the Manx words *fynney* (hair, fur)
and *oashyree* (stockings), possibly from the Swedish word *fjun* (down)
although this "hairy stockings" etymology may be conjectural. John Rhys
observes that *oashyr* was apparently borrowed from *hosur* (pl. of the Old
Norse *hosa*; compares with the German *Hose* "pants"). Fenodyree has
also been glossed simply as "the hairy one", or "something hairy" in Manx
by Joseph Train and J. F. Campbell after him. John Kelly's dictionary has
suggested an alternate etymology, stemming from *fenney* (invaders, wild
Irish). The term has also been used in the sense of "Satyr" in the 1819
Manx translation of the *Bible* (Isaiah 34:14) by Kelly. In one tale, the
Phynnodderee appears as a former Ferrish, a Knight of the Fairy Court.

He was transformed into a grotesque Satyr-like being as punishment, after falling in love with a human girl from Glen Aldyn, and skipping attendance of the royal high festivities.

Nimble mower
A tale attached to a round meadow in the parish of Marown held that a Phynnodderee had a habit of cutting and gathering the meadow grass there with a scythe, until a farmer criticized the job for not mowing the grass close enough to ground. The hairy Phynnodderee then ceased his mowing and *"went after him, stubbing up the roots so fast that it was with difficulty the farmer could escape, having his legs almost cut off by the angry sprite"*. Afterwards no one could succeed in mowing this meadow, until a knight devised a way to start at the center and clip the grass in a circular pattern.

Fépükar
Fépükar are money devils, in Icelandic lore, whose root lies in misers, who, when they die, cannot separate from their gold, money or possessions and therefore hide them in a certain place – which they then come to visit regularly. New Icelandic folktales tell how the Fépükar come every night to count their money and throw it over their heads in a playful manner. Like the *Alfr* and *Night-Trolls*, they do not want to be surprised by the daylight; at day break they prefer to abandon their money and sink into the ground. Sometimes a ghostly fire, a *vafurlogi* or *malmlogi* is seen burning at the place where they have hidden their treasures. In the sagas this is known under the name of *haugaeldr*.

Fiery-eyed horses
In British folklore there are several tales about *fiery-eyed horses, foals, donkeys* or *calves*. They are regarded as phantom-animals or shape-shifting *Bogies* who can take many forms. In Lincolnshire there was the *Shag-foal* who had a deep black color and could also appear as a dog, and the "shagg'd-looking" *Tatter-foal*, who liked to scare old ladies. Katharine Briggs also mentions the *Eli Twigg*, and the *Hedley Kow*, who could take the shape of a cow.

Fin(n)folk

In Orkney folklore, *Finfolk* or *Finnfolk* are sorcerous shapeshifters of the sea who regularly make an amphibious journey. The Finfolk were said to have two homes: the magical underwater world of Finfolkaheem where they lived in the winter, and the island of *Hildaland*. They were believed to wade, swim or sometimes row upon the Orkney shores in the spring and summer months, searching for human captives. The Finfolk (both *Finman* and *Finwife*) kidnap unsuspecting fishermen, or frolicking youth, near the shore and force them into lifelong servitude as a spouse.

Finmen are tall and thin with a stern, gloomy face. They have many magical powers, such as rowing between Norway and Orkney in seven oar-strokes, making their ship invisible and creating fleets of phantom boats. Finmen avoid human contact, but are extremely territorial and will wreak havoc on the boats of any fishermen trespassing in their waters. One could protect oneself against Finmen by drawing a cross on the bottom of a craft with chalk or tar, because Finfolk abhor the sign of the Christian cross above any other device.

Finwifes start their life as beautiful Mermaids, bent on acquiring a human husband. When they succeed, they take them to *Finfolkaheem*. In other stories a Finwife follows her human husband to live in his home instead. If she does not succeed to find a human male, the Finwife has to take a Finman husband and is often made to go ashore to work as a healer or spinner by her cruel Finman-husband, where she is forced to send all her silver home or risk a terrible beating. She often owns a black cat that can transform itself into a fish to deliver messages to her kin in Finfolkaheem. Another curse that befalls a Finwife should she marry a Finman, is that she loses both her beauty and mystical charm. As she ages (without a human husband), her ugliness increases in increments of seven years until she becomes the Finwife hag.

Unlike Selkies, the Finfolk are neither romantic nor friendly. Instead of courting the prospective spouse, Finfolk usually simply abduct them. The Finfolk's kidnapping attempt begins by approaching the prospective mate cautiously, floating ever closer, until it is possible to leap up and grab the victim. The Finmen often use another tactic, appearing in human form disguised as fishermen in a row boat, or a fishing boat propelled by oars. The Finwife prefers a more natural form, and often appears as a Mermaid with long, flowing golden hair, snow-white skin, incredible beauty, and, sometimes, a long fish tail. In some stories, she has a beautiful voice like that of the Greek Sirens. The Finfolk, in addition to their lust for humans, have a weakness for silver, including silver coins and jewelry. According to legend, a possible way to escape abduction is to exploit this Finfolk weakness by tossing silver coins away from oneself.

Finfolkaheem and Hildaland
The underwater dwelling of the Finfolk, known as Finfolkaheem (Finfolk's home) is regarded as the place of origin for the Finfolk, and their ancestral home. A fantastic under water palace with massive crystal halls, Finfolkaheem is surrounded, inside and out, by ornate gardens of multi-colored seaweed. It is never dark in Finfolkaheem, because it is lit by the phosphorescent glow of tiny sea creatures at night. Its great halls and vast rooms are decorated with draped curtains of which the colors move and dance with the underwater currents. Hildaland (Hidden Land), is a paradisiacal island that was said to either be invisible, hidden just underwater, or surrounded by magical fog. Nowadays, many people associate the very real island of Eynhallow with the magical Hildaland.

Fir darrig

In Irish mythology, the *Fir darrig*, *Far darrig* or in the Irish spelling *Fear dearg*, is described as a *Goblin* that is sometimes gigantic, sometimes tiny. They are also sometimes known as Rat Boys, as they are said to be rather fat, have dark, hairy skin, a long snout and a skinny tail. It is said that this Goblin has a tendency to force the inhabitants of a house to welcome him into their home reserving for him the best seat, by the fire. Then he will make himself comfortable and at home, even drying his filthy clothes soaked with his horrible odor, over the fireplace. If the inhabitants of the cottage do not comply, it is said that the Fir darrig will play all sorts of pranks on them and harass them relentlessly. The Fir darrig is described in particular as an entity that "engages in practical joking, especially with gruesome joking". One example of this is replacing babies with *changelings*. He is also said to have some connection to *Nightmares*. According to one folkloric tale, these Goblins are said to live in the cottages, between the ceiling and the thatched roof. Their role would usually be to play bad tricks on the inhabitants, but also, in case of danger, to protect them. Physically, the Fir darrig resembles his cousins,

the Leprechauns and the Cluricaunes, except that he often dresses in red
(Fear Dearg means "Red Man" in Irish and in Scottish Gaelic). With the
classic field-spirit, the Fir darrig had in common that whoever finished
shearing the sheep last had to feed the Goblin until the next harvest.

Flyðrumóðir

The *Flyðrumóðir*, or "Halibut Mother" (pl. *Flyðrumóðirin*), is a
representative of the Icelandic *Móðirin*, the "Mothers" of certain fish-
species. These creatures look like huge, monstrous versions of their
namesakes, and they protect their smaller kin fiercely. See also the
paragraph on *Skötumóðir* (Skate Mother). *There are also the* Salmon
Mother or *Laxamóðir* and Trout Mother or *Silungamóðir*. A Flyðrumóðir
looks like the halibut it protects, but it is much larger, growing to the
size of a fishing boat. Its body, which turns grey on both sides with age,
is covered with shells, barnacles, and seaweed, making it look like a
small island when it surfaces. The creature has supernatural powers and
messing with it is dangerous, or brings bad luck. A fishing boat, owned by
the Archdeacon Hannes Stephensen, by accident caught a Flyðrumóðir
on a coffin-nail hook and was capsized by the Halibut Mother whereby
all fishermen drowned. After the Halibut Mother of Breiðafjörður was
caught on a golden hook and filleted, the waters of the area abruptly
ceased to produce fish, and the angler who caught the giant halibut never
again caught a fish in his life.

Fossegrim or Grim

Fossegrim, also known simply as *the Grim* (Norwegian) or *Strömkarlen*
(Swedish), is a *water-spirit* or *Troll* in Scandinavian folklore. Fossegrim
plays the fiddle, especially the Hardanger fiddle. He has been associated
with a mill-spirit (*kvernknurr*) and as a water-spirit (*neck*) – he is
sometimes also called *Näcken* in Sweden. *Strömkarlen*, his Swedish name,
means *River Man,* and the Norse term *foss* means waterfall – a waterfall
being one of his favorite dwelling places. Fossegrim is described as an
exceptionally talented fiddler. He is said to be willing to teach his skills to
a human musician in exchange for:
• A food offering made on a Thursday evening and in secrecy: a white
  he-goat thrown – with its head turned away – into a waterfall that flows
  northwards,

• or smoked mutton (*fenalår*) stolen from the neighbors' storage four
  Thursdays in a row.

If there is not enough meat on the bone, he will only teach the supplicant
how to tune the fiddle. If the offering is satisfactory, he will take the
pupil's right hand and draw the fingers along the strings until they all
bleed, after which the student will be able to play so well that *"the trees
shall dance and torrents in their fall stand still"*. Famous fiddlers who were
rumored to have learnt from the Fossegrim include Torgeir Augundsson
(1801-1872), known as Myllarguten, and Ole Bull (1810-1880), whose
statue in the center of Bergen actually depicts a Fossegrim playing his
fiddle under the falling water.

Freybug

Freybug is a monstrous Black Dog that is said to originate from medieval
English folklore, specifically from Norfolk. Like most supernatural black
dogs, it was roughly the size of a calf, and wandered along country roads,
terrifying travelers. The English martyr Laurence Saunders mentioned
Fray-bugs in his letters to his wife in 1555. The word Fray-bug is defined
by the Oxford English Dictionary as "an object of fear; a bogy, a specter".
The quite similar word "fray-boggart" meant scarecrow. *Popular
Antiquities of Great Britain*, by John Brand, referenced Saunders' letters
and suggested that the Fray-bug was a Black Dog, similar to the *Barghest*.
Carol Rose seems to have drawn on Brand's work for her description of
the Freybug.

Fridean

Fridean (singular: *Frìde*) are small subterranean *Fairies* of Scottish
Highland folklore. They live in the Earth or under rocks and devour all
spilled milk or breadcrumbs. In contrast to this cleaning service they
have some nasty side effects; in a widely known story a piper and his
dog follow the Fridean into a winding cavern, his music still being heard
by mortals above ground; the piper never returns, but the dog returns
hairless and subsequently immediately dies thereafter.

Fuath

Fuath in Scottish Gaelic literally means "hatred" or "aversion", derived from the Old Irish fúath "hate, likeness", but in Ross-shire it is a common word to denote an apparition, ghost, specter. An alternative name for this class of monsters is the *Arrachd* or *Fuath-arrachd*. The plural is *Fuathan*, and as their name suggests, in Scottish Highland folklore, they are a class of malevolent spirits, mostly water-spirits. This is however criticized by John Gregorson Campbell in *Witchcraft & Second Sight in the Highlands & Islands of Scotland*:

> *"The attributes of the Fuath are different in different tales, and Mr. [John Francis] Campbell ("Tales of the West Highlands", [189] ii. 191) has fallen into the error of conjoining attributes ascribed in several stories, and representing the Fuath as a water-spirit, having web-feet, tail, mane, etc. The name of a desolate moor near Ullapool, in Ross-shire, "The Flat-stoned Declivity of Fuaths" (Leathad leacanta nam Fuath), is alone convincing it was not deemed particularly a water-spirit."*

In Sutherland was the so-called *Moulin na Fouadh*, "Mill of the Fuath", haunted by a female Fuath and her son, the *Brollachan*. The mill was along a stream off Loch Migdale, and belonged to the Dempster family (Skibo Castle) estate. A Fuath once seen at this mill was a nose-less *Banshee* with yellow hair wearing a green silk dress; in the story of its capture it was tormented into submission by use of a sewing needle, but it turned into a jellyfish-like mass when light was shone on it. A Fuath on the estate farm, encountered on a different occasion, had webbed feet. They sometimes intermarry with human beings (typically the female), whose offspring develop a mane and tail. In a poem of the so called *Muireartach* or *Muileartach*, ("Western Sea", a hideous female with a fish tail), we find an extended description of the Fuath:

> *"The name of the daring spectre (fuath)*
> *Was the bold, red, white-maned Westlin Sea;*
> *Her face was dusky, of the hue of coal,*
> *The teeth of her jaws crooked red;*
> *In her head there glared a single eye,*
> *That swifter moved than bait-pursuing mackerel;*
> *And on her head there bristled dark-grey hair,*
> *Like brushwood covered with hoar-frost."*

Fylgja

Fylgja (pl. *Fylgjor*), or (Norse) *Fylgjur*; Old Swedish *Fylghia*, modern Swedish *följa* (companion), from Old Norse *fylgja*, (protecting, to follow), was in Norse mythology a supernatural (female) being that protected and followed a specific human it felt connected with. Fylgjor appear as female guardian-spirits for individuals and for kindreds. The protector of the family is also called *Fylgjukona*, i.e. the female follower, or also *Ättefölja*, or the Norse *Hamingja*. The word *fylgja* means "to accompany", similar to *Fetch* in Irish folklore. In Icelandic lore sometimes, if someone dies, his *Fylgja* can pass to one of his close relatives. His *Hamingja*, very impersonally thought of as "happiness" in general, can also be transferred to another person already during his life.

In some literature and sagas, the Fylgjor can take the form of mice, dogs, foxes, cats, birds of prey, or scavengers, because these were animals that would typically eat their afterbirths. Other ideas of Fylgjor are that the animals they chose to be, reflected the character of the person they attached themselves to. Men who had a "tame nature" were accompanied by a Fylgja in the shape of an ox, goat, or boar. If they had an "untame nature" they would have a Fylgja resembling a fox, wolf, deer, bear, eagle, falcon, leopard, lion, or a serpent. The animal a Fylgja is said to appear as, in front of its owner, often in dreams, offer portents of events to come. Fylgjor are also linked to the were-animal phenomena and may also mark shape shifting between human and animal. In Egil's Saga, there are references to both Egil and Skallagrim transforming into (were)wolves or (were)bears, and there are examples of shape shifting in the Saga of King Hrolf Kraki, where Bodvar Bjarki turns into a (were)bear during a battle.

The evolution of the Icelandic Fylgja

In Iceland the *Fylgjur* underwent an evolution through the ages, whereby they got fused with all kinds of other spirits or beings. Gradually the Fylgjur as accompanying protective spirits developed into female guardian spirits; the *Hamingja* and *Disir* can also be considered as such. Of the original meaning of the Disir as the female guardian-spirits of a god, no trace remains in the sagas. The Disir have become a whole lineage of Fylgjur, who assist a single person or an entire family in worldly and spiritual matters. The beliefs about the Disir showed early signs of adapting to a Christian way of thinking. Þiðrandi e.g., who wants to convert to Christianity, is mistreated by dark-dressed Disir, who are very upset about this fact; the light-dressed women, who will follow this family from now on, however, chase the black ones away. Often only "the Fylgjur" is spoken of, without any further description. Later on, the Fylgjur became evil, harmful followers instead of protective forces, whom people tried to get rid of by all possible means. This development must be explained by the fact that in Christian times all representations connected with ancient folklore ran the risk of being considered daemonic (or devilish). Furthermore, the Fylgjur no longer belonged only to people, but also to certain places, houses, ships, etc. These spirits include, first of all, *Afturgöngur* and *Uppvakningar*, dead people who have been brought back to life by sorcery, in order to be sent to enemies – also called *Sendingar*. In addition, there is also an entity, that is not of the *Draugr*-type, namely the afterbirth. This was considered as being part of the soul, so as something sacred and related to someone's destiny. One therefore handled it very carefully. If one buried the afterbirth somewhere outside the farm, the Fylgja could become malicious, because the creature that first flew or stepped over the place where the afterbirth was buried, determined the nature of the Fylgya. For this reason, anxious parents often buried the afterbirth under the threshold or in the place where the mother first stepped over it. If the afterbirth was thrown out at random, it would be torn to pieces by one or another animal and become a Fylgya. Since burial was not always sufficient, the afterbirth was later burned.

In the later stories we can find under the name of Fylgjur:
1. *Afturgöngur*, *Uppvakningar* and *Sendingar*
2. all kinds of animals
3. *Will-o'-the-wisp*-like light phenomena known as *Mfraljós*

Skottur and Mórar

Before a guest, accompanied by such a Fylgjur, arrives at a farm, people at the farm feel sleepy, often become restless, horses become skittish, dogs start barking, sometimes even cattle die. Either one hears all kinds of ghostly noises, and smells like a *fylgjulykt* (placenta smell). Of such sleepiness, caused by the *fylgjulykt* of an approaching enemy, we find examples already in the sagas as well: Svanr, complicit in the murder of Ósvifr's son, begins to yawn greatly when the wrathful father is on his way to avenge him. Conversely, Njall is unable to sleep when, in a kind of vision, he sees the spirits following Gunnar's enemies. Later all kinds of ghostly phenomena before a guest arrives are also explained simply by the fact that this person thinks very strongly of the farm to which he is on his way. According to the blacksmith Halldór Jónsson, when leaving home one should first walk for some time in the wrong direction and say prayers, then suddenly turn around and go forward again. The aforementioned evil Fylgjen in human form can be male as well as female, and are called *Skottur* (female) and *Mórar* (male), according to their appearance. The Skotta wears a dark brown cap on her head, which resembles the old-fashioned headgear of Icelandic women. Only the tip of the hat does not curve forward, but hangs back over the shoulders, almost like a tail. They wear red stockings and suck on their fingers. The Mórar wear a dark brown sweater and a broad-brimmed shallow hat; sometimes they carry a shepherd's staff. Almost every valley or farm has one such Skotta or Móri.

Fylgya as a Mare or an omen

Popular belief also ranks the Mare (Nightmare) among the Fylgyes; often a Mare or Alp can be regarded as the Fylgya of a coming guest. The Mare is sometimes depicted as a girl lying on top of the sleeping one (*alpdruk* in German) and trying to count his teeth. One then becomes powerless and cannot move; however, if one is able to give a cry, she disappears.

Mfraljós

Of the luminous *Fylgyes*, only the moon-shaped one is considered a bad Fylgya (e.g., the *Urdarmani*). After all, it has had a bad name from time immemorial. Icelandic lore tells of the farmstead Unaós that had a round fireball, as big as a fist, as a Fylgja. When it was in the barn, even in bad weather the cattle refused to enter the barn. *Mfraljós* (wandering lights) arise, people believed, when an afterbirth is thrown into the swamp. Finally, all kinds of animals, glowing balls, light phenomena and sounds often also announce bad weather. These are the so-called *Weather-Fylgyes*, something which fuses them with elemental spirits, like *Sylphs* or *Storm-Elementals*.

G

Gabble Ratchets

In British dialect *Gabble Ratchets* (as a plural) stood for a flock of birds (usually wild geese) making a noise in the nocturnal air, and imagined or represented as a gathering of supernatural creatures presaging death or misfortune, or as the souls of children that have died unbaptized. As a singular, *Gabble Ratchet* meant simply the noise made by these birds or creatures. In some parts of England the Ratchets or Gabble Rachets were phantom dogs, baying in the night and gathering in the sky above houses where someone was soon going to die. Given the geographical range of the belief, the exact nature of the Gabble Ratchets varied somewhat. In his *Notes on the Folk-Lore of the northern Counties of England and the borders,* 1879, folklorist William Henderson described them as *"monstrous human-headed dogs, who traverse the air, and are often heard although seldom seen."* Henderson adds that *"In the neighborhood of Leeds the phenomenon is held to be the souls of unbaptized children doomed to restlessly flit around their parents' home".* Gabble Rackets are often used as a synonym for *Gabriel Hounds.*

Gabriel Hounds

Gabriel Hounds are dogs with human heads that fly high through the air, and are often heard, but seldom seen. In his *Memoranda for 2nd March 1664,* reverend Oliver Heywood wrote: *"There is also a strange noise in the air heard of many in these parts this winter, called "Gabriel-Ratches" (sic) by this country-people, the noise is as if a great number of whelps were barking and howling, and 'tis observed that if any see them the persons that see them die shortly after, they are never heard but before a great death or dearth."* Popular conceptions of the Gabriel Hounds may have been partially based on migrating flocks of wild geese when they fly at night making loud honking noises. In other traditions their leader *Gabriel* is condemned to follow his hounds at night for the sin of having hunted on Sunday (much like the Cornish *Dando*), and their yelping cry is regarded as a death omen similar to the birds of folklore known as the *Seven Whistlers.* The Gabriel Hounds sometimes hover over a house, and this is taken as a sign that death or misfortune will befall those who dwell therein.

They are also known as *Gabriel Ratchets* (a ratchet being a hound that hunts by scent), or *Gabble Ratchets*, and also *Sky Yelpers*, and like the *Yeth Hounds* they are sometimes said to be the souls of unbaptized children.

Gally-Trot

Gally-trot is the name of an alarming apparition in the shape of a dog, that frightened many people in the neighborhood of Woodbridge, Suffolk. It was white in color, of the size of a bullock, somewhat shadowy or undefined of outline, and it would chase anyone that ran away from it in fear. The word *gally* is derived from *gaily*, "to frighten, scare".

Gapper-ginny

The *Gapper-ginny* is a phantom dog, which patrolled a lane between Ashmore and Tarrant Grenville in North Dorset, England.

Gast

The word *Gast* is used in large parts of southern Sweden as a collective name for alleged supernatural phenomena, such as *Ghosts*. They could be heard by the sea (Gastarop in Halland) and could be sailors who had left their earthly life but had not found a safe existence on the other side, because they had drowned and not been buried. Gast is derived from the Old Swedish *Gaster*, probably from the Frisian *Gást*. To be compared to the German *Geist* (part of the word poltergeist) and the English *ghost*. Further north, Gast refers to unbaptized murdered children and *Mylings* (displaced fetuses).

Gengångare

Gengångare are said to be people who have died in a violent or unfortunate manner. Gengångare are said to haunt those involved in their deaths and sometimes also the innocent. In the old days, special measures were taken to prevent the creation of ghosts – for example, the body of the dead person could be anchored, such as buried deep in the ground, or buried in a way that made it impossible for the body to leave the grave. A famous example of this is the *Bockstein man*.

Gestafluga

In Icelandic lore the *Gestafluga* is a fly that announces the arrival of a guest. The creature is mentioned in the Dutch folkloristic study *IJslands Volksgeloof* (Icelandic Folk belief) 1936, by Paula Catharina Maria Sluijter:

"Once in a while we hear that a fly, the so-called Gestafluga, announces guests. Anna is on her way to visit her friend Rannveig. On the way, she is caught in a storm, in which she would have been lost, if the light that Rannveig had put in the window sill had not shown her the way. Rannveig suspected the arrival of a guest, because a fly kept flying around her head."

Gille dubh

In the north-west Highlands of Scotland dwelled a solitary male *Fairy* called the *Gille dubh, Ghillie dhuor* or *Ghillie dhu* (the Black Boy). His hair was black and he dressed in moss and leaves, while haunting a birch forest at the southern end of Loch a During, near Gairloch. He was well known and often seen in the second half of the eighteenth century. It was a friendly spirit, yet sometimes wild in character, who once found a girl called Jessie MacRae wandering at night in the woods. He looked after her kindly and took her home in the morning. Jessie was the only person to whom the Gille dubh was ever known to have spoken. *Ghillie* is an English equivalent of the Scottish Gaelic word *gille*. Edward Dwelly, a Scottish lexicographer, lists *gille* as a "lad", "youth", or "boy", with *dubh* translating as "dark" or "dark-haired".

Gjenganger

A *Gjenganger* (Norwegian: *Gjenganger, Attergangar* or *Gjenferd*; Danish: *Genganger* or *Genfærd*; Swedish: *Gengångare*) in Scandinavian folklore was a term for a Revenant, the spirit or ghost of a deceased, risen from the grave. A Gjenganger could have several reasons to return from the afterlife. Murdered people and their murderers could seldom sleep peacefully in their graves. People who had committed suicide often came back as a Gjenganger. At other times, a deceased person came back from the grave because they had left something undone, or were just evil. Most often they needed someone to help them set things right, before they could finally rest in peace. The Gjenganger in the Scandinavian tradition took on an entirely corporeal form. It normally had no spectre-like qualities whatsoever.

In older traditions, the Gjenganger was malicious and violent in nature, coming back from the grave to torment its family and friends. Their relatives took extensive precautions to make sure the deceased stayed in their graves. This tradition of the violent Gjenganger goes back to the Viking Age, where they are present in many of the Icelandic sagas. There were several ways for both the defense against the Gjenganger, and stopping people from becoming one. Certain symbols were painted, especially a cross. A Gjenganger could also be warded off with crucifixes and Christian incantations, or when someone had died, the coffin was carried three times around the church before being buried. So called *varps* were also used. A varp was a pile of stones or twigs that often marked the place where someone had died. It was believed that when you passed this place, you should throw another stone or twig on the varp, to commemorate what had happened there. Doing so would sometimes bring luck on your further travels, while not doing so would result in bad luck and dangerous accidents. Many of these varps have now disappeared, but in a few places the varp is marked with a sign, or something similar.

Glaistig or Green Lady

The *Glaistig* is a ghost from Scottish mythology, a type of *Fuath*. It is also known as *Maighdean uaine* (Green Maiden), and may appear as a woman of beauty or as half-woman and half-goat, similar to a *Faun* or *Satyr*, or solely in the shape of a goat. The lower goat half of her hybrid form is usually disguised by a long, flowing green robe or dress, and the woman often appears to have grey skin, with long yellow hair. One version of the Glaistig legend is that she was once a mortal noblewoman, to whom a "Fairy" nature had been given, while another one states that she was cursed with goat's legs and immortality, after which she was known as *the Green Lady*. In some tales she was a woman who was murdered in a green dress, and then unceremoniously stuffed up the chimney by a servant.

Green Lady myths originating in the murder of a woman have been associated with a number of locations, mainly in Scotland:
• Green Lady of Ardnacallich
• Green Lady of Dunollie Castle
• Green Lady of Loch Fyne
• Green Lady of Muchalls Castle
• Green Lady of Caerphilly (Wales)

- Green Lady of Fyvie, a ghost that supposedly wanders the corridors of
  Fyvie Castle in Aberdeenshire, Scotland
- Green Lady of Ashintully Castle in the county of Perthshire, Scotland
- Green Lady of Ballindalloch Castle in Aberdeenshire, Scotland
- Green Lady of the Barony of Ladyland in North Ayrshire, Scotland
- Green Lady of Crathes Castle in Aberdeenshire, Scotland
- Green Lady of Knock Castle (Isle of Skye)
- Green Lady of Longleat in Somerset, South West England

The Glaistig appears in legend as both a malign and benign creature.
Some stories have her luring men to her lair via either song or dance,
where she would then drink their blood. Other such tales have her casting
stones in the path of travelers or throwing them off course. In other,
more benign incarnations, the Glaistig is a type of tutelary spirit and
protector of cattle and herders, and in at least one legend in Scotland, the
town of Ach-na-Creige had such a spirit protecting the cattle herds. The
townsfolk, in gratitude, poured milk from the cows into a hollowed-out
stone for her to drink. According to the same legend, her protection was
revoked after one local youth poured boiling milk into the hollow stone,
burning her. She has also been described in some folklore as watching
over children while their mothers milked the cows and their fathers
watched over the herds. In some Scottish tales, the cows are replaced
with deer, of which the Glaistig is fiercely protective. Also known as the
Scottish Goddess of the Hunt, the Glaistig was both help and hindrance
to hunters, going so far as to hide her herds if the hunters made the
mistake of killing a doe instead of a stag. Another name for this being,
used in Scottish tales, is the *Maiden of Callart*.

Glashtyn

The *Glashtyn or Glashtin* (Manx English: *Glashtin, Glashtan* or *Glashan*)
is a water-spirit from Manx folklore, that often appears as a weak foal or
a year-old lamb. The spirit is said to be a kind of *Goblin* that is notorious
for its habit of raping bathing women. Apart from a foal or lamb, some
people claim it took the shape of the Water-horse known locally as *Cabyll-
ushtey*. Yet another source describes the Glashtyn as a Water-bull (*Tarroo-
ushtey* in Manx), half-bovine and half-equine. He can also pretend to be a
handsome man but is betrayed by his horse-ears. The crowing of a rooster
wards the creature off, as is the case with many spirits.

Gloson

Gloson, also known as *Gloso or Gravson* (*Gravsoen* in Denmark) is a southern Swedish folklore phantom-animal in the shape of a pig or a wild boar. It used to appear during the 12 days of Christmas (25 December - 6 January). Gloson is related to the classical field-demons, like the *Roggensau* (Rye-sow) in Germany, or the *Sauzagel*. To insure a good harvest people offered her gruel and fish, so that she would not harm anyone. Once the harvest had been brought in, three blades of wheat were left in the field and the harvester spoke: *"These are for Gloson; one for Christmas Night, one for the night of New Year and one for King's Night."* (King's night is better known as Epiphany, or Theophany; the night of January 5th into the morning of January 6th).

Gloson ("gloso" in indefinite form) comes from glo, to stare or to glow, and so, a sow. It was said to have glowing eyes and a wonderful "snyte" (snout) with large tusks and/or fangs and a sharp saw-toothed back and run between people's legs and thus crack them open. A Gloson travelled through the sky as a flame, its bristles shooting sparks. According to Claude Lecouteux in *Phantom Armies of the Night* (1999) Gloson was sometimes interpreted as the specter of a murdered child that was never buried, or as a supernatural guardian of a church like the *Kirkegrim*. Gloson was also known as *Gluffsuggan, Galoppso* or *Gluppso* (Galloping sow) because it was galloping through the sky – relating it to animals that partook in the so called Wild Hunt. In Blekinge, it was said that Saint Thomas comes on December 21, or Christmas, armed with a powerful sword and riding *Gloussi* (Glosso) to rid the land of Trolls.

Goblin

Goblin is the English generic term small, usually malevolent and grotesquely ugly pests or ghosts, but it is also commonly used as a generic term for all kinds of – often dwarfish – spirit beings. Alternative spellings include *Gobblin, Gobeline, Gobling, Goblyn, Goblino*, and *Gobbelin*. The term *Goblette* has been used to refer to female Goblins. As with the *dwarves* and Goblins of myth and fairytale, the sizes of Goblins vary widely, from a few inches to child size. They are ascribed conflicting abilities, temperaments and appearances depending on the story and country of origin, varying from mischievous household-spirits to malicious, bestial thieves. They often have magical abilities similar to a Fairy or demon, such as the ability to shape-shift. In folklore, Goblins are sometimes contrasted with the friendly and helpful but teasing *Hobgoblins* or *Hobs*, who are similar to *Brownies*.

The origin and meaning of the English word Goblin is uncertain; probably a loanword from Old French *Gobelin*. The 12th century chronicle of *Ordericus Vitalis* mentions a *Gobelinus*, a spirit that haunted the Évreux area. Possibly there is a connection with the German word *Kobold*, or the Late Latin *Cabalus*, which in turn goes back to Greek *Kobalos*, or with the personal name *Gobel*. In England the word first appears in the 14th century. The Welsh *Coblyn*, a type of *Knocker*, derives from the Old French *Gobelin* via the English Goblin.

Grindylow

In English folklore, *Grindylow* or *Grundylow* is a supernatural creature that appears in the folklore of England, most notably the Lancaster and Yorkshire area. In appearance, they are like diminutive humans with scaly skin, a greenish complexion, sharp claws and teeth and long, wiry arms with lengthy fingers at the end. They dwell in ponds and marshes, waiting for children to come by. When they spot children, they grab them with their strong grip and drag them under the surface of the water. Grindylows have been used – like the Italian *Borga* or Sicillian *Marabbecca* – as a Bogeyman figure to frighten children away from pools, marshes or ponds where they could drown, but may have their origin in nature-spirits akin to the Russian Vodyanoy. Other British variants are *Nelly Longarms* (or Nellie Longarms), a hag and water-spirit in English folklore who dwells at the bottom of deep ponds, rivers and wells. Other names are: *Peg Powler* and *Jenny Greenteeth*. They will reach out with their long sinewy arms and drag children beneath the water if they get too close. These long sinewy arms are a consistent pan-European feature of these creatures.

Grogan

A type of solitary broad shouldered and very strong *household-spirit* or *Brownie* of about two feet high. He helps Irish farmers in harvesting, threshing, and other tasks, but takes offense if any recompense is offered to him. The *Grogan* can be compared to the Scots Gaelic *Brùnaidh*.

Gruagach

Gruagach means "The Long-haired One," from the Gaelic *gruag* (wig).
It is a solitary Fairy-creature of Irish and Scottish Gaelic traditions,
sometimes seen as a giant or *Ogre*. His characteristic long hair links the
Gruagach to the *Woodwose* or *Wild Man of the Woods*. In Scotland the
term Gruagach may sometimes also refer to a Fairy woman dressed
in green, or to a slender, handsome man. The term is also used as a
synonym for the Brownie. In this latter role, the Gruagach was a creature
with protective duties in Scottish legends, apparently of either sex, but
generally female. The Gruagach was particularly associated with cattle,
and milk was laid aside for him or her every evening – otherwise no milk
would be given at the next milking. Usually this being was of a beneficent
nature, although it occasionally made mischief by setting the cattle free so
that the herders had to get up, sometimes several times during a night, to
tie them up. This apparently caused the Gruagach much impish delight.
Among the many stories of Fairies, there are tales in different parts of
Scotland about the Gruagach. It seems that this Fairy commonly had long
hair and was well dressed, whichever gender it was.

Gruvrået

In Norse folklore, the *Gruvrået* (*Bergsrået* or *Gruvfrun*) is a (usually
female) creature that rules over places with mining deposits. She appears
as a witch, an animal, a grey-bearded old man or a bat and often scares off
people who want to exploit the ore. She could also appear as an elegant
lady, tall and handsome, often genteel in a light grey dress. If she was in
a really good mood, she could show where the appropriate ore deposits
were or warn of accidents. The Gruvrået, the *Skogsrået/Huldra* (forest-
spirit) and the *Sjörået* (sea-spirit) have in common that they rule over
their local natural habitat. Such a nature-spirit is usually of the female sex
and attractive to men. Tales of the Gruvrået circulated in communities
where mining was common. Other names for this creature were the
Bergrået (mountain-spirit) and Gruvfrun (mine-woman). She had a less
erotic character than the Skogsrået and the Sjörået, which some explain
by the fact that the miner usually did not work at the same distance from
home, wife or other women as the lumberjack and the fisherman.

Guardian Black Dogs

Guardian Black Dogs refer to those relatively rare black dogs that are neither omens nor causes of death. Instead they guide lost travelers and protect them from danger. Stories of this type became more widespread around the early 1900s. In different versions of one popular tale a man was journeying along a lonely forest road at night, when a large black dog appeared at his side and remained with him until the man left the forest. On his return journey through the woods the dog reappeared and did the same as before. Years later two convicted prisoners told the chaplain that they would have robbed and murdered the wayfarer in the forest that night but were intimidated by the presence of the black dog.

Gunna

The *Gunna* is a kind of Scottish Highland *Brownie* or *household-spirit*, who, like the *Gruagach*, cares for cattle and keeps them away from cliffs and out of the fields of growing crops. The creature is described as very thin, with long blonde hair, and is dressed only in a fox skin. He was only seen by people gifted with the second sight. A man once saw that he was not wearing any clothing and took pity on him. He however made the classic mistake of offering the Brownie a gift of shoes and breeches. Gunna departed and since then the people of Baugh had to look after their own herds themselves again.

Gurt Dog

The *Gurt Dog* (Great Dog) of Somerset is an example of a benevolent phantom dog. It is said that mothers would allow their children to play unsupervised on the Quantock Hills, because they believed the Gurt Dog would protect them. It would also accompany lone travelers in the area, acting as a protector and guide.

Gwiddonod

Gwiddonod are a shape-shifting kind of witches in Welsch folklore; old women who could cast spells over people and animals, ride broomsticks through the air, tell fortunes, and use charms to heal or cause diseases. They could take the form of a hare, and could only be killed with a silver bullet. Only *Y Dyn Hysbys* (The Wise Man) could undo the harm they caused.

Gwrach y Rhibyn

Gwrach y Rhibyn in the Celtic mythology of Wales is a spirit of death in the shape of an ugly old crone. The Gwrach is also associated with the *Cyhyraeth*, spirits said to announce a person's death with eerie howls. Like the Scottish *Cailleach* and the Irish *Banshee*, Gwrach and Cyhyraeth also lament the death of compatriots in foreign lands. This ghostly figure is said to have harpy-like features, like scrawny, leathery arms with bat wings, tangled hair, and long black teeth in a cadaverous face. When someone has to die, she knocks on this person's window at night and calls the name, or she accompanies the person invisibly and cries out at fords or crossroads, or a stream, where she is sometimes depicted as washing her hands there. Her call, depending on the person, sounds like *Fy ngŵr, fy ngŵr!* (My spouse, my spouse!), *Fy ngwraig! Fy ngwraig!* (My wife, my wife!) or F*y mhlentyn, fy mhlentyn bach!* (My child, my little child!). Other legends associate Gwrach with a *water-spirit* or with the Welsh goddess *Dôn*. According to Hanes Taliesin she is also said to be the wife of *Morfran*, the despised son of *Ceridwen* and *Tegid Foel*. A Welsh way of insulting a woman is: *Y mae mor salw â Gwrach y Rhibyn* (She is as ugly as Gwrach y Rhibyn).

Gwragedd Annwn

In Welsh folklore the *Gwragedd Annwn* (literally, "wives of the lower world, or hell") – singular Welsh: *Gwraig Annwn*) are beautiful female Fairies. The Gwragedd Annwn haunts lakes and rivers, but especially the wild and lonely lakes upon the mountain heights and they are counted among the *Tylwyth Teg* or Welsh *Fairy-folk*. They are also known as *Lake Maidens* and these lovely creatures often marry mortals and live happily. Legends state that the Gwragedd Annwn who lived in Llyn Barfog, or Crumlyn Lake, were once ordinary women, who were cursed by St Patrick for taunting him during a visit and were condemned by the saint to sink below the waters. They are also said to be the originators of Welsh Black Cattle, who are descendants of the legendary cow *Fuwch Gyfeiliorn*, that came from the land of the Gwragedd Annwn.

Gwyllgi

The *Gwyllgi* (compound noun of either *gwyllt* "wild" or *gwyll* "twilight" + *ci* "dog") is a mythical dog from Wales that appears as a frightful apparition of a 'shaggy mastiff or a huge black wolf larger than a steed nine winters old, with baleful breath and blazing red eyes'. It is also called *Cwn Annwfn* or *Cwn Annwn* (meaning "dog of the otherworld") and *Cwn Cyrff* (corpse dog) and like most black phantom dogs it is an omen of death if one crosses your path. The apparition's favorite haunt being lonely roads at night. There have been sightings of this beast in the north east of Wales. Specifically, the Nant y Garth pass, located near Llandegla in Denbighshire. It has even been spotted as far away as Marchwiel in Wrexham, also in recent times.

Gwyllion

Gwyllion or *Gwyllon* (pl. noun from the singular *Gwyll* or *Wyll* "twilight, gloaming") is a Welsh word with a wide range of possible meanings, including "ghosts, spirits" and "night-wanderers (human or supernatural) up to no good, outlaws of the wild. Gwyllion is only one of a number of words with these or similar meanings in Welsh. According to folklorist Wirt Sikes, the Gwyllion are female *Fairies* of frightful aspect who haunt lonely roads in the Welsh mountains and lead travelers astray. They are gloomy spirits, akin to *Hags* or witches, as distinct from the Welsh *Ellyllon* (Elves) that are more benevolent. Those who encountered them either by night or on a misty day would be sure to lose their way even if they were perfectly familiar with the road. One Gwyll in particular was known as the *Old Woman of the Mountain*, who haunted Llanhyddel Mountain in Monmouthshire, and the popular tradition in that district was that she was the ghost of a woman who had been regarded in life as a witch. She is known to utter strange cries and shouts throughout her mountain in order to frighten wayfarers. The Old Woman has also been encountered on Black Mountain in Breconshire. At an encounter one can pull a knife and point it at her, after which the creature vanishes. Welsh ghosts and Fairies are afraid of knives and can be banished by them. This exorcism by knife, according to Sikes, is a particularly Welsh tradition.

Gytrash

Gytrash, a legendary road-daemon known in northern England, was said to haunt lonely roads, awaiting travelers. Appearing in the shape of a horse, mule, or black dog, the Gytrash haunts solitary ways and lead people astray but they can also be benevolent, guiding lost travelers to the right road. They are usually feared. In some parts of Lincolnshire and Yorkshire, the Gytrash was known as the *Shagfoal* and took the form of a spectral mule, horse or donkey, with eyes that glowed like burning coals. In this form, the beast was believed to be purely malevolent. Gytrash appears in Charlotte Brontë's novel *Jane Eyre*, chapter 12:

> *"As this horse approached, and as I watched for it to appear through the dusk, I remembered certain of Bessie's tales, wherein figured a North-of-England spirit called a "Gytrash," which, in the form of horse, mule, or large dog, haunted solitary ways, and sometimes came upon belated travelers, as this horse was now coming upon me. It was very near, but not yet in sight; when, in addition to the tramp, tramp, I heard a rush under the hedge, and close down by the hazel stems glided a great dog, whose black and white colour made him a distinct object against the trees. It was exactly one form of Bessie's Gytrash — a lion-like creature with long hair and a huge head [...], with strange pretercanine eyes [...]. The horse followed, — a tall steed [...]. Nothing ever rode the Gytrash: it was always alone [...]."*

This spirit is also known as *Guytrash* and *Guytresh* according to *The English Dialect Dictionary* of Joseph Wright (1855-1930), where it is defined as a ghost that takes the form of an animal. These animals include a "great black dog" as well as "an evil cow" whose appearance was formerly believed to be a sign of imminent death.

H

Habetrot

Habetrot (also: *Habitrot*, *Habtrot* or *Habbitrot*) is a figure in the folklore of the border regions of northern England and Lowland Scotland, especially Selkirkshire, and is associated with spinning and the spinning wheel. She is an old, deformed woman who lives underground with a group of other spinsters, all disfigured by their work (some have splayed feet or flat thumbs). *Scantlie Mab* is Habetrot's principal assistant. She was the plainest member of the "spinster assembly", for besides her deformed lip she had staring eyes and a long, hooked nose among her so called "defects of the Fairies". Habitrot spun yarn for a local girl and then convinced the girl's new husband that she should never spin again. Habetrot could make life very complex, when we take into account a report of folklorist William Henderson about a respiratory illness and the need for a linen sack spun by Habetrot:

> *"According to the folklore of the borders, it was considered unlucky to step upon "unchristened ground" (the graves of stillborn or unbaptized children) and any who did were said to catch "grave-merels" (grave-scab), an illness that causes difficulty of breathing and trembling limbs as well as the burning of the skin as if touched by a hot iron. The only way to relieve this was for the afflicted to wear a sack made from linen grown in a field using manure from a farmyard that has not been disturbed for forty years, spun by Habetrot, bleached by an honest bleacher in an honest miller's milldam and sewed by an honest tailor."*

Hag

A *Hag* is a wizened old woman, or a kind of *Fairy* or goddess having the appearance of such a woman, often found in folkloric and children's tales – used as a *Bogey*-figure to frighten children into good behavior. Hags are often seen as malevolent, but may also be one of the chosen forms of shapeshifting deities, such as the *Morrígan* or *Badb*, who are seen as neither wholly benevolent nor malevolent. The term "hag" appears in Middle English, and was a shortening of *Hægtesse*, an Old English term for 'witch'; similarly, the Dutch *Heks* and German *Hexe* are also shortenings,

– of the Middle Dutch *Haghetisse* and Old High German *Hagzusa* or *Hagazusa*, respectively. All of these words are derived from the Proto-Germanic *hagatusjon* which is of unknown origin; the first element may be related to the word *hedge*. In folklore a Hag, or *Old Hag*, was a Nightmare-spirit in English and anglophone North American folklore. This variety of Hag is essentially identical to the Old English *Mæra* – a being with roots in ancient Germanic superstition, and closely related to the Scandinavian Mara.

According to folklore, the Old Hag sat on a sleeper's chest and sent nightmares to him or her. When the subject awoke, he or she would be unable to breathe or even move for a short period of time. This state is now called sleep paralysis, but in the old belief, the subject was considered *hagridden* (ridden by the Hag). Alhough capable of projecting her of his etheric double that can take a seat on another person's chest, a Hag is a different creature than a human projector, as in contrast to a projected etheric double. A Hag, like a Succubus or Incubus, has substantial materialization-dematerialization power. In modern days unacceptable to write such a thing – "irrational" and "unscientific" as it is. However Hag-attacks do happen up to this day and everyone who ever experienced one will be thankful I wrote these lines. (No you're not mad or imagining things...)

In Scotland, a group of Hags, known as the *Cailleachan* (Storm Hags) are seen as personifications of the elemental powers of nature, especially in a destructive aspect. They are said to be particularly active in raising the windstorms of spring, during the period known as *A Chailleach*.

Hairy Jack

An English phantom dog, known locally as *Hairy Jack*, is said to haunt the fields and village lanes around Hemswell, and there have been reported sightings throughout the county, from Brigg to Spalding. Ethel Rudkin – who collected many tales of ghostly black dogs in Lincolnshire for her 1938 publication *Folklore* – claimed to have seen Hairy Jack herself, and formed the impression that black dogs in Lincolnshire were mainly of a gentle nature, looked upon as a spiritual protector. Hairy Jack was also said to haunt lonely plantations, byways, and waste places where it attacked anyone passing by.

Hamingja

In Norse folklore, *Hamingja*, from *ham* (harbor) and *gengja* (walker), is a
type of female supernatural protective being, who oversees and rules over
human happiness until the Hamingja's protégé dies. The spirit then moves
to someone who was close to the dead person. In this way, the Hamingja
is a being that follows a lineage for generations. A Hamingja can also be
lent to someone who needs protection. In the past, the Hamingja was
usually associated with kings and successful individuals. In Ancient
Icelandic, Hamingja means "happiness". One can note similarities
between the concepts of the Norse Hamingja and the Swedish *Fylgja*.

Hamn and Huge

In Norse mythology, a *Hamn* or *Ham* is a figure in which the soul,
Huge, could manifest itself during a dream, or leave the body in a
state of ecstasy. The word comes from the Norse *hamr*: (an animal's)
outer protective covering. Huge is a thought or soul potency that, in a
dream-like state, could leave the body and pass into a Hamn. In modern
occultism the Huge would be translated as the conscious mind and the
Hamn as a created etheric double.

In a mythological story, where Thor meets the giant Utgårdaloke, they
have their two servants compete against each other in swiftness. Thor's
servant was called Tjalve and Utgårdaloke's was called Huge. When the
start signal was given, Huge was still standing, but as Tjalve was about to
cross the finishing line, Huge suddenly rushed past it, quick as lightning.
Huge was said to be the giant's thought (hug) and no one can run faster
than the thought.

Hazelrigg Dunnie

Hazelrigg Dunnie is a mischievous *Dunnie* (a small *Brownie*-like being
in the folklore of the Anglo-Scottish border areas). He frequented the
heights in the vicinity of Hazelrigg, near Belford Moor (now Belford
Mains), Northumberland. He takes occasionally the form of a dun-colored
horse or pony. At other times his dim form is seen about the Crags, where
he frequents a cave on the side of Cockenheugh, near Hazelrigg, called
the Cuddie's Cove. Another favorite haunt is Fowberry Bridge, and he is
seen at Collier (or Coller) braes, as well as at Bowden Doors.

The Dunnie has been known to take the form of a horse in order to trick a rider into mounting him before disappearing and leaving them in the muddiest part of the road. He also is said to disguise as a plough-horse, only to vanish when the ploughman takes him into the stalls.

Hedley Kow

The *Hedley Kow* is a local English shape-shifting *Goblin* or *Brag* of the village of Hedley on the Hill in Northumberland (related to the Dutch-Flemish *Kludde* and *Oschaert*). It was described by Joseph Jacobs in *More English Fairy Tales* (1894) and earlier by William Henderson in *Folk-Lore of the northern Counties* (1866). According to the latter:

"The Hedley Kow was a bogie or Brag, mischievous rather than malignant, which haunted the village of Hedley, near Ebchester. His appearance was never very alarming, and he used to end his frolics with a horse-laugh at the expense of his victims. He would present himself to some old dame gathering sticks, in the form of a truss of straw, which she would be sure to take up and carry away. Then it would become so heavy she would have to lay her burden down, on which the straw would become 'quick', rise upright, and shuffle away before her, till at last it vanished from her sight with a laugh and shout. Again, in the shape of a favourite cow, the sprite would lead the milkmaid a long chase round the field, and after kicking and routing during milking-time would upset the pail, slip clear of the tie, and vanish with a loud laugh. Indeed the 'Kow' must have been a great nuisance in a farmhouse, for it is said to have constantly imitated the voice of the servant-girl's lovers, overturned the kail-pot, given the cream to the cats, unraveled the knitting, or put the spinning-wheel out of order. But the sprite made himself most obnoxious at the birth of a child. He would torment the man who rode for the howdie, frightening the horse, and often making him upset both messenger and howdie, and leave them in the road. Then he would mock the gudewife, and, when her angry husband rushed out with a stick to drive away the 'Kow' from the door or window, the stick would be snatched from him, and lustily applied to his own shoulders."

Hefnivargar

In Icelandic lore *Hefnivargar* (Revenge Wolves) are evil inclined *Afturgöngur*, who haunt out of revenge, or because of having not been given the proper funeral rites, or because of some other unfinished business. In addition, we read stories about the dead, who are dissatisfied with the treatment of their bones. When digging a new grave one often encounters bones of previous corpses, which are then put back into the earth, but of which sometimes one is accidentally forgotten. In the dream or even in broad daylight, the dead then come and ask for this missing bone. Furthermore, violent quarrels, misfortune in love, etc., can become a reason to ghost after death; often the threat of revenge is already expressed before death. Sometimes people even commit suicide in order to speed up their revenge. After all, the dead possess superhuman strength! Of course, even those who have died or been murdered find no peace after their death. They haunt and follow entire generations like a family curse, just like the dead who have been robbed of gold, clothes or the like and remain angry about this.

Heimselskendur

In Icelandic lore the *Heimselskendur* are the deceased, who either come to haunt their former lovers, or the perished, who often stay for years at the place of the calamity which caused their death. People who have perished near a certain farm often become the *Fylgjur* or guardian of such a place. Folklore has it that one sometimes sees them before the current living owners of the farm appear.

Helhäst

Helhäst, Hels häst, Dödshästen (Hell horse, Hells horse or Death horse) is a supernatural creature in Danish folk tales and in Swedish folklore. It is usually depicted as a three-legged, black and sometimes headless horse, which heralds death for those who encounter it. It appears mostly near cemeteries. Death is also sometimes imagined to ride on this three-legged horse. Folklore has it that the whole horse arose from a horse that was buried alive in every cemetery, before any human being was allowed to be buried there. The stories of the Hell horse live on in Denmark, where the saying *"He walks like a Hell horse"* is still used. The origin of the Helhäst can be assumed to derive from pre-Christian Norse mythology, where the goddess of death Hel has a particular three-legged horse, also known as Heldrasill. The stories about Hel and her horse have probably been changed and adapted with the Christianization of the North.

Hob

The *Hob* is a small household and countryside spirit and is found on the Anglo-Scottish border and in the north and middle regions of England. He lives inside or outside the (farm)house and does chores for humans. Hobs are usually described as small, hairy, wizened men. If the creatures are offended, they can become very troublesome. The Hob shows similarities to a *Hobgoblin*, *Brownie*, *Tomte* or *Nisse*. See also the *Lubberkin*. One way to get rid of a Hob was to give him new clothes. However, there is no one way to get rid of the most troublesome Hobs. Near Runswick Bay in the county of North Yorkshire, parents brought their children to the Hob Hole to cure them of whooping cough. In doing so, the following rhyme was recited: *"Hob Hole Hob, My bairn's gotten t'kink cough, Tak it off, Tak it off."* Hob is a diminutive form of the name "Robin", which is itself a diminutive form of the name "Robert".

Hoberdidance

In old English folkore, *Hoberdidance* was a subordinate demon who harassed people. Shakespeare adopted the name as *Hobbididance* and also as *Hopdance*. The original form may have been Hob of the dance, then Hob o' the dance. A certain Sarah Williams, one of the possessed, stated that she had often heard such a being spoken of jestingly when she was a child. Hoberdidance, she said, used his cunning to make a lady laugh. The spirit also appears in *Declaration of Egregious Popish Impostures* (1603) by Samuel Harsnett (1561-1631) as the name of a devil.

Hobgoblin

A *Hobgoblin* is – like the Russian *Domovoy* – a spirit of the hearth, typically appearing in folklore, once it was considered helpful *household-spirit,* but since the spread of Christianity, that demonized all spirit creatures rooting in old local religions, it has been considered mischievous. Shakespeare identified the character of *Puck* in his *A Midsummer Night's Dream* as a Hobgoblin. The etymology of the

Hobgoblin is not completely sure. It could come from *Hob* (Elf), or a flat metal shelf called *hob* at the side or back of a fireplace, having its surface level with the top of the grate and used especially for heating pots and kettles on which is congruent with the idea of a spirit who lives behind the stove. "Goblin" is usually interpreted as "a mischievous and ugly Fairy". Then there is "Hob" as the name of that other household-spirit whose name is derived from Robin, Robert and "Robin Goodfellow". In *British Goblins: Welsh Folk-Lore, Fairy Mythology, Legends and Traditions,* author Wirt Sikes comes with the most simple explanation by arguing that the English term "Hobgoblin" was derived from the Welsh *hob,* which simply means "to hop". The earliest instance of the word can be traced back to about 1530, although it was likely in use for some time prior to that.

Hobgoblins are described as small, hairy little men who, just like their close relatives the Hobs and Brownies, are often found within human dwellings, doing odd jobs around the house while the family is asleep. Such chores are typically small tasks like dusting and ironing. Often, the only compensation necessary in return for these services is leaving them a bit of food. While Brownies are more peaceful creatures, Hobgoblins distinguish themselves by their fondness of practical jokes. They also seem to be able to shape-shift, as seen in one of Puck's monologues in *A Midsummer Night's Dream*. Robin Goodfellow is perhaps the most mischievous and notorious of the Hobgoblins, but many are less antagonizing. Like other Fairies, they are easily annoyed and react in mischievous, frightening, or even dangerous ways. As with many of these kind of creatures, attempts at giving them clothing will usually banish them. There are several kinds of Hobgoblins:

• **Billy Blind** (also: *Billy Blin, Billy Blynde, Billie Blin,* or *Belly Blin*) is an English and Lowland Scottish Hobgoblin, found in several ballads collected by Francis James Child. Billy Blind is described as clever and helpful, as he helps humans in dramatic situations by offering valuable information and advice.

• **Blue Burche** is the name of a shapeshifting Hobgoblin that pulled harmless pranks in the home of a cobbler and his family at Buckland St Mary, on the Blackdown Hills in the Devon-Somerset border area. His usual shape was that of an old man wearing baggy pants held up by blue breeches, but he also took the form of a white horse, a black pig or a wisp of blue smoke. The family took his presence in good stride but some clergymen learned of his existence and finally he was exorcised by a priest.

- **Robin Roundcap** haunted Spaldington Hall in Spaldington, East Riding of Yorkshire and was a hearth-spirit of the true Hobgoblin-type. He helped thresh the corn and performed other domestic chores, but when he was in the mood for mischief he would mix the wheat and chaff again, kick over the milk pail, and extinguish the fire. He is said to have been confined in a well for a stipulated number of years through the prayers of three clergymen. This well is known as *Robin Roundcap's Well*.

- **Dobie** or **Dobby** is a complex creature, but the name is much used as another term for Hobgoblin in Lancashire and Yorkshire. According to the folklorist Elizabeth Mary Wright, a Dobby is especially one that is a relentless prankster. Much like the Boggart, a Dobby's pranks may become so troublesome that a family decides to move elsewhere, only to find that the Dobby has followed them. Dobbies could be just as industrious as other Hobgoblins and Brownies, which led to the expression "Master Dobbs has been helping you" whenever a person has accomplished more than was expected.

- The **Bauchan** (Scottish: *Bòcan*; English: *Bauchan, Buckawn* or *Bogan*) is a type of domestic Hobgoblin in Scottish folklore. It is often mischievous and belligerent, but is also very helpful when the need arises. John Francis Campbell in his *Popular Tales of the West Highlands* tells the story of Callum Mor MacIntosh whose farm in Lochaber was haunted by a Bauchan. The relationship between Callum and the Bauchan was complex. While the Bauchan was belligerent and combative, he often provided assistance in various farm-related tasks. When Callum emigrated to New York City, the Bauchan went with him and helped him clear his new plot of land. In this tale the Bauchan is a shapeshifter and is able to transform into a goat.

- The **Boobach** or **Bwbach** is a Welsh domestic Hobgoblin that will perform household chores in return for bowls of cream. They are good-natured but mischievous and have a dislike of clergymen and teetotalers, upon whom they will play relentless pranks.

Hogboon

A *Hogboon* is a kind of Brownie in Shetland folklore. The Hogboon undertakes agricultural laboring tasks in return for some food. The name derives from the Norse *haug bui*, meaning "mound-dweller", because they were believed to inhabit the ancient burial mounds.

Hogmen

On the Isle of Man the *Hogmen* or *Hillmen* were the most feared Manx *Fairies*. They changed their quarters (Fairy hills) at Hollantide (November 11th) and people stayed indoors on that night to avoid meeting or disturbing them. They were propitiated with gifts of fruit.

Hoopers

Hoopers are a shy Cornish class of *Fairies* which hid in the mist, and would warn fishermen of pending storms.

Howlaa

In Manx folklore the *Howlaa* is a *Mountain-Fairy* which appears as an old man. His voice could be heard in the winter lamenting about a coming tempest and thus warning the people of storms.

Hrökkáll

Icelandic lore is very rich in stories about dangerous and deadly poisonous fish. One story tells of a malicious Icelandic sorcerer, who in some necromantic process revived a dead, half-rotted eel, giving rise to an evil and toxic creature. This was the first *Hrökkáll*, or "Coil-eel". The sorcerer is long dead, but the eel's descendants went on to infest mainly stagnant waters. A Hrökkáll is two feet long, and resembles an eel in appearance. It has flexible, iron-hard scales, and sharp saw-toothed fins. Captured Hrökkálls are believed to have "melted" their way through earth and rock to get back into the water. Hrökkálls lie in wait for someone who steps into the water. Then they coil around one of the person's legs and constrict it, slicing into flesh and bone alike, amputating a foot or part of the leg, either with their acidic venom or their bladed fins, or perhaps both. They also dismember horses in this way, but sheep are safe, as their legs are too narrow for the Hrökkáll to gain a good grip.

Hulder dancing with man (1933) by Ridley Borchgrevink(1898-1981)

Hrosshvalur

In Icelandic folklore the *Hrosshvalur* (Horse-whale) is a sea-monster, a
supernaturally large and strong creature, 15 to 40 meters (50 to 130 feet)
in length, with a higher intelligence than a normal whale. It can emit
a terrible stench and manipulate the weather, often in order to create
storms or other hazards to those who travel the sea. With the *Stökkull* and
Raudkembingur the Hrosshvalur belongs to a class of creatures called the
Illhveli (Evil Whales). The Hrosshvalur was believed to delight in chaos
and is associated with the dark arts, since its size and ferocity made it an
excellent accomplice for sorcerers and witches bent on destruction. In
the *Kormaks saga*, the witch Dorveig transforms herself into an image of
Hrosshvalur to attack the brothers Kormakr and Dorgils. They recognize
her by her eyes and drive her off by throwing a javelin into her back.

Hugh of the Little Head

Eoghan a Chinn Bhig, in English known as *Hugh of the Little Head* was the
best known and most dreadful specter in the Scottish West Highlands.
It was the phantom of a headless or almost headless horseman, which
made its appearance whenever any of the Maclaines of Lochbuy, in Mull,
were near their death. The spectral horseman is mounted on a small black
steed, with a white spot on its forehead, and the hoof marks of which are
not like those of other horses, but round indentations as if it had wooden
poles as legs. Whenever any of the people which he follows are on their
death-bed, Hugh is heard riding past their house, and sometimes even
shows himself at their door. He does not sit straight on his horse's back,
but somewhat to one side, and the appearance of the almost headless
body is that of a water-bag tied on the horse's back.

Hulder or Skogsrå(et)

A *Hulder* (or *Huldra*) is a seductive – usually beautiful – female forest
creature found in Scandinavian folklore. Her name derives from the word
for "covered" or "secret". In Norwegian folklore, she is known as *Huldra*
or *Huldran*. Her name suggests that she may originally be the same
being as the divine figure *Huld* and the German *Holda*. Huldra is the
same forest-spirit as the *Skogsrå* (forest-spirit). In Sweden she is mostly
known as the (*Skogsrået*; lit. "forest Rå"), but also as *Skogsrådan, Skogsråa*
(forest ruler), *Råan, Rådande* (ruler, ruling spirit), *Skogsjungfru* (forest

maiden), *Skogsfru, Skogssnuva* (forest woman), *Skogskäringen* (forest hag), *Skogsfrun* (mistress of the forest), *Skogsnymfen* (forest Nymph) or with a nickname such as *Grankotte-Maja* (Spruce cone-Maja), *Grankotte-Kari* (Spruce cone-Kari), *Talle-Maja* (Pine tree-Maja). She can also be called by a name that is local and not known outside a certain area, such as: *Gonna, Besta, Rånda, Skogela, Trasåsa-frun, Lanna-frökna* (Lady of Lanna) or *Ysäters-Kajsa, Kajsa,* or *Ysäter.* On the island of Gotland, there are records of a female Troll known as *Torspjäska,* that plays the same role and has the same function as the forest-spirit on the mainland. In Sámi folklore she is known as *Ulda.* Some names in the Finnish language, mainly from the west coast, also show a link to the Swedish traditions, for example, *Metsänpiika* (forest girl) or *Metsänneito* (forest maid), which are the most widespread words used in Finland for the female forest-spirit. There are also other localized names such as *Haapaneitsyt* (Aspen-maid) or *Sinipiika* (blue maid).

Although a solitary creature, folklore presupposes that there is an entire Hulder *race* and not just a solitary creature. In Norway, the word *Huldrefolk* or *Huldre* (pl.) derived from Old Norse *huldr* 'hidden' is used for all kinds of supernatural beings that are sighted and talked about by the people of that area. Hulder, or Huldra in the singular, signifies a female forest-spirit, even though she might as well appear in the mountains. The Huldra or Skogsrå may have originally belonged to a group of collective creatures similar to the South Swedish Trolls. In some records, she is also called a *trollet* (Troll), or *trollkäringen* (Troll's witch). Similar creatures are found in other parts of Scandinavia; in the northern parts of the pastoral regions she is represented by *Vittra*, in Norway by *Huldra*, in Denmark by *Elverpigen* (river-girl) or *Mosekonen* (Moss-woman). Compare the German *Moosweiblein* or *Moosfraulein* (lit. Little Moss-Woman). The word Hulder is only used for a female; a male Hulder is called a *Huldrekall* and also appears in Norwegian folklore. This being is closely related to other underground dwellers, usually called *Tusser* (or *Tusse*). The Huldre were held to be kind to charcoal burners, guarding their charcoal kilns while they rested.

The Skogsrå usually appears as a seductive female in the forest. She is the guardian of wild animals, which she sometimes bestows on those she pleases. She lures wanderers astray and seduces men she takes a liking to. She is flattering and affectionate, and has the ability to change her shape.

When it comes to sexual activities, the female forest-spirit plays the active part. She approaches and tries to seduce the man by different means. If all else fails, she pulls up her skirt and shows him her genitals, in an attempt to have intercourse with him. It was believed that anyone who had sexual intercourse with a Skogsrå was in danger of becoming a dull and useless introvert – his soul having stayed with her. If the one she seduced was a hunter, however, his love was rewarded with great hunting fortune, but if he became unfaithful to the Skogsrå, he would suffer constant misfortune. The authorities took severe measures when someone copulated with a spirit being. Folklorist Tommy Kuusela writes:

"The crown and the church viewed intimate relationships with the forest-spirit as a crime that could lead to catastrophic consequences. Men accused of having sexual relations with a forest-spirit, and women for having sexual relations with a water-spirit (or Neck), turns up several times in Swedish judicial records from the 1600s and 1700s. The trial records show that people could be (and actually were) sentenced to death for this crime."

The Skogsrå used to visit men in the woods at night. These erotic encounters often took place in the charcoal stacks (kilns) or by a campfire.

Local variations of the Skogsrå
If a man attracted by the Skogsrå got lost in the woods, it was believed in Småland that he could find the right path by turning his shirt inside out and reciting the Our Father. Another regional variation is that in Svealand and southern Norrland the Skogsrå was said to have cattle, which she herded in the forest and which she lured from passing shepherds flocks. In the same area she was also said to have had a dog. In Skåne there was a male Skogsrå called *Skogman*. This male Skogsrå was most common in south-eastern Skåne. The Skogsrå also had positive qualities. By blowing down a gun barrel she could make sure that the gun never missed, however, she made sure that the gun always missed things that were hers. She was said to have awakened people to warn them for a fire – a performance that was most common in Bergslagen. The Skogsrå also occasionally helped shepherdesses with their cattle. In some places, the Skogsrået is considered to have a human foot and a horse's foot. In Götaland and south-eastern Svealand she was beautiful and attractive from the front, but seen from

behind she often has a hollow back like an old tree, so she always had to be careful to show only her beautiful side. Further north, in Dalarna and other pastoral areas, she looks like an ordinary woman with a normal back, but usually has a cow's tail or a horse's tail, and sometimes a fox's tail.

Huldufólk

The Huldufólk (hidden people), also called *Högfolk*, is a mythical race of *Elves* in Icelandic and Faroese folklore. They are supernatural beings that live in nature. They look and behave similarly to humans, but live in a parallel world. They can make themselves visible at will. In Faroese folk tales, *hidden people* are said to be large in build, their clothes are all grey, and their hair black. Their dwellings are in mounds, and they are also called Elves. The term *Huldufólk* was taken as a synonym of *Álfar* (Elves) in 19th-century Icelandic folklore. Jón Árnason found that the terms are synonymous, except Álfar is a disapproving term. Konrad von Maurer contends that *Huldufólk* originates as a euphemism to avoid calling the Álfar by their real name. There is, however, some evidence that the two terms have come to be taken as referring to two distinct sets of supernatural beings in contemporary Iceland.

The Christianization of Iceland in the 11th century brought with it new religious concepts. According to one Christian folk tale, the origins of the hidden people can be traced to Eve in Paradise. God had announced He would visit Eve. As she did not have enough time to wash all her children she hid her dirty, unwashed ones from God, and lied about their existence. God then declared: "What (hu)man hides from God, God will hide from (hu)man." The result was that these children were condemned to an eternally hidden life. However, the Huldufólk can decide for themselves whether we can see them or not. Other Christian folktales claim that hidden people originate from Lilith, or are fallen angels condemned to live between heaven and hell. In succession of Christianization, official opposition to dancing may have begun in Iceland as early as the 12th century, and the association of dancing with Elves can be seen as early as the 15th century. One folktale shows the Elves siding with the common people and taking revenge on a sheriff who banned dance parties. Aðalheiður Guðmundsdóttir concludes that these legends "show that Icelanders missed dancing". Einar Ólafur Sveinsson writes in *Folk Stories of Iceland* (2003): "

According to Árni Björnsson, belief in hidden people grew during the
17th and 18th centuries when Iceland was facing tough times.
Of all the mythological creatures, the Huldufólk are the most similar
to humans, except that they are more beautiful, more talented, more
charming, and wiser. They make contact with people when they want to.
Sometimes they come to help people in times of need, as in the story of
the writer Tryggvi Emilsson who fell off a cliff as a young man. He was
rescued by a Huldufólk maiden, and never would he forget her beauty.
In other cases, the Huldufólk needs our help. In the past, the Huldufólk
has asked for help with difficult births with some regularity. They
are basically benign, but people who disrupt or destroy their homes,
accidents often happen to them or they die unexpectedly. You will also
die soon if you are asked by someone from the Huldufólk to come and
see their home.

Huldufólk – people conflicts in modern days
Many Icelanders take the Huldufólk quite seriously, especially their
habitats and the believe that these should not be disturbed.
- During road construction in Kópavogur in 1971, a bulldozer broke
  down. The driver placed the blame on Elves living in a large rock.
  Despite locals not having been aware of any Elves living in the rock,
  newspapers ran with the story, thus starting a belief that Icelandic road
  construction was often impeded by Elves.
- In 1982, 150 Icelanders went to the NATO base in Keflavík to look
  for "Elves who might be endangered by American Phantom jets
  and AWACS reconnaissance planes". In 2004, Alcoa had to have a
  government expert certify that their chosen building site was free of
  archaeological sites, including ones related to huldufólk folklore, before
  they could build an aluminum smelter in Iceland.
- Another example of misfortune that the Huldufólk can cause if you
  disturb their habitat dates back to 1999. During the construction of the
  new road to the Hvalfjarðargöng under the Hvalfjörður (whale fjord) to
  Akranes, things kept going wrong. Construction tools continually broke
  down when they were supposed to be used, and there were unforeseen

setbacks each time. When a construction worker died in an accident, a local resident was finally called in, who claimed to be in contact with the Huldufólk. She told them that the Huldufólk lived on the route of the new road and were in the process of moving, but needed more time. The work was temporarily halted, until the woman came to tell the authorities that all the Huldufólk had moved out. The work was resumed, after which nothing more went wrong.
- In 2011, Elves/Huldufólk were – believed by some to be – responsible for an incident in Bolungarvík, where rocks rained down on residential streets.
- In 2013, proposed road construction from the Álftanes peninsula to the Reykjavík suburb of Garðabær, was stopped because Elf supporters and environmental groups protested, stating that the road would destroy the habitat of Elves and local cultural beliefs. Something similar also happened during the construction of Iceland's first shopping center, Smáralind. The underground electricity cables were rerouted because otherwise they would disturb the homes of Huldufólk.

Hyllemor

In the folklore of southern Sweden and Denmark, the *Hyllemor* is believed to be a female spirit that either lives under the elder tree or is the very spirit of the elder tree itself i.e. the *elder-Dryad*. Other names for Hyllemor (-mora, -moran) have been *Hyllefroan* (-froen, -frun), in Denmark *Hyldefrue* (-mor, -woman), while in Germany the spirit sometimes fuses with *Frau Holle, Holda, Holla or Holder*. C.W. von Sydow, 1932, writes:

"Sacrificing to the Hyllemor is quite common in southern Sweden. It is usually for illnesses that one sacrifices, namely for illnesses that one believes to have been contracted by touching a Hyllemor, or breaking a twig from it without first asking permission. In such a case one gets a skin rash disease called 'hylleskåll', and it is cured by washing oneself in warm milk, which one then beats out at the Hyllemor and asks for forgiveness for what one has let happen to oneself."

Eva Wigström exemplifies:

"If someone has got hylleskåll, it is because the Hyllemor, who lives in the elder tree, has been angered by the person having

defiled next to the bush. Then the sick person shall wash himself three mornings in succession in unsalted milk, beat it into the shrub and say: 'I heal thy root, take away the evil from me!'."

Sometimes on Christmas Eve beer was sacrificed to the Hyllemor to prevent sickness and attract good fortune. It was also believed that during the flowering season the elder tree is dangerous to anyone who has in some way seduced the *Hyllefroan* who lives there. Sometimes people sacrificed coins who were buried under one of the roots of the elder tree, and both silver and copper coins could be used. In general the elder tree-spirit functioned as a protector of the farm.

Botanist Johan Lange argued that the belief that the tree was animated was fueled by the fact that both the trunk and the larger branches are hollow from the degenerated pith. It was these hollows that were thought to house the tree's spirit or lead down to her abode in the roots. Even the name of the tree may give a clue to this, as it may be related to the verb *hylle* (hide, conceal), or be derived from the adjective *hul* (hollow). (Compare the English hollow-tree.) What the Hyllemor might look like, is shown in the following note of Eva Wigström (in the magazine *De svenska landsmålen och svenskt folklif*, 1898):

"Elder trees should never be cut down, for then the Hyllemor will only make you miserable. My husband once saw a chicken sitting in an elder tree. She wore a green skirt and sweater and a black-striped apron. He had meant to cut down the old elder tree, but now he nicely left it alone."

Hyter sprites

In Norfolk folklore the *Hyter* or *Hikey sprites* are a benevolent small and elusive kind of *Fairies*, which are said to find lost children in the fens (and stray donkeys) and help them find their way home again. The very protective Hyter sprites would also scold those who mistreated children. Oddly, the threat of the sprites was actually more frequently deployed by parents as a sort of nursery bogie to get children to behave.

I

Illhveli

The *Illveli* are the so called "evil whales" of Iceland. They balance on the
border of giant sea creatures and nature demons. In the first case they
are described as inedible and poisonous whales who attack ships. In the
second case magical and supernatural qualities are attributed to them,
or they are even described as were-manifestations of witches. There are
several types of evil whales:

- the *Katthveli* or "Cat-whale"
- the *Taumafiskur*, or "Bridle fish"
- the *Nauthveli* or *Nauthvalur*, also: *Nautshval* (Ox-whale); *Nautfiskur*
  (Ox-fish); *Kýrhvalur* (Cow-whale); *Fjósi* (Byre-whale); *Baulhveli*
  (Bellow-whale); *Búrhvalur* (Sperm-whale)
- the *Hrosshvalr*, also: *Hrosshualar, Hrosshveli, Rosshvalur, Monoculus,
  Equinus Cetus* (Horse-whale); *Saehestur* (Sea Horse); *Stökkull* (Jumper,
  probably erroneously); *Stori Svinhvalur* (Large Pig-whale); *Pollur*
  (Tenacious One)
- the *Rauðkembingur*, also: *Raudkembingr, Rauðkembingr,
  Raudkempingur, Red-comb, Red-crest; Raudkembir* (Red-crester);
  Raudkinni (Red-cheek); *Raudkinnung, Raudkinnungur* (Red-cheeker);
  Raudgrani (Red-snout); *Raudhofdi* (Redhead); *Kembingur* (Crest);
  Kembir (Crester); *Faxi* (Maned)
- the *Stokkull*, also: *Stöckull; Blödkuhvalur, Blökuhvalur, Blodkuhvalur*
  (Flap-whale); *Bloejuhvalur* (Veiled-whale); *Springhvalur* (Springing-
  whale); *Stökkfiskar* (Jumping fish); *Sprettfiskur* (Sprinting fish); *Léttir*
  (Agile One); *Léttur* (Light One); *Dettir* (Falling One)
- the *Múshveli*, or "Mouse-whale"

Imp

An *Imp* or *Impet* is, in folklore and witchcraft traditions, a tiny, demonic
creature. Katharine Briggs noted that originally an *imp* or *ympe* is an
off-shoot or cutting. Thus an *ymp tree* was a grafted tree, or one grown
from a cutting, not from seed. 'Imp' thus properly means a "small devil",
an off-shoot of Satan, so to speak. However, Christianity fanatically
tried to demonize every non-biblical entity, especially spirits from

pagan traditions. Thus the distinction between *Goblins* and *Bogles* or all kinds of *Fairies* and Imps from hell got blurred, as the English Puritans regarded all Fairies as devils making the Fairies of tradition – to quote Briggs: *"often hover uneasily between the ghostly and the diabolic state."* Imps are described as restless mischievous beings, rather than serious threats, and occupy a lower position in the hierarchy of demonology. The Devil's helpers are sometimes referred to as "Imps" (*Diablotins* in French). They originally appear in Germanic myths, in which they are described as small, relatively weak and unattractive demons. They love to trick people, but usually do so just to get attention. Even if the imp succeeded in getting the friendship he sought, he would often still play pranks and jokes on his friend, either out of boredom, or because it was simply in the imp's nature. This trait gave way to the English usage of the expression "impish" for someone who loves pranks and tricks. Being associated with hell and fire, Imps derive great pleasure from playing with high temperatures. Although Imps are often considered immortal, many northern peoples believed that they could be harmed or destroyed by certain weapons and spells, or kept out of homes by the use of fences. Imps can be found in art and architecture throughout the Germanic and Anglo-Saxon world, usually carefully and skillfully hidden under the eaves of a church or in the foot of a ceramic goblet, so they can only be found by the most interested and skilled observer.

The Imps of Elizabeth Clarke

In the Middle Ages, Imps were believed to be a kind of *familiar spirit*, servants of witches and warlocks, where the little devils served as their spies and informants. During the time of the witch hunts, all manner of supernatural creatures such as the imp were sought as proof of witchcraft, though often the so-called "Imp" was typically a black cat, lizard, toad or some other form of out-of-the-ordinary pet. One of the most weird and controversial texts on the subject of Imps was written by the British witch persecutor Matthew Hopkins (? -1647), also known as the *Witchfinder General* in 1647. Several Imps or familiars are described, supposedly belonging to Elizabeth Clarke. Supposedly, as we have no direct access to the reality of this poor old woman – only what a psychopath wrote down two years after he tortured her for days *"for the benefit of the nation"*. Elizabeth Clarke (1565-1645), alias Bedinfield, was the first woman persecuted by the Witchfinder General Matthew Hopkins, in 1645 in Essex, England. At 80 years old, she was accused of witchcraft by local tailor John Rivet. Hopkins and John Stearne took on the role of investigators, stating that they had seen familiars while watching her. During the process, she was deprived of sleep for multiple nights before confessing and implicating other women in the local area. She was tried at Chelsford, before being hanged for witchcraft. Below is the "Imp-fragment" *(Querie 4.)* of Matthew Hopkins' *The Discovery of Witches*, published in 1647. The description of the Imps or familiars of Elizabeth Clarke includes their funny names:

"Querie 4.
I pray where was this experience gained? And why gained by him and not by others?

Answ.
The Discoverer never travelled far for it, but in March 1644 he had some seven or eight of that horrible sect of Witches living in the Towne where he lived, a Towne in Essex called Maningtree, with diverse other adjacent Witches of other towns, who every six weeks in the night (being always on the Friday night) had their meeting close by his house and had their severall solemne sacrifices there offered to the Devill, one of which this discoverer heard speaking to her Imps one night, and bid them goe to another Witch, who was thereupon apprehended, and searched, by women who had for many yeares knowne the Devills marks, and found to have three teats about her, which honest women have not: so upon command from the Justice they were to keep her from sleep two or three nights, expecting in that time to see her familiars, which the fourth night she called in by their severall names, and told them what shapes, a quarter of an houre before they came in, there being ten of us in the roome, the first she called was
1. Holt, who came in like a white kitling.
2. Jarmara, who came in like a fat Spaniel without any legs at all, she said she kept him fat, for she clapt her hand on her belly and said he suckt good blood from her body.
3. Vinegar Tom, who was like a long-legg'd Greyhound, with an head like an Oxe, with a long taile and broad eyes, who when this discoverer spoke to, and bade him goe to the place provided for him and his Angels, immediately transformed himselfe into the shape of a child of foure yeeres old without a head, and gave halfe a dozen turnes about the house, and vanished at the doore.

Ina Pic Winna

Ina Pic Winna was a local *Fairy* worshiped by fishermen at Worle, North Somerset, England. Folklorist Ruth Lyndall Tongue recorded that, when the fishermen went down to sea, they each put a white stone on the cairn or 'Fairy mound' on the hillside and said, *Ina Pic Winna, send me a good dinner!* And more times than not they came back with a load of fish.

J

Jack-in-Irons

In Yorkshire *Jack-in-Irons* is a *Night-Bogie*, a gigantic figure in clanking chains, which may at any minute leap out on a benighted wayfarer going by a lonely road.

Jenny-wi't lantern

Jenny-wi't lantern, Jenny's Lantern or *Jenny of the Lantern*, is the reputed Northumbrian name for a *Will-o'-the-wisp*, a form of atmospheric ghost lights, associated with leading travelers to dangerous places. A legend about Jenny-wi't lantern tells of a shepherd who, one night, is drowned in a bog whilst following a lantern lit by his wife Jenny to guide his return home from the inn at Eglingham. Jenny had become a Will-o'-the-wisp that bobbed above of the moors and was dangerous whenever a traveler did not immediately turn their jacket or apron inside out on seeing it.

Jimmy Squarefoot

According to Manx folklore, *Jimmy Squarefoot* was a legendary two-legged pig-headed creature, that haunted the Grenaby district. He had two great tusks, like a boar. It is usually a peaceful wanderer. His large feet are wrapped with coarse cotton strips and appear square, hence the name "Squarefoot". It is said that he was once ridden by one of the *Foawr* (a race of stone-throwing giants), who lived on Cronk yn Irree Lhaa. Elsewhere, it is described that Jimmy Squarefoot himself was initially depicted as a stone-throwing giant, riding a pig, and he seems usually to have thrown his stones at his wife, with whom he was on very bad terms.

Julbock

The *Julbock* in Swedish folklore is now translated as "Christmas goat", but has its origins in the feast of *Yule* (a feast of 12 days which started on December 21) and Old Germanic field-spirit traditions, where animals made of the last bunch of ears of the cornfield functioned as a temporary home for the local field-spirit or daemon that had to ensure a good harvest and protection of the crops. Yule (also called *Jul, Julblot, jól, jólablót, joulu*, meaning "Yule time" or "Yule season") is a festival – historically of the Germanic peoples. Scholars have connected the original celebrations of Yule to the *Wild Hunt*, the god *Odin*, and the pagan Anglo-Saxon *Mōdraniht* (Mothers' Night). Later departing from its pagan roots, Yule underwent Christianized reformulation, resulting in the term *Christmastide*. Some present-day Christmas customs and traditions such as the *Yule log, Yule goat (Julbock), Yule boar, Yule singing*, and others may have connections to older pagan Yule traditions. Cognates to Yule are still used in the Scandinavian languages as well as in Finnish and Estonian to describe Christmas and other festivals occurring during the winter holiday season. Yule is the modern version of Old Norse *Jól* and *Jólnir* one of the names for Odin. The Old English derivates *ġēol* or *ġēohol* and *ġēola* or *ġēoli*, indicate the 12-day festival of "Yule", or "Christmastide", the latter indicating the month of "Yule", whereby *ǣrra ġēola* referred to the period before the Yule festival (December) and *æftera ġēola* referred to the period after Yule (January). Both words derive from Gothic ᚷᛁᚢᛚᛖᛁᛋ (jiuleis); Old Norse, Icelandic, Faroese and Norwegian Nynorsk *jól, jol, ýlir*; Danish, Swedish, and Norwegian *Bokmål jul*, and are thought to be cognate with Proto-Germanic *jehwlą-*. The etymological pedigree of the word remains uncertain, although numerous speculative attempts have been made to find Indo-European cognates outside the Germanic group, too. The noun *Yuletide* is first attested from around 1475.

Julbock synonyms

The Swedish *Julbock*, also *Julgumse* (Yule-ram); Danish: *Julebuk*, *Juleged* (Yule-goat), *Nytårsbuk* (New Year's goat); Norwegian: *Julebukk*, Finnish: *Olkipukki* (Straw goat); Estonian: *Joulosak*; Latvian: *Joulopuk*, today is primarily an object instead of a "field-spirit container". In appearance it is still a goat figure, made of straw, which is a popular Christmas ornament, especially in Denmark, Norway and Sweden. In the past, the Julbock brought the presents, before being replaced by *Santa Claus* (Danish: *Julemand*, Norwegian: *Julenisse*, Swedish: *Jultomte*). In Finland today, *Joulupukki* is synonymous with Santa Claus. By the middle of the 19th century, various Yule rituals were common throughout Scandinavia. In Denmark and Sweden there were also Julbock-cakes. The billy goat as a Christmas symbol with its roots in Germanic religion stood for the annually recurring fertility of the earth (grain goat) and where Yule itself was linked to Odin, the billy goat was originally an embodiment of the thunder god *Thor* or *Donar*. In Germany it has its equivalent in the *Habergeiß* of the Alpine region, the *Klapperbock* on the Baltic island Usedom, or the *Capra* in Transylvania. According to the various Scandinavian legends, the Julbock was imagined as a demonic creature with horns that "generally resembled a goat", only much larger than a goat. In summer he hides in deep forests or inaccessible mountains, and then, in the course of Advent, he comes a little closer to the farms every day, until on Christmas Eve he enters people's homes. His arrival is usually preceded by strange light apparitions and in the house he often first took a seat behind the stove (like a house ghost). Even though the Julbock was originally thought to be a fearsome demon – who, for example, resented imitations by humans and would take small children if not appeased with a sacrifice – he was nevertheless a positive symbol of fertility.

Relation to Krampus

Knecht Ruprecht, who is called *Krampus* in the German-speaking Alpine countries, also takes on a role similar to that of the Julbock. The appearance of a Krampus has similarities with the Norwegian *Julebukklaufen*. However, the Krampus appears on St. Nicholas Day

(December 6th – in the Netherlands December 5th), while the Julbock
runs between the homesteads between "Jul" and New Year's Eve.

The oldest origins

The Julbock tradition is to be seen in connection with the widespread
worship of the goat (and the ram) among many Indo-European peoples as
the embodiment of the annual fertility given by the gods. Corresponding
indications go back to the Bronze Age. The billy goat was either attached
to a mother deity like the Roman goddess *Juno*, who appears everywhere
with a goat, or was itself considered a goat-shaped embodiment of a god.
The Basques, although not Indo-European, worshipped the billy goat
Akerbeltz as a separate god, but also as a manifestation of the goddess *Mari*.
According to the investigations of Franz Rolf Schröder, the Germanic
god Thor formerly had the shape of a goat. Later he is also called by the
epithet *Hafra dróttin* (Lord of the goats). Analogous to the deity *Nerthus*
or *Njörd* his chariot is pulled by two he-goats, known as *Tanngrísnir* and
Tanngnjóstr (Tanngrisnir in Old Norse means "teeth thin", or "one that has
gaps between the teeth" and Tanngnjóstr means "teeth grinder" or "one that
grinds teeth"). According to one tale, they are slaughtered for the meal, but
are resurrected afterwards. In addition to this recurring fertility, various
relationships to lightning and thunderstorms are also attested, of which
goat horns are symbolic. Goats killed by lightning were not allowed to be
eaten, they were considered as sacrifices to Thor. After the Christianization
of the Germanic tribes, the goat is outlawed as an animal of the Devil,
as part of an ongoing policy of overwriting all old pagan traditions and
customs with Christian ones, or eradicating them altogether.

K

Katthveli

In the folklore of Icelandic sailors and fishermen the *Katthveli* (Cat-whale), is one of Iceland's evil whales or *Illhveli*. It is generally smaller and of a less harmful nature than its larger brethren. Like the other Ilhveli, it is inedible. It does not tolerate anyone who mentions its name. Speaking about it at sea is considered as highly foolish.

Kelpie

A *Kelpie* (also *Kelpy*; in Scottish Gaelic *Colpach*, "heifer") is a water-spirit that appears in Scottish folklore. It is not to be confused with the Each Uisge (water-horse), which is said to live on Scottish sea coasts and in inland lochs. The Kelpie does not inhabit the sea, but the flowing waters of the Highlands.

According to the *The Folk-Lore of the North-East of Scotland* by Walter Gregor 1881, the Kelpie or *Water-kelpie* was a creature that lived in the deep pools of rivers and streams, which had commonly the form of a black horse. He appeared at night, and often travelers, in passing through fords or over old bridges, have heard him go splash, splash through the water. At times he approached a traveler, and by some means or other induced him/her to mount him. He rushed to his pool, and carried the unsuspecting victim to its death. The creature pulls its victim into the depths and eats it. If you throw a veil over a Kelpie's head, or if someone manages to snaffle it, it is obliged to be of service to that person. In Celtic folklore, the Kelpie is described as a strong and powerful horse. Its coat is originally black, or white in some stories. It usually looks like a stray pony, but can often be identified by its dripping mane or by the blue sheen next to the actual color of its coat. The skin resembles that of a seal, soft and cold as death when touched. Kelpies are reported to transform into beautiful women to lure men into their trap. They create illusions as shapeshifters to keep themselves hidden. You can only see their eyes above the water surface. According to Walter Gregor a Kelpie could be killed:

"A blacksmith had a small croft. He sent his wife, family, and cow to the sheeling during summer. When the blacksmith was employed in his work, Water kelpie took advantage of his absence, and paid frequent visits to the sheeling, much to the terror and annoyance of the family. At last the wife told the husband. He resolved to kill him. The wife took fright at the proposal, and tried to dissuade him, under the fear that the Kelpie would carry him off to his pool, but to no purpose. The smith prepared two long, sharp-pointed spits of iron and repaired to the sheeling. He put a large fire on the hearth, and laid the two spits in it. In a short time Kelpie made his appearance as usual. The smith waited his opportunity; and with all his might drove the red-hot spits into the creature's sides. It fell as a heap of starch, or something like it."

Kern baby

The term *kern* had a lot of overlapping meanings: corn; grain; kernel; the last handful or sheaf reaped at the harvest; a doll or figurine decorated with corn (or grain) flowers, etc., carried in harvest festivals, or harvest-home in celebration of a successful harvest as the *Kern baby*, also called *Harvest Queen*. Kern comes from the Middle English *curn*, *cooren*, variant forms of English and Middle English *corn*, and also Dutch *koren*, *kern*, Old High German *kerno*, *cherno*, Middle High German *kerne*, *kern*, German *Kern* (core, kernel), the Old Norse *kjarni*, Icelandic *kjarni*, Danish *kjerne*, Swedish *kärna* (core, kernel); see also *kernel*.

The Kern baby was the last English remnant of the ancient Ceres-festivals and the ritual is related to the many German field daemon rituals at the end of the harvest, whereby often puppets made of grain were made to house the good daemon of the field – like the *Roggensau* or one of the many variants – to ensure a good and fertile season the next year. Sometimes a person chosen from the village was also carrying the daemon through the winter months. The last of the Kern babies were made in Northumberland in Whalton. There, a two feet high doll was taken to the church as the presiding genius of the festival. In the northern part of Northumberland at the close of the reaping, not the ingathering, the sickle was laid down and when the last sheaf set on end, the men shouted they had *"got the kern"*. Then a curious image was produced, dressed in a white frock with colored ribbons and crowned with corn ears. It was stuck on a pole and held aloft by the strongest man of the party while the other villagers circled around it. Subsequently it was taken to the barn, set on high and the merrymakers fell to on the harvest supper.

Kilmoulis

In the regions of the Anglo-Scottish border, the *Kilmoulis* is an ugly kind of *Brownie* who is said to haunt mills. The creature is described with a huge nose and no mouth. This lack of a mouth forces him to inhale his food through the nose. The Kilmoulis works hard for the miller, but like most Brownies and household-spirits he also delights in tricks and pranks. While his pranks may be a nuisance, he offers generally enough help to offset the food he eats and the disturbances he causes.

Klippe

Klippe is the Forfarshire name for a *Fairy*. A well-known minister of the Church of Scotland related, not so long ago, at a dinner in Edinburgh, how his father had met a Klippe in a bare moor-land in Forfarshire, a little brown-faced *Elf*, who started up on the path before him, walked before him awhile and then vanished.

Knockers

According to M. A. Courtney (in *Cornish Feasts and Folk-Lore*, 1890) *Knockers*, also *knacker*, *tommyknockers* (USA) are *Mine-Fairies*, under Christian influence popularly believed to be the souls of the Jews that crucified Christ, sent by the Romans to work as slaves in the tin mines. In proof of this, they are said never to have been heard at work on Saturdays, nor other Jewish festivals. They are also compelled to sing carols at Christmas time. Small pieces of smelted tin found in old smelting-works are known as *Jews' bowels*. The name derives from their habit of knocking on the walls of mines. Their knocking is interpreted as hammer blows to make the tunnels collapse. In Cornwall's many tin mines, there were always serious tunnel collapses, and so the miners always left a few bites of their meal in the tunnel as thanks for this warning. Knockers are described as up to six feet tall, they always live underground, and are usually dressed like miners. They especially haunt the richest tin mines, and many are reputed to have been discovered by their singing and

knocking underground; miners think when they hear them, it is a sign
of good luck, because when following their noises they often chance on
lodes of good ore. When a miner goes into an "old level" and sees a bright
light, it is a sure sign that he will find tin there.

Knockers like *Spriggans* are very ugly beings, and, if you do not treat them
in a friendly spirit, very vindictive. "As stiff as Barker's knee" is a common
saying in Cornwall. One miner named Barker had in some way angered
the Knockers, either by speaking of them disrespectfully or by not leaving
behind a bit of his dinner on the ground for them (for good luck). In
revenge they threw all their tools in his lap, which crippled him for the
rest of his life. There is a similar story of a man named Tom Trevorrow,
who when he was working underground heard the Knockers just before
him, and roughly told them "to be quiet and go." Upon which a shower of
stones suddenly fell around him, which gave him a dreadful fright.

Kraken or Hafgufa

The *Kraken*, (Danish: *Krake, Kraxe, Krabbe*) is a legendary mythical
sea monster of gigantic size, a cephalopod mollusk known from the
descriptions of Icelandic sailors, from whose language its name is derived.
According to the Norse sagas, the Kraken dwells off the coasts of Norway
and Greenland and terrorizes nearby sailors. The English word *kraken*
is taken from the modern Scandinavian languages, originating from
the Old Norse word *kraki*. In both Norwegian and Swedish, *Kraken* is
the definite form of *krake*, a word designating an unhealthy animal or
something twisted (cognate with the English *crook* and *crank*). After
returning from Greenland, the anonymous author of the Old Norwegian
natural history work *Konungs skuggsjá* (circa 1250) described in detail
the physical characteristics and feeding behavior of these creatures. The
narrator proposed there must be only two in existence, stemming from
the observation that the beasts have always been sighted in the same parts
of the Greenland Sea, and that each seemed incapable of reproduction, as
there was no increase in their numbers. He does not use the term *Kraken*
but *Hafgufa* (Sea mist):

> *"There is a fish that is still unmentioned, which it is scarcely advisable
> to speak about on account of its size, because it will seem to most
> people incredible. There are only a very few who can speak upon it*

*clearly, because it is seldom near land nor appears where it may be
seen by fishermen, and I suppose there are not many of this sort of
fish in the sea. Most often in our tongue we call it hafgufa. Nor can
I conclusively speak about its length in ells, because the times he has
shown before men, he has appeared more like land than like a fish."*

In the late13th-century version of the Old Icelandic saga *Örvar-Oddr*
is an inserted episode of a journey bound for Helluland (Baffin Island),
which takes the protagonists through the Greenland Sea, and here they
spot two massive sea-monsters called *Hafgufa* (sea mist) and *Lyngbakr*
(heather-back). The Hafgufa is believed to be a reference to the Kraken:

*"Now I will tell you that there are two sea-monsters. One is
called the Hafgufa, another Lyngbakr. It [the Lyngbakr] is the
largest whale in the world, but the Hafgufa is the largest monster
in the sea. It is the nature of this creature to swallow men and
ships, and even whales and everything else within reach."*

In Olaus Magnus' (1555) work *Historia de Gentibus Septentrionalibus*
(History of the northern Peoples), he describes the Kraken as a serpent so
bold that it would come out from its underwater cave on bright summer
nights to feast on calves, lambs and pigs. This beast was said to be 200 feet
long and 20 feet wide and was believed to live outside Bergen. Kraken
were extensively described by Erik Pontoppidan, bishop of Bergen, in
his *Det første Forsøg paa Norges naturlige Historie* (Copenhagen, 1752).
Pontoppidan made several claims regarding Kraken, including the notion
that the creature was sometimes mistaken for an island and that the real
danger to sailors was not the creature itself but rather the whirlpool it left
in its wake. Anticipating on the work of Pontoppidan, Swedish author
Jacob Wallenberg described the Kraken in 1781 in his work *Min son på
galejan* (My son on the galley):

*"Kraken, also called the Crab-fish, which is not that huge, for heads
and tails counted, he is no larger than our Öland is wide [i.e., less than
10 miles/16 km] ... He stays at the sea floor, constantly surrounded by
innumerable small fishes, who serve as his food and are fed by him in
return: for his meal lasts no longer than three months, and another three
are then needed to digest it. His excrements nurture the following army of
lesser fish, and for this reason, fishermen plumb after his resting place ..."*

According to Pontoppidan, Norwegian fishermen often took the risk of trying to fish over the Kraken, since the catch was so plentiful (hence the saying *"You must have fished on Kraken"*.

Part of the Kraken remains a legendary monster, lurking in the depths of the northern seas and fjords, part of it remains an unsure factor within the field of cryptozoology, as it is mostly described as an octopus-like being of a size far exceeding the largest known specimen of the species, and finally part of it is debunked by sea-biologists as the colossal squid (Mesonychoteuthis hamiltoni) or giant squid (Architeuthis dux), as disappointing as their sizes may be.

Kvarngubbe

In later Swedish folklore, *Kvarngubbe* was a spirit-being that lived in mills and either helped the miller or worked against him. This creature shared traits with both *Näcken* and the farmer, as like Näcken he was a skilled violinist, while like the farmer he was very strong and helped his master, the miller. He was also known as *Bäckahästen* in Skåne (although Bäckahästen is normally used for the Scandinavian version of the British-Celtic water-horse), *Strömkarl*, common in Småland, Västergötland, Värmland and Uppland, while further north he was called *Forskarl*, *Kvarngubbe* or *Kvarnrå*. The term Kvarngubbe is most common in northern Sweden.

L

Lagarfljótsormurinn

The *Lagarfljótsormurinn* (Lagarfljót worm) is a *Vatnaormur* or *Lyndorm*, a mythical water serpent-like animal that is said to live in Lagarfljót, a lake near the Icelandic town of Egilsstaðir. Seeing it's body come out of the water was regarded as bad luck. The Lagarfljótsormurinn is described as a type of sea serpent, with information on its length varying from 10 to 90 meters. The idea of the Lagarfljótsormurinn goes back to a legend contained in Jón Árnason's collection of Icelandic folk tales and legends. This collection, published between 1862 and 1864, contains the story of a girl who lived near Lagarfljót. She put a golden brooch together with a small worm in a box, hoping to increase the gold in this way. Instead of the gold, however, the worm grew and the girl threw the box in panic into the Lagarfljót. There the worm continued to grow, but was able to be chained with head and tail to the bottom of the lake by Lapp sorcerers. Occasionally it arches its back over the water, and that is an ill omen. Sightings of the worm were first written down in 1345, and also in 1479, 1555, 1589 (by bishop Oddur Einarsson), 1594, 1749-1750 and 1819, appearing as a great snake with humps or spikes on its back, or a monstrous horse. Sometimes it stretches itself onto the riverbanks while spewing massive amounts of poison. Over the centuries, the worm has been described, among other things, as a giant monster that destroys ships or even houses, or as a harbinger of coming misfortune. In the 20th century, the worm continued to be reportedly seen in various places in and also near the water. After having dwelt for a long time on the threshold of ancient myth and a cryptozoological possibility, on February 2, 2012, the local farmer Hjörtur Kjerulf filmed a large serpent-like creature, swimming slowly like a huge water-snake in a river flowing into Lagarfljót. The video gained notoriety on the internet and in international media, after being broadcast by the Icelandic television station Ríkisútvarpið. He filmed it again on March 8. Alas, as a YouTube video is never 100% airtight evidence, what remains is that one can choose to believe in the Lagarfljótsormurinn or not.

Last corn cut

The last corn cut was called the *Mell*, the *Kirn*, or the *Churn* in various parts of England, Scotland, and Ireland, the *Maiden* in the Highlands of Scotland, or the *Clyack sheaf*, in Aberdeenshire. All over the European continent the same ritual meaning was attached to the last cut of corn, wheat, rye, barley etc. The last ears were usually kept – often braided in the shape of some animal, like a pig or other form – to house the field-spirit (responsible for the fertility and protection of the fields) during the autumn and winter months.

Lazy Laurence

According to folklorist and storyteller Ruth Lyndall Tongue (1898-1981), *Lazy Laurence* was a guardian spirit of the orchard, in Hampshire and Somerset. In Hampshire, he sometimes took the form of a foal and chased orchard thieves. In Somerset, Lazy Laurence seems rather to afflict thieves with what is described in one of the so called "night spells" in British Museum MS. 36674 as: *"Crampe and crookeing and fault in their footing"*.

Leannán sídhe

The *Leannán sídhe* (lit. Fairy lover; Scottish Gaelic: *Leannan sìth*; Manx: *Lhiannan shee*) is a figure from Irish Folklore. She is depicted as a beautiful woman of the *Aos Sí* (People of the Barrows) that takes a human lover. Lovers of the Leannán sídhe are said to live brief, though highly inspired, lives. The name comes from the Gaelic words for a sweetheart, lover, or concubine and the term for the inhabitants of Fairy mounds. While the Leannán sídhe is most often depicted as a female *Fairy*, there is at least one reference to a male Leannán sídhe troubling a mortal woman. A version of the myth was popularized during the Celtic Revival in the late 19th century. The Leannán sídhe is mentioned in Jane Wilde's writings as "Speranza", in her 1887 *Ancient Legends, Mystic Charms and Superstitions of Ireland*. W. B. Yeats popularized his own 'newly-ancient' version of the Leannán sídhe, emphasizing the spirit's almost vampiric tendencies. As he imagined it, the Leannán sídhe is depicted as a beautiful muse who offers inspiration to an artist, in exchange for their love and devotion; although the supernatural affair leads to madness and eventual death for the artist;

*"The Leanhaun Shee (fairy mistress) seeks the love of mortals. If
they refuse, she must be their slave; if they consent, they are hers,
and can only escape by finding another to take their place. The fairy
lives on their life, and they waste away. Death is no escape from
her. She is the Gaelic muse, for she gives inspiration to those she
persecutes. The Gaelic poets die young, for she is restless, and will
not let them remain long on earth—this malignant phantom."*

Leprechaun

The Anglo-Irish word *Leprechaun,* used for the most popular dwarfish,
humanoid spirit of Ireland, has a complex etymology. Scholars
maintained that Leprechaun descended from Old Irish *Luchorpán* or
Lupracán, via various (Middle Irish) forms such as *Luchrapán, Lupraccán,*
(or *Luchrupán*). Leprechaun or *Lepricaun* was derived from the Irish
leith brog i.e., the *One-shoemaker*, since he is generally seen working
at a single shoe. It is spelt in Irish *leith bhrogan*, or *leith phrogan*, and
is in some places pronounced *Luchryman* (O'Kearney in *Feis Tigh
Chonain*). Another theory states that "Leprechaun" may come from the
Irish root *lú*, meaning "smaller," and from the Irish root *chorp*, derived
from the Latin word "corpus", meaning "body", but the latest academic
research concluded that Leprechaun is originally not an Irish word.
Research published in 2019 by a team of five academics, from Cambridge
University and Queen's University Belfast, suggests that although
Leipreachán has been in the Irish language for a long time, it comes from
Luperci, a group linked to the Roman festival of *Lupercalia*. The feast
included a purification ritual involving swimming and, like the *Luperci*,
Leprechauns were also associated with water in what may be their first
appearance in early Irish literature.

The earliest known reference to the Leprechaun appears in the medieval
tale known as the *Echtra Fergus mac Léti* (Adventure of Fergus son of
Léti) of which there are two widely divergent versions: one from the 7th
or 8th century, and a burlesque, Rabelaisian one from the 13th. The text
contains an episode in which Fergus mac Léti, the legendary King of
Ulster from 26-14 BC, falls asleep on the beach and wakes to find himself
being dragged into the sea by three *water-sprites* or *lúchorpáin*. He
captures his abductors, who grant him three wishes in exchange for their
release.

Features and appearances

Although originally a water-sprite, William Butler Yeats classed the Leprechaun as a "solitary Fairy", although clearly to be distinguished from the *Aos Sí* (good people) of the Fairy mounds (sidhe). Folklorist Diarmuid Ó Giolláin however observes that the dwarf of Teutonic and other traditions as well as the household familiar are more amenable to comparison. This is underlined by modern comparisons of the Leprechaun with the German *Kobold*, French *Lutin*, Dutch *Kabouter*, etc. One has to keep in mind however, that the modern image of the Leprechaun sitting on a toadstool, having a red beard and green hat, etc. is clearly a modern invention. John O'Donovan's supplement to O'Reilly's Irish-English Dictionary defines *Lugharcán, Lugracán, Lupracán* as *"a sprite, a pigmy; a fairy of a diminutive size, who always carries a purse containing a shilling"*. According to David Russell McAnally (*Irish Wonders*, 1888) the Leprechaun is the son of an "evil spirit" and a "degenerate fairy" and is *"not wholly good nor wholly evil"*. Concerning their clothing Yeats stated that the solitary Fairies, like the Leprechaun, wear red jackets, whereas the "trooping Fairies" wear green. The Leprechaun's jacket has seven rows of buttons with seven buttons to each row. On the western coast, he writes, the red jacket is covered by a frieze one, and in Ulster the creature wears a cocked hat, and when he is up to anything unusually mischievous, he leaps onto a wall and spins, balancing himself on the point of the hat with his heels in the air. McAnally describes the Leprechaun as *"about three feet high, and dressed in a little red jacket or roundabout, with red breeches buckled at the knee, gray or black stockings, and a hat, cocked in the style of a century ago, over a little, old, withered face. Round his neck is an Elizabethan ruff, and frills of lace are at his wrists. On the wild west coast, where the Atlantic winds bring almost constant rains, he dispenses with ruff and frills and wears a frieze overcoat over his pretty red suit, so that, unless on the lookout for the cocked hat, ye might pass a Leprechawn on the road and never know it's himself that's in it at all."* This dress could vary by region, however. In McAnally's account there were differences between Leprechauns or *Logherymans* from different regions:

- The *Northern Leprechaun* or *Logheryman* wore a *"military red coat and white breeches, with a broad-brimmed, high, pointed hat, on which he would sometimes stand upside down"*.
- The *Lurigadawne* of Tipperary wore an *"antique slashed jacket of red, with peaks all round and a jockey cap, also sporting a sword, which he uses as a magic wand"*.

- The *Luricawne* of Kerry was a *"fat, pursy little fellow whose jolly round face rivals in redness the cut-a-way jacket he wears, that always has seven rows of seven buttons in each row"*.
- The *Cluricawne* of Monaghan wore *"a swallow-tailed evening coat of red with green vest, white breeches, black stockings, shiny shoes, and a long cone hat without a brim, sometimes used as a weapon.*

David Russel McAnnaly wrote that in regions Galway and Clare:

"[…] the favorite amusement of the Leprechawn is riding a sheep or goat, or even a dog, when the other animals are not available, and if the sheep look weary in the morning or the dog is muddy and worn out with fatigue, the peasant understands that the local Leprechawn has been going on some errand that lay at greater distance than he cared to travel on foot. Aside from riding the sheep and dogs almost to death, the Leprechawn is credited with much small mischief in the house. Sometimes he will make the pot boil over and put out the fire, then again he will make it impossible for the pot to boil at all. He will steal the bacon-flitch, or empty the potato-kish, or fling the baby down on the floor, or occasionally will throw the few poor articles of furniture about the room with a strength and vigor altogether dis-proportioned to his diminutive size. But his mischievous pranks seldom go further than to drink up all the milk or despoil the proprietor's bottle of its poteen, sometimes, in sportiveness, filling the bottle with water, or, when very angry, leading the fire up to the thatch, and then startling the inmates of the cabin with his laugh as they rise, frightened, to put out the flames."

Leprechauns liked the company of people and could also get very attached to a family, only leaving them for good when deeply insulted; for instance when the dog ate the food leftovers that were put there for him. According to William Butler Yeats, the great wealth of the Leprechauns comes from the "treasure-crocks, buried of old in war-time", which they have uncovered and appropriated. They are however unwilling to share their treasures with humans. In later fairytales the Leprechaun appears with his pot of gold at the end of the rainbow. The association of the Leprechaun with a dwarfish shoemaker is kept alive in folk etymology, which derives the word Leprechaun in the alternative spelling *Leithbrágan* from *leith* (half) and *bróg* (brogue), because of the frequent portrayal of the Leprechaun as working on a single shoe.

Lhiannan-Shee

Katharine Briggs describes the *Lhiannan-Shee* of Manx folklore as a
vampiric spirit who attaches herself to a man, to whom she appears
irresistibly beautiful, while staying invisible to everyone else. If he yields
to her seduction, he is ruined, body and soul. The Irish *Leanan-sidhe* is
more favorably regarded, as a life-giving spirit, the inspiration of poets
and minstrels, though also fatal in the end. The confusing thing here is
that both names mean 'the fairy sweetheart'. Like *Melusine*, the Lhiannan-
Shee haunted wells and springs.

Lí Ban or Muirgeilt

Lí Ban or *Liban'* (from Old Irish *lí* "beauty", and *ban* "of women", hence
"paragon of femininity"), was a woman turned into a *Mermaid* in the
legend surrounding the formation of Lough Neagh, who inhabited
the area before the great lake gushed up on dry land. Her family was
drowned, but she survived in an underwater chamber in the lake for a
year, after which she was transformed into a being that was half-human,
half-salmon. Many legends and folktales surround Lí Ban. The oldest was
written down in the *Annals of the Four Masters*, which was compiled in
the 17th century: Liban, the daughter of Eochaid, was captured in the
year 558 AD on the bank of "Ollarbha" (River Larne, or Inver River in
Larne), in the net of a fisherman from St. Comgall of Bangor. Her capture
is also given brief notice in the year 571 in the *Annals of Ulster*.

An account of Liban's life story is found in the tale *Aided Echach maic
Maireda* (Death of Eochaid son of Mairid), preserved in the 12th century
Lebor na hUidre (Book of the Dun Cow). According to this old tale, the
Mermaid was free to roam the seas for 300 years, while maintaining her
dwelling under the same Lough, together with her lapdog, which had
assumed the form of an otter. During the time of St. Comgall, her angelic
singing causes her to be discovered by a passing boat (coracle), and she
agreed to come ashore. The Mermaid was then baptized *Muirgen* (Sea-
born), but died immediately and ascended to heaven. Another legend
has solidified Lí Ban into a Catholic saint; in her Mermaid-form, she was
spotted by the ship carrying a messenger sent by St. Comgall to Rome.
She promised to meet at the seaport inlet of Inbhear nOllarbha (Larne
Lough) in Ireland after one year, and was captured in a fishnet. There she
was baptized by St. Comgall, and given the Christened name *Muirgein*

Kraken by Pierre Denys-Montfort (1766-1820) engraved by Étienne Claude Voysard in 1801

(Sea-born) or *Muirgeilt* (Sea-wanderer). She appears to be canonized as *St. Muirgen* in genealogies of Irish saints, her day of celebration assigned to January 27 and she is venerated by both the Eastern Orthodox Church and Roman Catholic Church.

Llamhigyn Y Dwr

In Welsh folklore the Llamhigyn Y Dwr ("Water Leaper" in English) is a malevolent Fairy, described as a giant frog with bat's wings instead of forelegs, no hind legs, and a long, lizard-like tail with a stinger at the end. It jumps across the water using its wings, hence its name. It was blamed for problems ranging from snapping fishing lines to eating livestock or even fishermen.

Loireag

In the folklore of the Hebrides and western Scotland the *Loireag* or *Lorreag* is a kind of *Water-Nymph* or *Sprite* famous for the unparalleled talent that she shows in the art of spinning and weaving, for which she takes care of the strict respect of the traditions and the rites. She is related to the *Habetrot* of the Low Lands. When Loireags catch a woman spinning or weaving without respecting customs and rites, they will show a clear resentment towards her, sometimes going as far as canceling all her work in order to force her to start again from scratch. A Loireag will be particularly annoyed if the woman allows herself to sing the same song twice during the washing of the raw wool, or if she sings out of tune or has a hoarse or metallic voice.

In terms of appearance, the Loireag resembles a young girl with a pale complexion, dressed in white, but with the size of a newborn. Her clothes are said to be those of the inhabitants of the west of Scotland. She is fond of milk and of milk produce, and she is said to suck the goat, the sheep, and the cow when she gets the opportunity, placing a spell upon the creatures to refrain them from moving while she was drinking. To prevent her from sucking and cursing their animals, the inhabitants of the Hebrides offered the Loireag a libation of milk.

Lubberkin

The *Lubberkin, Lubber fiend, Lob, Lurdane* or *Lob Lie-By-The-Fire* is a male *household-spirit* of English folklore. He has been related also to *Robin Goodfellow* and *Hobgoblins*. He is best known for being mentioned by John Milton. The Lubberkin is typically described as a large, hairy man with a tail, who performs housework in exchange for a saucer of milk and a place in front of the fire. One story claims he is the son of a witch and the Devil. A special version is the *Abbey Lubber* that haunts the wine cellars and kitchens of abbeys, tempting the monks into drunkenness, gluttony and lasciviousness.

Luideag

The *Luideag* is a murderous female *water-demon* of the Scottish Gaelic oral tradition, related to the fearful *Athach*, a mythical giant in Scottish lore. Squalid in appearance, as she was evil, the Luideag haunted several pools on the Isle of Skye, especially the Lochan of the Black Trout.

Lunantishee

In Irish lore the *Lunantishee* are a class of Moon-worshipping *Fairies* that guard the sloes (blackthorn trees) and will not allow any branches to be cut from those trees on 11 November (originally All Hallows Day) or on 11 May (originally May Day). If you cut blackthorn on those days, some misfortune will befall you.

Ly Erg

Ly Erg is a death related *Fairy* from Scottish folklore, particularly associated with the area in and around the Glenmore Forest, part of the present-day Cairngorms National Park. He is dressed as a soldier, and distinguishable from a real soldier only by his diminutive size and red right hand, said to be stained with the blood of its victims. While out walking, it will stop near water and by raising its right hand challenge passersby to fight. Writing in 1847, the antiquarian Joseph Robertson reports that in the 17th century, for instance, three separate men encountered Ly Erg, fought him and died forthwith. By all accounts any adversary to Ly Erg will not live longer than two weeks. Ly Erg's act of raising his red hand to a person is a portent of death for that unfortunate soul. Ly Erg shares the affinity for water with the *Banshee*, who is seen by the riverbanks washing clothes – but only by those for whom death is nigh. If you encounter the Scottish Ly Erg, the best thing to do is make a calm retreat and hope he doesn't raise his right red hand.

Lyktgubbe

The *Lyktgubbe* (Lantern man) or *Lyktgubbar* is the name given in Swedish folklore to the *Irrblossen (Will-o'-the-wisps)*, out in nature that were often associated with a creature carrying a lantern. For example, the more general idea might be that the Will-o'-the-wisp was the soul of some dead person. Will-o'-the-wisps have been reported from cemeteries and gallows, and the Lyktgubbe could be a ghost that had not been laid to rest in its grave. In some parts of Sweden, this creature was the ghost of a man who, lantern in hand, watched over money that had been wrongly buried, or over someone who had moved landmarks without legal permission.

M

Maggy Moulach

Maggy Moulach (also known as: *Meg Mullach, Maggie Moloch, Maug Moulack, Maug Moulach, Mieg Moulach, Maug Vuluchd, May Moulach, Meg Molloch, Manch Monlach* and *Hairy Meg*) is a character from Scottish folklore said to be a Highland Brownie. According to the folklore, Maggy Moulach had a son named *Brownie-Clod*, who was said to be a *Dobie*. A Dobie is a somewhat dull-witted, though well-intentioned, variety of Brownie. Maggy Moulach is described as a two feet tall creature with an impressive head of hair or (and), as told in other lore, with hairy hands; that's why she was sometimes called *Hairy Meg*. In some later versions of the story, it is said that she reached down chimneys and stole children. She was also capable of shape-shifting into a grasshopper.

In the earlier legends, it is said that Maggy and her son were living in Tullochgorm castle, which belonged to the *Grant family*. She performed the usual labors of a Brownie, but also helped the clan chief beat his opponents at chess. She also functioned as a *Banshee*, announcing the deaths of members of this family.

Mallt-y-Nos

Mallt-y-Nos or *Matilda of the Night*, is an ugly and vicious old crone from the Celtic mythology of Wales. The Welsh term *mallt* goes back to the Welsh noun *malltod*, which means "curse, blight, rot, decomposition" or "blast of wind". *Nos* is the noun for "night". Thus Mallt-y-Nos can be translated as "curse of the night".

Mallt-y-Nos rides in the *Wild Hunt* together with *Arawn* and the *Cŵn Annwn*, the hounds from the Otherworld. She drives the hounds with her wailing cries and screams, who then hunt the lost souls for Annwn. It is also said that she was once a beautiful but godless Norman noblewoman, who came with Fitzhamon of Gloucester to subdue South Wales. She loved hunting above everything else. Her cry, *"If there is no hunting in heaven, I never want to go there!"* came true, which is why she now cries so wailingly as she rides through the night. When she died, the Welsh god of the Otherworld, Arawn, appeared and took care of her soul. During her lifetime she had been an extremely beautiful woman, but after her death she was transformed into a terrible and ugly witch. Matilda was condemned by Arawn to hunt for all eternity.

There is a second story which also tells of a young Welsh lady who loved hunting, but her fiancé thought nothing of it for women. At her wedding, he promised never to hunt again and she also agreed. However, she missed hunting very much. For over a year she longed for it, but her husband forbade it. Once when he was absent for a while, she seized the opportunity. For a whole day she rode with a hunting party, forcing everyone to keep quiet about it. Unfortunately, on the way back, she was thrown from her horse and broke her leg. When her husband returned, he immediately guessed what had happened and that she had broken her promise not to hunt. He stormed out of the house and consulted a *dyn hysbys* (wise man, sorcerer). The two men returned to the castle and uttered imprecations that caused the young woman to rise from the ground into the air and throw her to the wind. As a whirlwind sucked her upward, she was rescued by Arawn, who placed her in a chariot to lead *Annwn's hunt*.

Mandragora

According to Rosemary Ellen Guiley (in *The Encyclopedia of Demons and Demonology*) *Mandragoras* – apart from a name used for the mandrake – are demons that appears in the shape of little beardless men with thin hair. Mandragoras also are small puppets, or dolls, that are inhabited by the Devil and used in spell-casting. Mandragoras would predict the future by nodding their head, and can converse with their owners. They bestow good health, curing of disease, and protection of homes against evil.

Marmennill

In Icelandic folklore, *Marmennill* is a male sea creature that, like the *Mermaid*, has a human upper body and a fish tail as its lower body. The creature was believed to have the ability to predict the future. The female equivalent, a creature with long golden blond hair, was called *Margygur* and a similar creature in Sweden and Denmark was called *Havmannen*. Sometimes they are fished alive from the sea. They then want to be released the same way as they were caught. Marmennills can see humans' and animals' inner emotions and see through physical objects, and if one is displeased, it might reveal you things you really, really did not want to know. They herd beautiful sea-green cows with a blister between the nostrils, which must be broken in order to obtain them. The cattle of the Icelandic *Mermen* and Mermaids (*Scevar-büar* or *Vatna-büar*) also include the *Nykur* or *Nennir*, a gray horse with its hooves turned outward. It lives in fast-flowing rivers and can assume all kinds of forms. It offers to carry people over wild mountain streams. If, however, a person sits on its back, it will jump into the water and pull its rider down with it.

Marool

The *Marool* (also: *Angler-fish, Carrachan, Devil-fish, Keddle-man, Kethrie, Kettach, Kilmaddy, Marmaid, Mareillen, Marsgum, Masgum, Merlin-fish, Molly Gowan, Monk-fish, Plucker, Shoemaker, Toad-fish, Weever, Widegab*) was regarded as a malicious fish shaped sea-devil and perhaps the most malevolent of the Shetland sea-monsters. It is described by Jessie Saxby in *Shetland Traditional Lore* as having a crest of flickering flame, and eyes all over his head. He often appeared in the center of *mareel* (seafoam when it is phosphorescent). He delighted in storm, and was heard to shout his wild exultant song when some luckless bark went under.

Melsh Dick

Melsh Dick is a *wood-demon* and *Orchard-Fairy* that protects the unripe nuts from children in the West Riding of Yorkshire. The importance of nut thickets in earlier rural economy may be judged by the number of supernatural beliefs surrounding them, such as the appearance of the Devil to Sunday nut-gatherers, and the fertility value ascribed to nuts. "*So many cratches* [baskets]*, so many cradles*" is a Somerset proverb.

Merrow

The *Merrow*, or as it is written in Irish, *Moruadh* or *Murúghach*, from *muir* (sea) and *oigh* (a maid), is the Irish equivalent of the Mermaid, inhabiting the wilder coasts of the island. Like them they are beautiful, although with fishes' tails and little webs between their fingers. The fishermen do not like to see them, because they appear before coming gales, but they are gentler than most Mermaids and often fall in love with mortal fishermen. The offspring of these marriages are sometimes said to be covered with scales. The male Merrows have green teeth, green hair, pig's eyes, and red noses; but their women are beautiful, for all their fish tails and the little duck-like webs between their fingers. Sometimes female Merrows prefer good-looking fishermen to their sea lovers. Near Bantry, in the last century, there is said to have been a woman covered all over with scales like a fish, who was descended from such a marriage. Sometimes they come out of the sea, and wander about the shore in the shape of little hornless cows. They have, when in their own shape, a red cap, called a cohullen druith, usually covered with feathers. If this cap is stolen from them, they cannot again go down under the waves.

Moddey Dhoo

The *Moddey Dhoo* (Manx Gaelic for: "black dog") is a black phantom hound in Manx folklore that reputedly haunted Peel Castle on the west coast of the Isle of Man. The Manx name Moddey Dhoo was transcribed as *Mauthe Doog* by the influential 18th century English topographer and poet George Waldron, which led to a history of misspellings of the proper name. Waldron was however the first to put a description of the phantom on paper (*History and Description of the Isle of Man* (1st ed. 1731) 1744 edition, p.23):

> *"They say, that an apparition called, in their language, the Mauthe Doog, in the shape of a large black spaniel with curled shaggy hair, was used to haunt Peel Castle; and has been frequently seen in every room, but particularly in the guard-chamber, where, as soon as candles were lighted, it came and lay down before the fire in presence of all the soldiers, who at length, by being so much accustomed to the sight of it, lost great part of the terror they were seized with at its first appearance."*

According to the same author:

> *"There used to be a passage connected to the Peel Castle, traversing the church grounds, leading to the apartment of the Captain of the Guard, and the Mauthe Doog was always seen to come from that passage at the close of day, and return to it again as soon as the morning dawned."*

Waldron reports that one drunken guard of the castle, who in defiance of the dog, went against the usual procedure of locking up the castle gate in pairs, and did this all alone. Emboldened by liquor, he *"snatched up the keys"* when it wasn't even his turn to do so. The watchman, after locking up, was supposed to use the haunted passage to deliver the keys to the captain. Some noises were heard, the adventurer returned to the guard-room, ghastly frightened, unable to share the story of what he had seen, and died three days later. That was the last sighting of the dog. But the passage was sealed up and never used again after the haunting, and a different pathway constructed. The dog was made known to the world at large when Sir Walter Scott introduced the *"Manthe Dog – a fiend, or demon, in the shape of a large, shaggy, black mastiff"* in *Peveril of the Peak* (1823), an installment of his Waverley novels. Here he freely adapted the folklore to suit his plot, but Scott derived knowledge of this folklore through Waldron's work. Note how Scott took the liberty to scale up the size of the dog in his novel.

Moddey Dhoo became more or less in use as a generic term for Manx phantom dogs ever since. Manx scholar, folklorist and poet William Walter Gill (1876-1963), preserved some of the local lore regarding *Black Dogs* appearing in the Manx landscape, as well as firsthand eyewitness accounts: A field near Ballamodda, near a field named *Robin y Gate* (Robin of the Road) was haunted by an *"ordinary Moddey Dhoo"*, in contrast to Ballagilbert Glen or Kinlye's Glen, where stood a farmhouse on the east side, and in the lane leading to it *"lurked a Moddey Dhoo, headless like that at Hango"*. Gill also reports sightings of Moddey Dhoo at a spot called Milntown corner, close to Ramsey: In 1927, a friend saw it turning towards Glen Auldyn, and it was *"black, with long shaggy hair, with eyes like coals of fire,"* and a doctor while driving the road beyond the corner 1931 encountered *"a big black dog-like creature nearly the size of a calf, with bright staring eyes"*.

Modyrmi

In Iceland the *Modyrmi* (hay wormling) is a canine variant of supernatural cat-like creatures like the *Skoffin* and *Urdarköttur*. A Modyrmi is supposedly created when puppies born with their eyes open sink into the ground and reappear after three years as wretched, virulent monsters.

Mooinjer veggey

In Manx folklore *Mooinjer veggey* is (like *Sleig beggey*) a term for *Little people*, the *Fairies* or *Faeries* in Gaelic lore. The equivalents in Irish and Scottish Gaelic are *Muintir Bheaga* and *Muinntir Bheaga*. The Mooinjer veggey are small creatures of two to three feet (60 to 90 cm) in height, but otherwise very like mortal humans in appearance. They wear red caps and green jackets and are most often seen on horseback, followed by a pack of little hounds in all the colors of the rainbow. They are rather inclined to be mischievous and spiteful. They are visible to people only when they choose to. Some of them are benevolent, curing men of diseases and delivering them from misfortune. Others are malevolent, stealing children, even abducting adults, and bringing misfortune.

It was an old custom to keep a fire burning in the house during the night, so that the Mooinjer veggey might come in and enjoy it. It is said that on dark, dismal and stormy nights, in the mountain parts of parishes, the people would retire to rest earlier, in order to allow the weather-beaten Mooinjer veggey the unwatched enjoyment of the smoldering embers of the turf fire. It was also customary to leave some bread out for these Fairies and to fill the water crocks with clean water for them, before going to bed. This water was never used for any other purpose, but was thrown out in the morning. Manx-women would not spin on Saturday evenings, as this was deemed displeasing to the Mooinjer-Veggey, and at every baking and churning a small piece of dough and butter was stuck on the wall for their consumption. Both salt and iron were considered efficacious against a Mooinjer veggey that behaved malevolent.

Mothan

The Scots believed that a herb called *mothan* protected humans against Fairy-spells. The milk of a cow that had eaten from the mothan was similarly efficacious. This folk-remedy was recorded on paper by Donald Mackenzie in his *Scottish Folk-Lore and Folk Life – Studies in Race, Culture and Tradition* (1935).

Muilearteach

The *Muilearteach* is the watery form of the *Cailleach Bheur*. As a sea-spirit, she had a reptilian as well as a human form. But on land, she appeared as an old hag. In some stories she is begging to be allowed to warm herself at a fire and then gradually swells in size and ferocity. She raised winds and sea-storms. She had a blue-black face and only one eye, and is distinguished only from the Cailleach Bheur by her connection with the sea.

Myling or Myrding

A *Myling* or *Myrding* in Swedish folklore was, like the Slavic *Poroniec* a Revenant of an unbaptized, newborn child who had been murdered and hidden by its mother. According to some traditions, the dead child was even buried under the wooden floor of a house or shed, to hide the child's unwanted birth. Folk tales tell how the murderous mother is revealed when the Myling sings a song about its fate. Mylings were believed to be found in places where young mothers might have hidden their killed child, for example under bushes of dog roses, in compost heaps, in bogs, on forest slopes or in storerooms. From these places, one could sometimes hear children's cries. The unbaptized child could also be heard calling for help with the words, *"Give me a name!"* and one could save the child by replying, *"You can have mine, my name is NN."* One could also help by searching for its body and then burying it in consecrated ground in the cemetery.

One legend tells of an old day laborer who was on his way from the pub and was approached by a young boy with the following words: *"Grandpa, Grandpa, can I have pappa?"* (The word "Pappa" is dialectal and means "to breastfeed"). The old man refused to engage in the question, but the boy kept asking the question until the old man replied, *"If you have pappa let it feed you, but you won't be breastfed by me."* The boy disappeared. When the old man finally came home to his parlor, he found his daughter, still living at home, dead on the pull-out sofa full of blood flowing from her breasts. The old man's response gave the boy the opportunity to take revenge on his mother. When the boy was given permission to be breastfed, he knew where to go.

N

Na fir ghorma

Na fir ghorma are creatures capable of raising storms and capsizing boats, inhabiting the waters between the Scottish mainland and northern Outer Hebrides, looking for sailors to drown and stricken boats to sink. They appear to be localized to the Minch Strait (a strait that separates the northwest Highlands of Scotland and the northern Inner Hebrides from the northern Outer Hebrides), and surrounding areas to the north and as far east as Wick, and are unknown in other parts of Scotland. The Na fir ghorma are also known as the *Blue men of the Minch*, or *Storm-Kelpies*. Their appearance is anthropomorphic, including their size, but they have blue skin. The Scottish folklorist Lewis Spence thought they were the *"personification of the sea itself"* as they took their blue coloration from the hue of the sea. Their faces are gray and long in shape and some have long arms, which are also gray, and they favor blue headgear and at least one account claims they also have wings. In other versions they are portrayed as Storm-Kelpies. As the most common water-spirits in Scottish folklore, Kelpies are usually described as powerful horses, but the name is also used for different spirit-forms in tales throughout the country. The Na fir ghorma swim with their torsos raised out of the sea, twisting and diving as porpoises do. They are able to speak, and when a group approaches a ship, its chief may shout two lines of poetry to the master of the vessel and challenge him to complete the verse. If the skipper fails in that task then the Na fir ghorma will attempt to capsize his ship. When the weather is fine they sleep or float on – or just below – the surface of the water.

Näcken or Nøkk

The Scandinavian *Näcken*, *Näkki*, *Nøkk* were dangerous male *water-sprites* who played enchanted songs on the violin, luring women and children in order to drown them in lakes or streams. This enthralling music of the Nøkk was most dangerous to women and children, especially pregnant women and unbaptized children. He would scream at a particular spot in a lake or river, in a way reminiscent of the loon, and on that spot, a fatality would later take place. He was also said to cause drownings, but

swimmers could protect themselves against such a fate by throwing a bit of steel into the water, just as the female water-spirit, the *Sjörået*, could be chased away by throwing a fishing line in front of her feet. However, not all of these spirits were necessarily malevolent. Many stories indicate at the very least that *Nøkker* were entirely harmless to their audience, and attracted not only women and children, but men as well with their sweet songs. It was believed that if a person offered the Nøkk a treat of three drops of blood, a black animal, some *brännvin* (Scandinavian brandy) or *snus* (wet snuff) dropped into the water, he or she would be taught his enchanting form of music. He was thought to be most active during Midsummer's Night, on Christmas Eve, and on Thursdays. Stories also exist wherein a Nøkk, called the *Fossegrim*, agreed to live with a human who had fallen in love with him, but many of these stories ended with the Nøkk returning to his original home, usually a nearby waterfall or brook. The Nøkker were said to become depressed unless they had free, regular contact with a water source. The Norwegian *Fossegrim*, or Swedish *Strömkarl*, is a related figure who, if properly approached, will teach a musician to play so adeptly *"that the trees dance and waterfalls stop at their music"*.

Appearance

It is difficult to describe the appearance of the *Näcken*, as one of his main qualities was shape-shifting. Perhaps he did not have any true shape. He could show himself as a man playing the violin in brooks and waterfalls. These days he is often imagined as fair and naked, but in folklore he was more frequently described as wearing more or less elegant clothing. However, he could appear as whatever he wanted to be, including various kinds of floating objects, a treasure, or an animal – most commonly in the form of a *Brook-horse*. Modern Scandinavian names are in fact often derived from the Old Norse *Nykr*, meaning *"river horse"*. Thus, it is likely that the figure of the Brook-horse preceded the personification of the Näcken. Fossegrim and derivatives were almost always portrayed as very handsome young men.

Nattramnar

In Swedish folklore, *Nattramnar* (Night Ravens) are the Revenants of suicides or dead unbaptized children. They were believed to appear at night in the form of birds, mainly ravens. In his description of folklore

in southern Småland, Gunnar Olof Hyltén-Cavallius describes the
Nattramnar as a *Gast* (ghost) of a child that has been carried into the
forest. The Nattramnar only appears at night and then usually only at
major festivals. It flies through the air in bird-like flight and emits a
squeaking sound, similar to the squeaking of an unoiled wagon wheel.
It always flies from West to East and never closer to the ground than
an ox carries its yoke. According to medieval belief, the Nattramnar is
constantly on its way to Christ's tomb, but can only travel at night and is
not allowed to rest until it arrives.

The word Nattramnar comes from *ramn*, which is an older Swedish word
for "raven". The corresponding word in Old Swedish is *rampn*, in Old
Norse and Icelandic *hrafn*, in Danish and Norwegian *bokmål ravn*, and in
Nynorsk *ramn*. The oldest form of the word is documented from the 6th
century on the Järsberg stone, where it is spelled as *HarabanaR*. Compare
also the English *raven* and the German *Rabe* (m). In German speaking
regions the creature is mostly known as the *Nachtkrabb*.

Niägruisar

The *Niägruisar* of the Faroe Islands are described by George Landt in
1810, as a kind of *Hobgoblins* or *Brownies* who wore red caps and brought
good luck. J.G. Campbell describes them as *household-spirits*. They take
care of the fire, the sheep, the maintenance of the boats. In the wild, they
live in streams and lakes (especially Lake Sørvágsvatn). They may be
connected to the *Niðagrísur*, the soul of a murdered unbaptized child,
which returns to haunt people in the shape of a round creature no bigger
than a ball of yarn.

Nicneven

Nicneven, Nicnevin or *Nicnevan* is a witch or *Fairy-queen* from Scottish
folklore, first mentioned in 1580 by Alexander Montgomerie (1550-1598).
According to some folklorists it is the same figure as the *Gyre-Carling* or
Hecate. Although other scholars disagree with this. After collecting a lot
of data about these entities, it seems most likely they are actually one and
the same, but can differ from each other locally. It is debated whether
the name originally referred to a real woman or a mythical goddess.
The name may derive from a Scottish Gaelic surname *Neachneohain*,

meaning "daughter(s) of the divine" and/or "daughter(s) of Scathach"
or *NicNaoimhein*, meaning "daughter of the little saint". Other theories
propose that the name derives from the Irish war goddess *Neamhain*, or is
connected to *water-sprites* such as the *Nixie*, *Nokke* or even *Neptune*. After
Montgomerie's 1580 poem, the next known mention of Nicneven date
from the early 1800s. In 1801, John Caspar Leyden (1775-1811) wrote
that Nicneven was one of the *"popular appellations of the gyre-carlin, the
queen of Fairies, the great hag, Hecate, or mother-witch of the peasants"*.
Robert Hartley Cromek (1770-1812), in his *Remains of Nithsdale and
Galloway song: with historical and traditional notices relative to the
manners and customs of the peasantry* (1810), gave a more colorful
description, linking her to Samhain (Halloween) and the supernatural
traffic on that day, known as the *Hallowmas Rades* in a role that reminds
one of figures like *Perchta*, *Herodias* or *Hellequin*:

> *"We will close our history of witchcraft with the only notice we could
> collect, of a celebrated personage, called the Gyre Carline; who is
> reckoned the mother of glamour, and near a-kin to Satan himself.
> She is believed to preside over the 'Hallowmass Rades' and mothers
> frequently frighten their children by threatening to give them to
> McNeven, or the Gyre Carline. She is described as wearing a long
> gray mantle, and carrying a wand, which, like the miraculous rod
> of Moses, could convert water into rocks and sea into solid land."*

During the Hallowmas Rades, a kind of *Wild Hunt*, all good folk who did
not want to fall prey to the depredations of evil spirits or the unhallowed
dead – or to experience the unimaginable fate of being swept up into
the rade itself, stayed safely inside their locked and darkened homes. Sir
Walter Scott (1771-1832) conflated Nicneven not only with Hecate, but
with other queens of *Fairies* and witches like *Diana* and Herodias.

The historical Nicneven and the Gyre-Carling
It is possible that Nicneven as a spirit being has her roots in one or more
historical figures. In May 1569 an accused witch known as *Nicneven* or
Nic Neville was condemned to death and burnt at the stake at St. Andrews.
Sir Walter Scott considered the possibility that multiple women were
nicknamed in honor of this legendary figure. Nic Neville told her
interrogators that the apothecaries had caused her arrest because of
her superior healing powers. This woman may have been the same as

Nikneveing of Monzie, mentioned in the 1643 witchcraft trial of John Brughe of Fossoway. Brughe's teacher, *Neane NcClerith*, was Nikneveing's niece. On the one hand the *Gyre-Carling* is an *Ogress*-like figure, with variants such as *Gyre-Carlin*, *Gy-Carling* and *Gay-Carlin;* on the other hand she is a synonym for "witch". *Gyre* is possibly a cognate of the Norse word *geri* and thus has the meaning "greedy," or it may be from the Norse *gýgr* meaning "Ogress"; *carling* or *carline* is a Scots and northern English term for "old woman", which is related to the Norse word *kerling* (of the same meaning). In Scotland, Gyre-Carling was frequently used as a generic term for witches.

In his response to Montgomerie, Patrick Hume of Polwarth (c.1550-June 1609) wrote *"Leave boggles, brownies, gyr-carlings and gaists."* Similarly in 1793, Robert Heron (1764-1807) wrote that Fairies and "Gyar-Carlins" roamed on Halloween and other nights to stop those they were displeased with, and could be heard curling on the ice on winter nights. In the East of Scotland, however, especially in Fife, the Gyre-carlin or Gy-carling is not a witch, but a female Fairy who's particularly linked to cloth-making. It used to be said that, if unspun flax was not removed from the distaff at the end of the year, she would steal it all. Conversely, if asked by a woman for the endowment of skill in spinning, the Gyre-carling would enable the recipient to do three to four times as much work as other spinners. Despite these humble domestic aspects, though, the Gyre-carlin had a more fearsome side to her character as the Lowland equivalent of the *Cailleach*, or *Hag*, being well-armed, violent and partially cannibalistic.

Nissir

In Icelandic folklore, ships have guiding spirits in the form of *Nissir*, benevolent *dwarfs*, who indicate the places where fish are to be found and protect the ship from dangers. In storms they are cheerful, but before a death case they are sad. They also leave the ship when they know it will perish.

Nuckelavee

The *Nuckelavee* or *Nuckalavee* is a horse-like demon from Orkney-mythology that combines equine and human elements. It has its origins in Norse mythology, and British folklorist Katharine Briggs called it *"the nastiest"* of all the demons of Scotland's Northern Isles. The Nuckelavee's breath was thought to wilt crops and sicken livestock, and the creature was held responsible for droughts and epidemics on land – despite being predominantly a sea-dweller.

The creature resembles a *Centaur*, with an enormous gaping mouth and a single huge eye that burns with a red flame. The most gruesome detail of his appearance is the fact that he has no skin. Black blood flows through his yellow veins and his pale tendons and powerful muscles are visible as a pulsating mass. He has an aversion to running water and those who are chased by him only have to cross a watercourse to get rid of him. Some reports claim that he is just a big head on two small arms, but with all the above characteristics. Another aversion of the Nuckelavee is the burning of seaweed to make kelp. This enrages him and causes him to unleash a raging plague, killing cattle and other animals and destroying crops. When this happens, he can only be stopped by the *Mither-o'-the-Sea*, another god-like being from Celtic and Orkney mythology.

Nuggle

The *Nuggle*, *Njuggle*, or *Neugle*, is a mythical *water-horse* of primarily Shetland folklore, where it is also referred to as a *Shoepultie* or *Shoopiltee*, particularly in the northernmost islands. Karl Blind, a 19th-century folklorist who regularly wrote about the lore of Shetland, asserts that after extensive inquiries he had only ever heard of the Nuggle in Shetland; there may however be tentative references to it around the lochs and watercourses of Hoy and at Muckle Water on Rousay, that are both part of the Orkney archipelago. (Karl Blind, *Scottish, Shetlandic and Germanic Water Tales*, 1881.) Tales of Nuggles were never recorded on the islands of Yell and Fetlar, parts of the Shetland archipelago.

The Nuggle is a nocturnal spirit that is always of male gender and lives in rivers, streams and lochs. The creatures were also found beside watermills and they never strayed very far from water. The entity was capable of assuming many disguises but generally favored the form of an attractive horse. It never assumed a human form. Nuggles were always male water-horses or ponies and were never portrayed as mares. His overall proportions were like those of a generously fed and well-conditioned Shetland pony or horse. The color of his sleek coat ranged from a deep bluish-gray to a very light, almost white, gray. Similar equine type creatures are: the evil *Each-uisge* from the Gaelic folklore of the Scottish Highlands; the *Tangies* that haunt the coastline and sea shores, but reside in the ocean depths; and the Norwegian *Nøkk*. Folklorist Ernest Marwick considers the demonic *Nuckelavee*, which features in Orcadian folk tales, to also be a relative of the Nuggle. Among the characteristics distinguishing the Nuggle from his counterparts was his tail, which resembled a wheel. With this special tail as his 'trademark' he was easily recognizable, despite his attempts to hide it between his hind legs so he tended to stay out of sight except at night, or at "the hour of power"; just as the sun set in the twilight hours. Additionally, unlike other corresponding creatures, he was of a gentle disposition, more likely to instill fear rather than attacking islanders, although some tales suggest otherwise; according to the author and folklorist Jessie Saxby *"he was a more feeble sort"*. He liked playing practical jokes and making mischief, but was deceitful and not very brave. Spitefulness was not a part of his character and his pranks were tempered with a degree of mercy.

Etymology

The *Scottish National Dictionary* attributes the word *neugle* and its variant spellings like *ni(o)gle*, *nyogle*, *nyugl* etc., as coming from the Old English *nicor*, the Old Norse *nykr*, the Middle Low German or the Middle Dutch *necker*. The same publication gives *Shoopiltee* and its spelling variations as adaptations of the Old Norse *sjó* and *piltr* meaning "sea" added to "boy" or "lad". In *An Etymological Glossary of the Shetland and Orkney Dialect,* Thomas Edmondston lists the creature as a *niogle*, crediting a Gothic derivation from *gner* for horse and *el* for water.

Child Bogey

Saxby suggests fear of the Nuggle prevented children venturing too close to deep water or watermills and that parents embellished the tale by adding that the creature was capable of producing a pleasant tune providing a child stood well away from the water (compare the East Frisian *Busebeller*). John Spence, a resident of Lerwick and author of the 1899 publication *Shetland Folk-lore*, agrees that many of the legendary tales of spirits were told as a precaution to keep children out of danger. He further explains the tales originated in bygone times, when oral traditions were passed down the generations by grandparents retelling the stories. Writing in the *Journal of American Folklore* during 1918, the anthropologist James Teit hypothesizes that, as is common with most supernatural creatures, Nuggles were thought to be fallen angels.

Nykur

In Faroese, the word *Nykur* refers specifically to a supernatural horse, described in one Faroese text thus: *"The Nykur dwells in water; at the bottom, down in the depths, he has his lair; from here he often goes onto land and it is not good to meet him"*. Sometimes he is like a beautiful little horse which seems to be good and tame, and thus he lures people to draw near to him to pat him and stroke him along the back. But when they come to touch the tail, they become stuck fast to him and then he releases no-one, but he drags them with him to the bottom of the water. Sometimes he encounters people in human form, as a handsome youth, to lure young women to himself, and promises them joy and gladness in his hall if they want to go along with him. But if they get a suspicion of who he is, when they are giving themselves away, such that they can call him by his true name – Nykur – then he loses the power over them and must release them and go along into his waters.

It is said that the Nykur can equally well change itself into the form of all quadrupedal animals, except that he does not know how to create the horn-points of a ram or a male lamb on himself. But when he hasn't changed his form, he is like a horse, and it has come about that people gain power over him by carving a cross into his back and then they have been able to have him drag great stones by his tail down from the mountains to homesteads or houses. Some are still seen in Húsavík in Sandoy and on Eiði in Eysturoy and the big rocks that are gathered together there bear witness to how strong he is. At Takmýri in Sandoy, lies one huge rock, which they wanted to have him draw to Húsavík, but his tail broke here, and the stone remains there. One part of the Nykur's tail, which was attached to the stone, is visible on it still.

O

Oakmen

Although the oak once was a very important sacred tree in both Celtic and Germanic traditions, the tree's related spirits, the *Oakmen* do not seem to play a serious role in British folklore for quite some time. Folklorist Katherine Briggs wrote:

> *"There are scattered references to Oakmen in the North of England, although there are very few folktales about them: there is no doubt the oak was regarded as a sacred and potent tree. Most people know the rhyming proverb 'Fairy folks are in old oaks'; 'The Gospel Oak' or 'The King's Oak' in every considerable forest had probably a traditional sacredness from unremembered times, and an oak coppice in which the young saplings had sprung from the stumps of felled trees was thought to be an uncanny place after sunset; but the references to 'Oakmen' are scanty."*

No doubt, considering the enormous importance of the oak in the Celtic and other traditions, the oaks had their spirits, but the only serious references to *Oakmen* (apart from the fiction of Beatrice Potter) can be found in a list of *Bogey-spirits* composed by Reginald Scott (c. 1538-1599) in his *The Discoverie of Witchcraft; Book VII, Chapter XV*, who listed *"the man in the oke"*, and in *Letters on Demonology and Witchcraft; Letter VI* (1830): of Sir Walter Scott (1771-1832): "[…] *and I might conjecture that the man-in-the-oak was the same with the Erl-König of the Germans"*.

Oberon

Oberon is the legendary king of the *Fairies* in medieval and Renaissance literature. He is best known as a character in William Shakespeare's play *A Midsummer Night's Dream*, in which he is king of the Fairies and spouse of *Titania*, queen of the Fairies. The name Oberon is derived from *Alberich* (from Old High German *Alb* (Elf) and *rîh* (ruler, king), the name of a treasure guarding dwarf mentioned in the *Nibelungenlied*, a Burgundian poem written around the turn of the 13th century. In Old French, the Alberich became *Alberon* and then *Auberon* (pronounced "Oberon"). The name Auberon is first attested to in the early 13th century chanson de geste, entitled: *Les Prouesses et faitz du noble Huon de Bordeaux*, wherein it refers to an *Elven* man of the forest. Huon, son of Seguin count of Bordeaux, passed through the forest inhabited by Auberon. He was warned by a hermit not to speak to Auberon, but his courtesy had him answer Auberon's greetings and so gain his aid in his quest. Huon had murdered Charlot, the Emperor's son, in self-defense, and so he had to visit the court of the Emir of Babylon and perform various feats to win a pardon. He succeeded only with Auberon's help. Auberon is described as dwarfish in height, although very handsome. He explains that, at his christening, an offended Fairy cursed him to this dwarfish size but relented and gave him great beauty as compensation. He is given some Celtic trappings, such as a magical cup that is ever full for the virtuous. *"The magic cup supplied their evening meal; for such was its virtue that it afforded not only wine, but more solid fare when desired"*, according to Thomas Bulfinch. In this story, he is said to be the child of Morgan le Fay and Julius Caesar.

Oberon in Elisabethan magic

Oberon is mentioned as a very powerful spirit ruler in a compilation of Elisabethan magical documents, beautifully restored and republished as *The Book of Oberon* (2016) by Daniel Hars, James A. Clark and Joseph H. Peterson. In this work he appears as a crowned king *"under the government of the Sun and Moon"*. He is the king of the Fairies and can teach men about the secrets of stones, herbs, trees and metals. He can teach how to become invisible and how to obtain hidden treasures. He can also bring treasures out of the sea and tell about things of the past and future. The book contains a long ritual text to evoke Oberon, who presides over several spirits of whom the sigilli are also given.

P

Padfoot

In Wakefield, Leeds, Pudsey and some areas of Bradford a local phantom creature is known as *Padfoot*. A death omen like others of its type, it may become visible or invisible and exhibits certain characteristics that give it its name. It is known to follow people with a light padding sound of its paws, then appearing again in front of them or at their side. It can utter a roar unlike the voice of any known animal, and sometimes the trailing of a chain can be heard along with the pad of its feet. It is best to leave the creature alone, for if a person tries to speak to it, or attacks it, then it will have power over them. One story tells of a man who tried to kick the Padfoot and found himself dragged by it through hedges and ditches all the way to his home and left under his own window. Although usually described as black, another tale concerns a man who encountered a white Padfoot. He attempted to strike it with his stick, but it passed completely through, and he ran home in fear. Soon afterward the man fell sick and died.

Peg o' Nell

Peg o' Nell is an evil spirit of Lancashire folklore, which haunts the river Ribble near Clitheroe, and Waddow Hall in particular. She is described by the folklorists William Henderson and Katharine Briggs. Every seven years she claims a victim for the river, and if a cat or dog has not been drowned at this Peg o' Nell's Night, the Ribble will claim a human victim. A well in the grounds of Waddow Hall is named after her, and a headless stone figure standing near it is supposed to represent her. It seems likely that she was originally the Nymph of the Ribble; if so, tradition has replaced her by a human ghost. Long ago, it is said, there was a maidservant named Peg o' Nell at Waddow Hall, who was cursed by her mistress and broke her neck by falling into a frozen well. A curse was on the place. Misfortunes to the stock and the illness of children were all blamed on the angry ghost of Peg o'Nell.

Peg Powler

Peg Powler is a *Hag* and *water-sprite* in English folklore, who inhabits the River Tees. Similar to the *Grindylow, Jenny Greenteeth*, and *Nelly Longarms*, she drags children into the water if they get too close to the edge. She is regarded as a *Bogeyman* figure who is invoked by parents to frighten children into proper behavior. The 19th century folklorist William Henderson describes Peg Powler as having green hair and *"an insatiable desire for human life"* and she is said to lure people into the river to be drowned or be devoured. The foam or froth which is often seen floating on certain parts of the Tees is called "Peg Powler's suds" or "Peg Powler's cream". A similar creature, named *Nanny Powler*, is said to haunt the River Skerne, a tributary of the Tees. Michael Denham regards her as either the sister or daughter of Peg Powler.

Elliott O'Donnell paints a somewhat different picture of Peg Powler in his 1924 book *Ghosts, Helpful and Harmful.* He describes her as a spirit who lures men and boys to their doom in the river Tees by appearing as a beautiful young woman with green hair pretending to drown, so that her victim will enter the water in an attempt to save her. She may even appear on land on foggy nights and lead men astray until they stumble into the river.

Pillywiggins

According to most books on folkloric creatures the *Pillywiggins* are tiny peaceful *spring flower-Fairies* in English and Welsh folklore. Pierre Dubois, in his *La Grande Encyclopédie des Fées* (1996) attaches insect antennae to them and mentions intermarriages with insects. They were described as able to ride on the back of bees and living on honey and nectar. *Ariel* is mentioned as their queen.

Pisky or Pixie

Pisky (pl.: *Piskies*; also *Pixy, Pixi, Pizkie, Piskie* and *Pigsie*) is a mythical creature of British folklore. Piskies are considered to be particularly concentrated in the high moorland areas around Devon and Cornwall, suggesting some Celtic origin for the belief and name. The origin of the word Pisky or Pixie is uncertain. E. M. Kirkpatrick (*Chambers 20th Century Dictionary*, 1983) has speculated that it comes from the Swedish dialectal *pyske* meaning "small Fairy". Others have disputed this, given there is no

ROBIN
GOOD-FELLOVV,
HIS MAD PRANKES AND MERRY IESTS.

Full of honeſt Mirth, and is a fit Medicine
for Melancholy.

Printed at *London* by *Thomas Cotes,* and are to be ſold by
Francis Grove, at his ſhop on Snow-hill, neere the
Sarazens-head. 1639.

plausible case for Nordic dialectal survivals in southwest Britain. Piskies or *Pixies* are believed to inhabit ancient underground ancestor sites such as stone circles, barrows, dolmens, ringforts or menhirs.

In traditional regional lore, Piskies are generally benign, mischievous, short of stature and childlike; they are fond of dancing and gather outdoors in huge numbers to dance or sometimes wrestle, through the night, demonstrating parallels with the Cornish *Plen-an-gwary* and Breton *Fest Noz* (Cornish: *Troyl*) folk celebrations originating in the medieval period. According to some writers *Piskies* and the *Small People or Pobel Vean* are one and the same; according to others, they are different. In Cornwall unbaptized children were, at the beginning of the century, said to turn, when they died, into Piskies; they gradually went through many transformations, getting smaller with each change, until at last they became *Meryons* (ants) and finally disappeared. Another tradition holds that they were ancient Druids, who, because they would not believe in Christ, were for their sins condemned to change first into Piskies; gradually getting smaller, and they too, as ants, at last were lost. It is on account of these legends considered unlucky to destroy an ant's nest, and a piece of tin put into one could, in bygone days, through Pisky power be transmuted into silver, provided that it was inserted at some varying lucky moment about the time of the new moon. Moths were in Cornwall formerly believed to be departed souls, and are still, in some districts, called Piskies. There is also a green bug which infests bramble-bushes in the late autumn that bears the same name, and one of the reasons assigned for blackberries not being good after Michael's Mass is that Piskies spoiled them. Pisky is in some places invoked for luck at the swarming of bees. It was once a common custom in East Cornwall, when houses were built, to leave holes in the walls by which these little beings could enter; to stop them up would drive away good luck. And in West Cornwall knobs of lead, known as Pisky's paws or Pisky feet, were placed at intervals on the roofs of farm-houses to prevent the Piskies from dancing on them and turning the milk sour in the dairies. Country people in East Cornwall sometimes put a prayer book under a child's pillow as a charm to keep away Piskies. M.A. Courtney in her *Cornish Feasts and Folklore* describes a poor woman, near Launceston, who was fully convinced that one of her children was taken away and replaced by a Pisky-changeling. The woman believed the disaster was due to the absence of a prayer book on one particular night. Small round stones, known as *Pisky Grinding Stones*, are occasionally found in Cornwall; they are most probably parts of old spindles.

Plant Annwn

Plant Annwn are Welsh *Fairies* of the underworld, whose entrance to the human world is by the lakes. These Fairies are regarded as the children of the Underworld-god Arawn and they are chiefly known to men through their *Lake-Maidens*, the *Gwragen Annwn*, by their white or speckled *Lake-Cattle*, the *Gwartheg Y Llyn*, and by their swift white hounds, the *Cwn Annwn*, who were sometimes seen with their Fairy mistresses, but more often heard on summer nights in full cry after the souls of men who had died soiled and impenitent. The Lake Maidens made loving and docile wives, until the taboo attached to them was violated; the Lake Cattle brought wealth and prosperity to any farmer who was lucky enough to keep these animals.

Plentyn cael

In Wales the *Plentyn cael* (singular), or *Plant cael* (pl.) was the name of a changeling child which initially resembles the human child for which it has been substituted, but gradually grows uglier in appearance and behavior; ill-featured, malformed, ill-tempered, given to screaming and biting. It may be of less than usual intelligence, but may equally well be identifiable on account of its more-than-childlike wisdom and cunning. The common means employed to identify a Plentyn cael is to cook a family meal in an eggshell. The child will exclaim, *"I have seen the acorn before the oak, but I never saw the likes of this"*, and vanish, only to be replaced by the original human child. Alternatively, or following this identification, it is supposedly necessary to mistreat the child by placing it in a hot oven, by holding it in a shovel over a hot fire, or by bathing it in a solution of foxglove – all in the hope one was not mistaken about the identity of the child, of course...

Pobel Vean

Pobel Vean (Small People) are local *Fairies* or *Piskies* of Cornwall. In the old days almost everyone in Cornwall believed in their existence and most people feared them. There are many types of Piskies in Cornwall:

those in rags who dance merrily on the moors, those who conjure up storms to protect their treasure, those who dwell in the darkest places underground and those who steal children. Like the sea itself, that surrounds Cornwall on three sides, the folklore of this land is capricious. Piskies are capable of helping humans and also causing them great harm. Piskies do seem especially fond of helping on farms, and like the Brownie they disappear when given new clothing. Walter Yeeling Evans-Wentz (1878-1965) regarded the Pisky as being of the Fairy-race of the Pobel Vean:

"The Pobel Vean or Small People, the Spriggans, and the Piskies are not really distinguishable from one another. Bucca, who properly is but one, is a deity not a fairy, but the only true Cornish fairy is the Pisky, of the race which is the Pobel Vean or Little People, and the Spriggan is only one of his aspects. The Pisky would seem to be the 'Brownie' of the Lowland Scot."

Miss M.A. Courtney (in *Cornish Feasts and Folklore*, Beare and Son, Penzance, 1890) does not agree with Evans-Wentz and writes that the Fairies of Cornwall may be divided into four classes, the *Small People*, the *Pixies* (pronounced Piskies or Pisgies), the *Spriggans*, and the *Knockers*. According to her, the *"Small People are said to have been half-witted people who had committed no mortal sin, but who, when they died, were not good enough to go to Heaven. They are always thought to have lived before."* The difference between a Pisky and the Pobel Vean, according to Courtney, lies in the social context of these creatures. While the Small People or Pobel Vean always appear in groups, the Piskies appear as solitary creatures – this opinion however is not unanimously shared by other folklorists. Spriggans or sprites she regards as spiteful creatures, never doing a good turn for anyone, while the Knockers are distinguished explicitly as Mine-Fairies.

Poldies

Poldies are *Wood-Fairies* of the Cheshire, Lancashire region. Children were told by their parents to come home before dark, as the Poldies came out at night. They were guardian spirits who would defend the woods and punish anyone who did damage to the trees.

Pooka or Púca

Pooka, *Púca*, also *Puka*, *Phooka*, *Phuka*, Cymric *Pwca* or *Bwca*, Cornish *Bucca*, in Manx *Glashtyn*, is a creature from Celtic mythology. He is a mischievous and sorcerous but relatively harmless spirit or *Goblin*, related to the *Nightmares*, who lives underground along with *Gnomes* and *dwarfs* on solitary mountains and among old ruins. Some say he derived his name from *poc*, a he-goat; and speculative people consider him the forefather of Shakespeare's *Puck*. In Ireland he belongs to the *Fairies* and *Leprechauns* from the Síde, in Scotland to the *Brownies*. He can be associated with the Gallic god *Bugius* and the German Puk. Púcas are said to appear to people in Ireland especially at Samhain. The Welsh/Cornish *Knockers* are very similar to the *Púcas*. Púcas are shapeshifters, now and then they appear to people in the form of different animal shapes, e.g. as a dog, goat or horse, but always with black fur. Their preferred form of appearance is that of a black pony. Púca likes to invite careless travelers to a ride on his back, which for the unsuspecting traveler then quickly turns out to be a horror trip over hill and dale and sometimes through thorny bushes. Most of the time Púca throws his "guest" off somewhere in the moor and disappears under resounding laughter. Since Púcas know the language of humans, they can sometimes warn of mischief. When the harvest is brought in, everything that remains in the fields after Samhain is the property of the Púcas. The beings were regarded as November-spirits and the November-day is sacred to the Pooka/Púca. Halloween was sometimes called "Púca night".

Portune

Portunes are small agricultural *Fairies* or *household-spirits*, first described by Gervase of Tilbury (1150-1220) and later by Katherine Briggs. It was their habit to labor on farms, and at night when the doors were shut they would blow up the fire, and, taking frogs from their bosoms, they would roast them on the coals and eat them. Gervase describes them as only half an inch in height, but Keightley, taking this "frog eating" into account, suggests that by a copyist's error *pollicis* was substituted for *pedis* and that therefor they must have been considerably larger. They were like very old men with wrinkled faces and wore patched up coats. If anything had to be carried into the house or any arduous labor had to be undertaken, they would perform it, however hard it was. In fact they were all for good and never for ill, except for one mischievous trick. If any man was riding alone on a dark night, a Portune would sometimes take his horse's bridle, lead it into a pond or muddy swamp and make off with a loud laugh. In fact, the Portune was very like *Robin Goodfellow*, except that he seemed to be a gregarious creature rather than a solitary being.

Puck or Puk

– See under *Robin Goodfellow* and in *Spirit Beings in European Folklore*, compendium 2

Puddlefoot

Scottish folklore tells of a special Brownie called *Puddlefoot*. He lived in the County of Perth (Siorrachd Pheairt) in a small burn on the road between Pitlochry and Dunkeld. He used to splash and paddle about in the burn, and then would go up with very wet feet to a farm nearby and do a certain amount of household work, but rather more mischief. What was tidy he untidied, and what was untidy he tidied. People were afraid of passing the burn at night because they heard the Brownie. Puddlefoot didn't like it to be called Puddlefoot or to be given a name whatsoever. Legend has it that one night he left his burn for good, when a passer-by who was not afraid of him, asked how he was doing and called him by his hated name.

Q

Quhaip

The *Quhaip* is a dwarf-sized Scottish *Goblin* or evil spirit who supposedly goes about under the eaves of houses after night fall. He has a long beak resembling a pair of tongs for the purpose of carrying off evil doers. The name *Quhaip* seems to be derived from *curlews*, a group of nine species of birds in the genus *Numenius*, characterized by their long, slender, down-curved bills and mottled brown plumage. They can harass horses and act as an *Alp* or *Nightmare*.

R

Rå

According to Swedish folklore, a *Rå* is a brute and an impersonal mythical creature that rules and guards over a specific domain, such as a mountain, lake or forest area, where it also rules the animals. It may act on visitors by warning or appear in animal form, or as a man or a woman. Dialectal forms include *råd, ro, råa, rådi* and *råä*. The word is probably derived from *råda*, and originally refers to *something or someone who rules over something*. *Råd* is thought to be the older form from which Rå is formed. Sami has a term for similar beings called *Radie*, and in Old Norse there was *Råð*.

In ancient belief, all objects, animals and plants were considered to have a *rå*, or "spirit", watching over them, and great care was taken to stay on friendly terms with these spirits. A Rå was associated with a certain part of nature in particular, and folklore therefore spoke of the *bergsrået* (mountain rå), *skogsrået* (forest rå) or *sjörået* (sea rå). Sometimes a Rå could also be associated with human places, such as the *skeppsrået* (ship rå) and the och *gruvrået* (mine rå). Leprechauns can also be counted among the Rå. The Rå was thought to have power over the animals and forces of nature that belonged to its domain. It could sometimes use this power to bring people luck, but more often the opposite was true.

Raudkembingur

Of all the *Illhveli*, or "Evil whales" that inhabit the Icelandic waters the *Raudkembingur* (also: *Raudkembingr, Rauðkembingr, Raudkempingur, Raudkembir, Raudkinni, Raudkinnung, Raudkinnungur, Raudgrani, Raudhofdi, Kembingur, Kembir,* or *Faxi*) was regarded as the most dangerous, wild and bloodthirsty. Its name means "Red comb" or "Red crest" and it was not only notorious for its size (10 to 20 meters) but also for its ferocity in attacking boats. As with all Illhveli, the Raudkembingur is an abomination, and eating its inedible flesh is forbidden. Boiling its meat causes it to disappear from the pot. Accounts describing its appearance refer to a crest of bristly hair, a mane like a horse, or even a row of finlets; its extent varies from depiction to depiction. The crest is

a bright red on a coffee-brown body with a pink belly; other accounts say
it is reddish all over, or has red cheeks or a red head. Sometimes there
are red streaks from the mouth to the trunk, as if drawn in blood. The
head itself is sometimes depicted as almost saurian in appearance, with
sharp teeth. It either has a small dorsal fin or none at all. Their movement
is accompanied by massive amounts of foam. This, along with the red
mane, makes the Raudkembingur confusable with the *Hrosshvalur*, and
the two have become interchangeable over time. Hrosshvalurs, however,
can be easily distinguished by their dappled coloration, horse's tail, and
enormous eyes. Like the Hrosshvalur, the demonic Raudkembingur is
also associated with sorcery and metamorphoses.

Raw Head & Bloody-Bones

In English folklore a *Bogie* or *Hobgoblin*, usually called *Raw-head and
Bloody-Bones*, used to frighten children – as in *"Go to sleep or raw-head
an' bloody-bones fetch thee!"* In Lincolnshire, it is a spirit that haunts wells
and in Warwick, it is said to pull naughty children playing on the edge of
dangerous water into the pool. The name is found twice in *Hudibras*, an
English mock-heroic narrative poem from the 17th century written by
Samuel Butler.

Redcap

The murderous *Redcap* or *Powrie* inhabiting the border region of
Northern England and Scotland is one of the most malignant of British
Goblins. According to Katharine Briggs, Redcaps lived in old ruined peel
towers and castles where wicked deeds had been done, and delighted to
re-dye his red cap in human blood. Sir Walter Scott also stated that the
Redcap is a class of spirits that haunts old castles, and that every ruined
tower in the south of Scotland was supposed to have one of these spirits
residing within. William Henderson gives a full account of him in *Folk-
Lore of the Northern Counties*. He describes the Redcap as a short thickset
old man, with long prominent teeth, skinny fingers armed with talons
like eagles, large eyes of a fiery-red color, grisly hair streaming down his
shoulders, iron boots, a pikestaff in his left hand, and a red cap on his
head. Human strength can avail little against him, but he can be routed by
scripture or the sight of a cross. If this is held up to him, he gives a dismal
yell and vanishes, leaving one of his long teeth behind.

Legend has it that the notorious Sir William de Soulis of Hermitage Castle had a Redcap *(Robin Redcap)* as his familiar, who made him weapon-proof. Tradition maintains that this thoroughly evil individual was a practitioner of the Black Arts who kidnapped the children of the neighborhood and used their blood in his sinister rituals, during which Robin Redcap was conjured. Eventually the local people petitioned King Robert de Bruce, begging to be relieved from the scourge of their wicked lord, who replied *"Boil him if you must"*. The locals stormed the castle, wrapped de Soulis in lead, and plunged him head first into a cauldron with boiling oil on Nine-stone Rig. His ghost now wanders the castle, a malevolent specter, whose nebulous meanderings are often accompanied by the sobs of children echoing along the crumbling corridors. The ruin of Blackett Tower, a border fortress that was owned by the Bell family in the parish of Kirkpatrick-Fleming in Dumfriesshire, was haunted by a more traditional ghost known as "Old Red Cap" or "Bloody Bell". A description of the tower and ghost was given by William Scott Irving in the poem "Fair Helen" in which the *"ghastly phantom"* holds a bloody dagger beneath a red eastern moon.

Not all Redcaps are monsters. The term redcap is also used in a more general sense. For example, in the village of Zennor in Cornwall *Fairies* were often referred to as "Red-caps" (including the more benevolent trooping Fairies) because of their fondness for wearing green clothing and scarlet caps. The folklore of Perthshire also describes a more friendly Redcap. The little man lives in a room high up in Grantully Castle and it brings luck to see or hear him.

Robin Goodfellow

Robin Goodfellow, "drudging fiend", is a merry domestic Fairy, famous for mischievous pranks and practical jokes. At night-time he will sometimes do little services for the family over which he presides. The Scots call this domestic spirit a *Brownie*; the Germans, *Kobold* or *Knecht Ruprecht*. Scandinavians called it *Nissë God-dreng*. *Puck*, the jester of Fairy-court, is the same. In the 16th century *Robin Goodfellow* appears as a synonym for Puck or *Hobgoblin*, in which *Hob* may substitute for *Rob* or *Robin*. The name Robin is Middle English in origin, deriving from the Old French Robin, the pet form for the name *Robert*. Similar to the use of "the good folk" in describing *Fairies*, it reflected a degree of wishful thinking and an attempt to appease the Fairies, recognizing their fondness of flattery despite their mischievous nature. Puck, in medieval English folklore, is a malicious Fairy or demon. In Old and Middle English the word meant simply "demon." In Elizabethan lore he was a mischievous, Brownie-like Fairy also called Robin Goodfellow, or Hobgoblin. As one of the leading characters in William Shakespeare's *Midsummer Night's Dream*, Puck boasts of his pranks of changing shapes, misleading travelers at night, spoiling milk, frightening young girls, and tripping venerable old dames. The Irish *Pooka*, or *Púca*, and the Welsh *Pwcca* are similar *household-spirits*.

The earliest reference to "Robin Goodfellow" cited by the *Oxford English Dictionary* is from 1531. Anthony Munday mentions Robin Goodfellow in his play *The Two Italian Gentlemen*, 1584, and he appears in *Skialtheia, or a Shadowe of Truth* in 1598. An early 17th century broadside ballad *The Mad Merry Pranks of Robin Goodfellow* describes the character as the emissary of *Oberon*, the Fairy King of the Night, inspiring night-terrors in old women but also carding their wool while they sleep, leading travelers astray, taking the shape of animals, blowing out candles to kiss the girls in the darkness, twitching off their bedclothes, or making them fall out of bed on the cold floor, tattling secrets, and changing babes in cradles with Elflings. John Milton, in *L'Allegro* tells *"how the drudging Goblin swet / To earn his cream-bowle"* by threshing a week's worth of grain in a night, and then, *"Basks at the fire his hairy strength"*. Milton's Puck is not small and sprightly, but nearer to a *Green Man* or a hairy *Woodwose*. An illustration of Robin Goodfellow from 1639 represents the influence of Pan imagery giving Puck the hindquarters, cloven hooves and horns of a goat. In the aftermath of the Protestant Reformation, as with other supernatural beings, Robin Goodfellow became the subject of negative texts written by Protestant polemicists. Reginald Scot referred to him as the *"great and ancient bull beggar"*, Edward Dering blamed him for the *"idle superstitions"* of medieval religion and Edmond Bicknoll claimed he was born from the *"fruit of infidelity"* and was a conspirator of the Devil. After Meyerbeer's successful opera *Robert le Diable* (1831), neo-medievalists and occultists began to apply the name Robin Goodfellow to the Devil, with appropriately extravagant imagery.

S

Sea Mither & Teran

Sea Mither (Sea Mother) is a *nature-spirit* of Orkney and Shetland folklore. Sea Mither is a spirit of summer days that quells the turbulent sea waters around the northern isles of Scotland. During summer months the Sea Mither keeps the demonic Nuckelavee confined, empowers aquatic creatures with the ability to reproduce, warms and calms the seas, and creates the gentle summer breeze. In winter time control of the seas is maintained by *Teran*, until Sea Mither arrives around the days of the vernal equinox in mid-March. The two spirits fight bitterly, often for weeks on end, as Sea Mither tries to gain control. Their struggle causes gale-force winds and heavy tumultuous seas. Teran's screeches are carried by the howling gales as the two spirits try to oust each other. This period of the spring combat is termed the *Vore Tullye* or "Spring Struggle". Eventually Sea Mither always overcomes Teran, relegating him to the depths of the ocean. Inclement summer weather is caused by Teran's attempts to escape. In the Autumn they battle again and this time Teran triumphs in the conflict, now termed the *Gore Vellye*. Control of the ocean and weather is returned to Teran and Sea Mither is forced to leave until the next Spring. Stories of the Sea Mither and Teran are among Orkney's oldest legends. Shetland islanders, particularly fishermen, seek her protection from the Devil.

Sea-witches

In the book *Water-beings in Shetlandic folk-lore, as remembered by Shetlanders in British Columbia* (1918), James A. Teit writes that:

"in the belief of some people, the sea was possessed of a powerful being or witch-like spirit capable of doing harm. As it could hear what was said, it was pleased with sincere praise, but resented insincere praise and mockery. One could not, without incurring danger, speak disparagingly of, or mock the sea. It could bewitch people and cause their destruction. It claimed certain people as victims, who were therefore doomed to be drowned. For this reason, it seems, there was formerly an aversion among some to save people who were drowning in the sea, as the sea

would before long avenge itself on the rescuer for being cheated of its prey. Stories are told of men who rescued others, and invariably were themselves drowned within the next twelve months. Probably for the same reason some people were averse to helping shipwrecked men, and it is said that in some cases obstacles were actually put in the way of their being saved. Some spoke that a certain witch living in the sea who made winds and storms, and wrecked ships and boats, and of another witch or being, also living in the sea, who grind salt to keep the ocean salty."

Selamóðir

The *Selamóðir*, or "Seal Mother", is the protective Genius of the harbor seals and gray seals of Iceland. She can be compared to other supernatural creatures of the unique Icelandic class of *Móðirin* (Mothers), just like the different kinds of Icelandic *Fish Mothers*. It is called by seals when they are persecuted, or it may appear of its own accord to defend them. Unlike most seals, the Selamóðir can be found inland as well as at sea, in freshwater and saltwater. In appearance a Selamóðir looks like a seal of *"unusual large dimensions"*, or she has the size of a large dog with short legs. It has a strange reddish-pink color or a red neck, with flashing eyes and a tuft of hair between its eyes. A Selamóðir can leave the ocean and swim upriver. One was inhabiting the Lagarfljót river. It slept under the waterfall, and was much feared, until it was vanquished and transfixed to a rock.

Selkie

In Celtic and Norse mythology, *Selkies* (also *Silkies*, *Sylkies*, *Selchies* or *Selkie folk*; Scots: *Selkie fowk*), meaning "seal folk", are mythological beings capable of changing from seal to human form by shedding their skin. They are found in folktales and mythology originating from the northern Isles of Scotland like the Shetland Isles, the Orkney's and the Faeroe Islands, but they extend to Iceland and Ireland. Selkies, according to the myths, can be either men or women. Most stories about Selkies are romantic tragedies in which people fall in love (sometimes without realizing it themselves) with a Selkie in human form. Male Selkies in human form are said to have a strong attraction to women, especially women who are dissatisfied with their lives. According to the myth, a woman who wants to contact a Selkie must cry seven tears into the sea.

If a man steals the skin of a female Selkie, she is in his power and must
become his bride. She will then become a perfect wife and can even
have children with her human husband, but if she ever regains her skin,
she will immediately return to the sea and will basically seek no further
contact with her husband. In stories originating in the Shetland Islands,
Selkies sometimes deliberately lure people into the sea. These people then
never return to land.

Folk-tales often revolve around female Selkies being coerced into
relationships with humans by someone stealing and hiding their sealskin,
thus exhibiting the tale motif of the swan maiden type. There are
counterparts in Faeroese and Icelandic folklore that speak of seal-women
and seal-skin. The Icelandic folk-tale "Selshamurinn" (Seal-Skin) published
by Jón Árnason offers an Icelandic analogue of the Selkie-folk tale. The
tale relates how a man from Mýrdalur forced a woman transformed from
a seal to marry him after taking possession of her seal-skin. Another tale
was recorded by Jón Guðmundsson the Learned in 1641. According to
him these seal folk were sea-dwelling Elves called *marmennlar* (mermen
and Mermaids). His tale is of a man who comes across the dancing and
celebrating of Elves within a cave by the ocean. The cave is lined with the
seal skins of the dancing Elves. As soon as the Elves take notice of the
man, they rush to don their skins and dive back into the ocean. However,
the man is able to steal the smallest of the skins, sliding it underneath his
clothes. The owner of the skin tries to retrieve her skin from the man but he
quickly takes hold of the young Elf and takes her to his home to be his wife.
The man and the Elf are together for two years, producing two children, a
boy and a girl, but the Elf harbors no love for the man. During this time,
the former Elf woman's Elf husband swims along the shore by the couple's
home. One day, the Elf woman finds her skin, and runs away, never to be
seen again. A more distant echo of Selkie-type stories may be found in the
medieval story of the demonic woman *Selkolla* (whose name means "Seal-
head"). There are hundreds of seal bride type tales that have been found
from Ireland to the Isles north of Scotland to Iceland.

Selkolla

Selkolla (seal-head) is a *Succubus*-like being in Icelandic folklore. She is
described as a fair woman who sometimes appears with the head of a
seal. The main medieval sources for stories about Selkolla is an episode,

now referred to as *Selkollu þáttr* ('the Selkolla episode') in version B and D of the *Guðmundar saga biskups* or *Guðmundar saga Arasonar*, an Icelandic bishops' saga, recounting the life of Bishop Guðmundur Arason (1161-1237). Since the saga survives in different versions, it is common to speak of it in the plural, as *Guðmundar sögur* (rather than Guðmundar saga). Selkolla is most prominently attested as an antagonist of Bishop Guðmundur Arason and in the sögur/sagas Christian ideas are combined with concepts found in pagan Scandinavian traditions. The medieval story of Selkolla has been shown to share motifs with post-medieval Scandinavian folklore about *changelings* and *ghosts* or other hauntings by dead children, the *Skogsrå* or *Huldra*, and folklore about seals. The summary below is adapted from that of Gunnlaugur Bjarnason, *Tveir heimar mætast: Guðmundur Arason biskup, hetja og vörður gegn illsk.* (unpublished BA dissertation, University of Iceland, 2017), pp. 10-11, citing Biskupa sögur, ed. by Jón Sigurðarson and Guðbrandur Vigfússon, 2 vols (Copenhagen: Møller, 1858–78), II 78-81:

The events of Selkollu þáttr take place in the Westfjords, and begin when a man and a woman are taking a baby girl to be baptized. On the way, they indulge in an "immoral rest" beside a large stone, fittingly called *Miklisteinn* (large stone) and *"turn onto the alternative road of fornication"*. Once they have finished having sex, they return to the child, who they had set down, and find that it is now *"black, dead, and hideous"*. The couple decides to leave the child behind and walk away, but as they do so they hear a cry. They return to the child and find that it is still alive, but it is now so *"terrifying that they dare neither touch it nor come near"*. They go to the farm to fetch more people, but when they return to the stone, the child has vanished. It is then said that a certain woman is *"newly arrived in the district, sometimes with an ordinary face but sometimes with a seal's head. This devil walked about as boldly by day as by night, for which reason this midday-devil was called 'Selkolla' in the district"*. What follows is an account of the assaults of Selkolla at a farm which is never localized in any more detail. First, in the guise of the farmer's wife, she tries to entice him into having sex. When he realizes what is actually going on, he attempts to leave, but Selkolla bars his way, such that he gets home to the farm *"tired and exhausted"*, and lies in bed *"on account of that sickness, which the deceitful trick of the Devil had afflicted upon his virility. He could not have any thereafter, because the same unclean spirit seeks him day and night with enthusiasm"*.

Forest-troll (1890) by Theodor-Kittelsen (1857-1914)

No-one wants to be near the farmer to provide him with any solace, *"except for one diligent kinsman of his, who lies beside him until Selkolla overcomes him in the night and bursts out his eyes"*. Guðmundr, who is wandering the Westfjords, is called in and asked to tackle the fiend. He decides to stay at the farm which Selkolla is afflicting, and once he has gone to bed for the night he sees that a woman *"takes him by surprise"* and tries to pull off his shoes, which his servants have forgotten to do. Guðmundur realises immediately who it is and drives Selkolla away with the words *"far niðr, fjandi, ok gakk ei framarr!"* (go down, devil, and don't come back!). The next day, Guðmundr and Selkolla meet again and he drives her down once more, this time by setting up seven crosses. So ends Guðmundr's dealings with Selkolla. She rears her head once more on board a ship which is on the way *"over the fjord, or bay"* which separates the country's dioceses. But the crew have received the blessing of Guðmundr for the journey, and the blessing prevents Selkolla from harming them.

Seonaidh (Shoney)

In the folklore of the Hebrides, the *Seonaidh*, anglicized as *Shoney* was originally a Celtic sea god who took offerings of ale from the inhabitants of Lewis. Like with many pagan gods the Seonaidh was reduced to a local nature-spirit. The spirit-ritual was described by the Scottish writer Martin Martin (Màrtainn MacGille Mhàrtainn, ? -1718). Martin says that the inhabitants of Lewis used to propitiate Seonaidh by a cup of ale in the following manner. They came to the church of St. Mulway (Mael rubha), each man carrying his own provisions. Every family gave a pock (bag) of malt, and the whole was brewed into ale. One of their number was chosen to wade into the sea up to his waist, carrying in his hand the cup full of ale. When he reached a proper depth, he stood and cried aloud: *"Seonaidh, I give thee this cup of ale, hoping that thou wilt be so good as to send us plenty of seaware* (seaweed used as a fertilizer) *for enriching our ground during the coming year."* He then threw the ale into the sea, in a ceremony performed at night. On his coming to land, they all repaired to church, where there was a candle burning on the altar. There they stood still for a time, when, on a given signal, the candle was put out, and straight-away, they adjourned to the fields where the night was spent mirthfully over the ale. Next morning, they returned to their respective homes, in the belief that they had ensured a plentiful crop for the next season.

Shellycoat

In Scottish and Northern English folklore, a *Shellycoat* is a type of
Bogeyman that haunts rivers and streams. The name comes from the coat
of shells these creatures are said to wear, which rattle upon movement.
Many places on the coast of Scotland have names that refer to the
Shellycoat. Supposedly, Shellycoats are particularly fond of the area
around the River Hermitage. Shellycoats are considered to be relatively
harmless; they may mislead wanderers, particularly those they think are
trespassing upon the creature's territory, but without malice. A common
tactic of a Shellycoat would be to cry out as if drowning and then laugh at
the distracted victim. The Shellycoat shares many of the traits of the *Brag,
Kelpie* and *Nix.* Jacob Grimm stated in his *Deutsche Mythologie* that the
Scottish *Goblin* Shellycoat is one and the same as the German *Schellenrock*
– literally meaning *bell-coat*: *"A pück (house-spirit) served the monks of a
Mecklenburg monastery for thirty years, in kitchen, stall and elsewhere; he
was thoroughly good-natured, and only bargained for 'tunicam de diversis
coloribus, et tintinnabulis plenam.'* (a "multi-coloured coat with tinkling
bells"). *In Scotland there lived a goblin named Shellycoat, and we saw that
the dwarfs of the Middle Ages also loved bells (Schellen; and Schellenkappe*
is German for cap and bells). *The bells on the dress of a fool still attest
his affinity to the shrewd and merry goblin."* Within this context Thomas
Keightly quoted Grimm and classified the Shellycoat as a type of brownie:
*"Another name by which the domestic spirit was known in some parts of
Scotland was Shellycoat, of which the origin is uncertain."* The domestic
nature of the Shellycoat emphasized by Grimm and Keightly stands in
contrast to the wild nature of the water-sprites mentioned in other sources.

Shopiltee

The *Shopiltee* (also: *Shoepultie, Shoopiltee, Nuggle, Njuggle, Njogle,* or
Neugle,) is a male *water-horse,* local on the Shetland Islands and Orkneys.
It is described as similar in size and shape to a horse or pony of the
Shetland type, well proportioned, and of great strength and fleetness.
Generally the creature looked well fed but sleek, and of handsome
appearance; but occasionally he appeared as a very skinny, worn-out,
old horse. His color was gray, usually a rather dark gray, but sometimes
lighter, and approximating to white or black. He differed from ordinary
horses in that his hair grew and lay in the opposite direction to the hair of
other horses; his fetlocks grew upwards instead of downwards; his mane

was stiff and erect; his hoofs were also reversed and pointed backwards; and his tail was shaped like the rim of a wheel. Some people claim that his naturally very long tail was dragged behind, and occasionally rolled up like a hoop or the rim of a wheel, between his legs, or on his back. He could roll it up at will. Blue lights or flames are described emerging from his nostrils or hoofs. Unlike other corresponding water-horses, he was of a gentle disposition, more likely to instill fear rather than attacking islanders, although some tales – which equal him to the *Cabyll-ushtey* – suggest otherwise. According to folklorist Jessie Saxby *"he was a more feeble sort"*. He liked playing practical jokes and making mischief, but was deceitful and not very brave. Spitefulness was not a part of his character and his pranks were tempered with a degree of mercy. Contrary to the *Fuath*, the Shopiltees never take on a human form.

Sianach

The *Sianach* is a creature of the Scottish Gaelic oral tradition. It is described as a large, ghostly, malevolent, predatory and carnivorous deer with large, serrated teeth, and glowing eyes and hooves.

Silky

Silkies, according to Katharine Briggs, are female Brownies – except for the *Gruagachs*, who were as much female as male – who are always dressed in silk. In some lore the term *Silky* seems to switch from nature-spirit to the ghost of a woman. The Northumbrian and Border Silky is always female, like the *Banshee*. She is a spirit dressed in rustling silk, who does domestic chores about the house and is a terror to idle servants. The Silky of Black Heddon, mentioned by William Henderson in *Folk-Lore of the Northern Counties*, was the most famous of them all, and more mischievous than helpful, for though she tidied what was left in disorder, she would often throw about anything that had been neatly arranged. She would spend a great part of the night sitting in an old tree near an artificial lake. The tree was long called *Silky's Chair*. From this position she often used to stop carts and halt horses, and could only be countered by somebody wearing a cross made of rowan wood. One day a ceiling in Heddon Hall suddenly gave way and a large, rough skin filled with gold fell into the room below. The Silky never haunted Heddon Hall after that, and it was thought that she was the ghost of someone who had hidden this treasure and died without disclosing it.

Sjörået

Sjörået is the name of a Norse female water-spirit. In medieval ballads she is often referred to as the *sea-woman* or *Mermaid*. In Old Norse tradition, the sjörået is the equivalent of the sea-goddess *Rán*. She was considered to be nature's ruler over the lake, or lake system that was part of her territory. Like the *Skogsrået*, she was a seductive creature, despite having a hollow back. She appeared, however, almost exclusively to lonely men who stayed near the lake, where she used to sit and comb her long, sweeping hair with delight. To avoid close contact, she could easily be frightened away with a metal object. One such trick was to throw a fishing knife at her feet, and in a flash she would be gone.

Sjörået sometimes took the appearance of a perch or pike belonging to her lake. Anyone who caught a really big pike should therefore be careful that it was not the lake's Sjörået that was captured. By sharing one's food with the Sjörået, one could get good fishing luck in return, which could be seen as a kind of sacrificial gift. A popular tale is that of a fisherman who gives a mitten (or stocking) to the Sjörået and in return receives good fishing luck or is warned by her of an approaching storm. The story is recounted by Olaus Magnus in his *History of the Nordic Peoples*.

Skoffín

In Icelandic lore the *Skoffín* is a strange creature which – like the *Basilisc* – can kill a person just by looking at him or her. The creature is also known – with sometimes slight variations – as *Skuggabaldur, Finngalkn, Fingal; Urdarköttur, Naköttur* or *Modyrmi*. In later texts the creature is described as being born from a male Arctic blue fox and a female tabby cat, thus born as a kitten, that is directly recognizable because it leaves the womb of its mother with its eyes open. If not destroyed immediately, these kittens sink into the ground and emerge after three years of maturation. It is therefore imperative with kittens born this way to kill them before they manage to do so. When a litter of three sighted kittens was born at a farm in Súluholt, they were placed in a tub of urine to prevent their descent into the earth, and were drowned by placing turf on top of them. The entire tub was then tossed onto a pile of manure and hay and set on fire. The mother cat was also killed. The appearance of the adult Skoffín varies; it may even change color with the seasons, like the Arctic fox. Reports suggest that Skoffíns are short-haired, with bald patches throughout.

In older folklore, the Skoffin is much closer to the *Basilisc*, as we can read in *Icelandic Beast and Bird Lore* (1906) by Vilhjálmur Stefánsson:

"When a rooster is allowed to get very old he often lays an egg, but one which may always be told from hens' eggs by being smaller. This egg should be destroyed. If it is allowed to hatch, there is born from it a monster known as Skoffin, a thing with such baleful eyes that whatever it looks at immediately drops down dead. A story is told of a Skoffin which took its position near the doors of a church during service. When people began to leave the church they dropped dead one after the other. Those behind kept crowding out and no one noticed the state of affairs until there was quite a pile of dead bodies in front of the church door. Then the deacon, who was a shrewd man, noticed what was happening, and called to the people to remain in the church. He then took a small mirror, bound this on the end of a long stick and thrust it out through the door. After holding it here a moment he told the people that they might now safely go out, and they did so. When they came out they found the Skoffin dead. The wily deacon had induced it to look at its own reflection in the mirror and thus to kill itself.

The Skuggabaldur or Finngalkn has the same parentage as the Skoffín, but is born of a tomcat and a vixen. It has very dark fur, shading to black, sometimes has a deadly gaze, and preys on livestock.

Skogsrået

The *Skogsrået* (forest Rå) or *Skogsrå* is a female woodland *rådare* (spirit) in Swedish folklore. She is the same creature as the *Hulder* or *Huldra* (See under Hulder).

Skötumóðir

In Icelandic folklore the *Skötumóðir* (Skate Mother), also: *Vatnsandi* (water-spirit), *Vatnaskratti* (water-devil) or *Fluxuskrímsl* (flow-monster) are mysterious creatures that are intimately connected to the number nine. (Skates are cartilaginous fish belonging to the family of *Rajidae* in the superorder *Batoidea* of rays.) A skate was believed to have nine good qualities and nine bad. It will watch over a drowned man for nine nights, and spend the next nine nights eating him. A skate will carry its young within her for nine months, then lie upon them for nine weeks, during which a stone grows within them. This stone, the "skate-stone", could make a man invisible for one hour, or relieve labor pangs.

Icelandic lore knows a special kind of nature-spirits called the *Móðirin*, the "mothers" of certain kinds of fish. These creatures are linked to a special species, like a sort of "species-daemon or -genius". These Móðirin look like a specimen of that animal class but are much larger in size and manifest supernatural abilities. The most terrifying of these "Mothers" is the Skötumóðir, or Skate Mother. Like the other Icelandic "Fish mothers", they are not necessarily skates themselves; in fact, some accounts describe them as evil whales that resemble skates. They are enormous and toxic to eat, with backs like mud-covered islands, and with nine tails instead of one. Unlike regular skates, they have been found inland, in freshwater, and even on dry land. There is always a swarm of skates swimming around a Skötumóðir. As they are caught by fishermen, the sea seems to get shallower as the Skötumóðir rises to the surface. Finally, the vengeful Skate mother hooks her wings onto the gunwales of the boat, and drags it below the waves. An enormous ray, thought to be a Skötumóðir, was one of three monsters terrorizing people around Lagarfljót, lying in wait at ferry crossings until – according to folk-tales – it was transfixed to the bottom of the river by a powerful sorcerer.

Skriker or Trash

The *Skriker* or *Shrieker*, a Goblin of Lancashire and Yorkshire folklore, is a canine death portent like many others of its type, but it also wanders invisibly in the woods at night uttering loud, fearful screams. It may also take visible form like *padfoot*, a huge dog with saucer eyes and enormous paws that make a splashing sound when walking, like old shoes in soft mud. For this reason the Skriker is also known as *Trash*, another word for "trudge" or "slog". The name Skriker is derived from a dialect word for "screech" in reference to its frightful utterances.

Sleih beggey

In Manx folklore *Sleig beggey* (Little people), also *Sleigh veggy*, *Sleigh beggey*, *Beggys* and *Ferrishyn* is used as a blanket term for the Manx *Fairies* in general. A wide variety of individual mythical creatures come under the umbrella of Sleih beggey. With both benevolent and malevolent Fairies.

Sluagh

In Irish and Scottish folklore, the *Sluagh* (Old Irish: *Slúag*; English: "host, army, crowd") were in Scottish Gaelic folklore the hosts of the restless, unforgiven dead. Sometimes they were seen as sinners, or generally evil people who were not welcome in heaven or hell, or even in the other worlds, who had been rejected by the Celtic gods and by the Earth itself. Their story was told from family to family. Whatever the underlying belief, they were almost always described as troublemakers and destroyers. They were seen flying in groups like swarms of gray birds or clouds, coming from the west, and were known to try to enter the homes of dying people to take their souls with them. In Irish legend the Sluagh preyed on the dying while they were still in bed and weak. The living prayed that the dying person would die quickly to prevent the Sluagh from coming to take their soul, which would place them in a perpetual hell. The Sluagh would strike at night and the souls that were taken away screamed in terror. When someone was found dead in a forest, a field or a river, it was believed that the Sluagh had taken the soul of this person. Windows facing West were sometimes kept closed to prevent them from entering. However, in other Gaelic lore they came from the East, and the exclamation *"O shluagh!"* was uttered as a cry for help against the demons. They were believed to be able to approach and pick up a person from any direction and then transport them far away through the air, from one island to another. Although they could sometimes rescue humans from dangerous rock clefts, they were generally portrayed as dangerous to mortals.

Appearances

In the beginning, the Sluagh could take any form. He took on a human appearance in the second stage. The Sluagh was often described as a flying, swirling shadow with long, skinny, webbed fingers and deformed legs that ended in long claws. Sluagh flocks produced a shadowy sight and flapping sound and gave off a smell of rotting meat. In the Middle Ages, it was said that the Sluagh was pale and fed on rotten food that humans could not eat. They had no teeth. It was assumed that some lived in caves or sewers.

Spittal Hill Tut

In Lincolnshire *Tut* is a generic term for a *phantom, sprite* or *Fairy*. The following is taken from *County Folk-Lore* by Gutch and Peacock (1908), who stated their source was *The History and Antiquities of Boston in the County of Lincoln*, by Pishey Thompson (1856):

"There is a curious superstition relative to a place in the parish of Freiston called Spittal Hill (from a hospital which was formerly there), that a hobgoblin or sprite frequents the spot at midnight in the shape of a small rough horse. This sprite has been named the Spittal Hill tut and sometimes the shag-foal. It is said to have frequently followed a traveler, mounted his horse behind him, and almost hugged him to death with its forelegs. It accompanies him to a certain distance and then vanishes. Different causes are assigned for this appearance by those who believe in it. One is, that a murder was committed near the spot where the 'shag-foal' appears, another, that a treasure is secreted there, and that this hobgoblin is appointed to watch over and protect it."

Spriggan

A *Spriggan* is a legendary creature from Cornish *Fairy*-lore. Spriggans are particularly associated with West Penwith in Cornwall. Spriggan is a dialect word, borrowed from the Cornish plural *spyrysyon* "spirits". Spriggans were depicted as grotesquely ugly wizened old men, with large childlike heads. They were said to be found at old ruins, cairns and barrows, guarding buried treasure. Although small, they were usually considered to be the ghosts of giants and retained gigantic strength, and in one story collected by Robert Hunt, they showed the ability to swell to enormous size. Hunt associated these spirits with the hillfort known as Trencrom Hill in Cornwall. Spriggans were notorious for their unpleasant dispositions, and delighted in working mischief against those who offended them. In some tales they can trigger storms to destroy crops, or were blamed if a house was robbed or a building collapsed, or if cattle were stolen. Spriggans were notorious for stealing babies from destitute mothers, when they had been obliged to leave them alone for a few hours in order to work, putting their own ugly, peevish brats in their cradles, who would never thrive under the foster-mother's care, in spite of all the loving care they might bestow upon them. They are said to be scared of women who openly demonstrate their sexuality, as in one tale, where an elderly woman scares a gang of Spriggans away by lifting her skirt and placing her hands on her behind. In one story, an old woman got the better of a band of Spriggans by turning her clothes inside-out (inside-out clothing being supposedly as effective as holy water or iron in repelling Fairies) to gain their loot.

Sprite

The generic term *sprite* is derived from the Latin *spiritus* (spirit), via the French *esprit*. Variations on the term include *spright* and the Celtic *Spriggan* – the latter also being a term for a specific entity. The term is chiefly used in regard to *Elves* and *Fairies* in European folklore, but in modern English is rarely used in reference to spirits. The belief in beings such as sprites, *Elves*, *Fairies*, etc. has been common in many parts of the world, and still is. The sprite is sometimes believed to be an *air-spirit* or *Elemental,* identical to the *Sylph*. Elemental spirits are nature-spirits dwelling in an Elemental realm, like the *Salamanders* in Fire, The *Undines* in Water and the *Gnomes* in Earth and mountains. According to alchemist Paracelsus, a *water-sprite* (also called a *Water-Fairy* or *water-faery*) is a general term for an Elemental spirit associated with water. Water-sprites are said to be able to breathe water or air and sometimes they can fly. They are considered mostly harmless, unless threatened. These creatures exist in mythology of various parts of the world. Ancient Greeks divided *Water-Nymphs* in several types, such as *Naiads* (or *Nyads*), which were considered to be divine entities that tended to be fixed in one place, so differed from gods or physical creatures. Slavic mythology knows them as *Vilas*. Water-sprites differ from corporeal beings, such as *Selkies* and *Mermaids*, as they are not purely physical and are more akin to local deities than animals.

Spunkie

Spunkie is a solitary *Goblin* of the Scottish Lowlands, related to the *Will-o'-the-wisp*, that delights in playing tricks on lost travelers. To lure its victims to their destruction it manifests a light that is perceived like a distant window.

Strandvaskare

In Swedish folklore, a *Strandvaskare* (beach washer) or *Strandgast* (beach ghost) is a drowned person who walks again. Among these were dead sailors whose bodies were never found and therefore did not receive a Christian burial. When it stormed, their unholy spirits could be heard gasping from the sea.

Svartálfar

In Nordic mythology, *Svartalfer* or *Black Elves* – usually translated as *Black* or *Night Elves* – are the counterparts of the *Light Elves*. The Light Elves live in *Alfheim*, the *Svartalfer* in *Svartalfheim*. According to Nordic mythology, *Svartalfer* are evil. They look like humans, but are as black as night. *Svartalfer* are often confused with *dwarfs*. Yet there are clear differences. For example, dwarfs – unlike Night Elves – are generally benign. Also, dwarfs live in *Nidavellir*, not *Svartalfheim*. In English folklore, the Night Elves were called *Goblins*. After the Christianization of the Vikings, with which their mythology also fell into oblivion, the English Goblin continued to exist, but his malice diminished over time, until he became just an annoying prankster.

Svipir

In Icelandic lore – as analyzed by Dutch folklorist P.C.M. Sluijter – the *Svipir*, in most cases, are phantoms of non-present persons who are in mortal danger or have already died. In any case they are absolutely harmless spirits. Reason for their appearance might be that people who have died in an accident often appear to their next of kin to let them know that – and how – they lost their lives. In the sagas, the harmless – as well as the harmful – spirits usually appear in their former human form. In the later folktales, however, we also find the Svipir described as a kind of perceptible soul, grayish in color, often stretched very long and in the form of a column of smoke or luminous specks and stars. Since such descriptions do not occur at all in antiquity, this representation of the soul as a kind of mist probably arose under the influence of Christian concepts, or of strange fairytales, etc. In the case of the dead appearing in their human form, one sees them in the state in which they were at the moment of death. This then shows how they died. In the sagas the drowned appear in soaking wet clothes; those who have died in battle appear all bloodied and the beheaded "spinning Klaufi" was seen beating his enemies in battle with his own bloody head. We find this same motif in new Icelandic literature. The Svipur of a woman, who died in a fire, is regularly seen with singed hair and a burnt cheek. Those who have been caught in a snowstorm also return to the living snowed in, etc.

T

Tangie

In the folklore of the Orkney and Shetland Islands in the British Isles, a *Tangie* or *Tongie* is a shape-shifting sea-spirit or Trow, that takes on the appearance of either a *(water)horse* or an aged *(mer)man*. Usually it is described as being covered with seaweed, its name derives from *tang*, or seaweed, of the genus *Fucus*. The Tangie is known for terrorizing lonely travelers, especially young women on roads at night near the lochs, whom he will abduct and devour underwater. Similar yet distinctive from the smaller and less harmful *Nuggle*, a Tangie is able to cause derangement in humans and animals. The Tangie plays a major role in the Shetland legend of *Black Eric*, a sheep rustler. The Tangie he rode gave him supernatural assistance when he raided and harassed surrounding crofts. In his final battle with crofter Sandy Breamer, Black Eric fell to his death in the sea. The Tangie then continued to terrorize the area, particularly the young women he was hoping to abduct.

Tarbh uisge

The *Water bull*, also known as *Tarbh uisge* in Scottish Gaelic, is a mythological Scottish creature similar to the Manx *Tarroo ushtey*. Generally regarded as a nocturnal resident of moorland lochs, it is usually more amiable than its equine counterpart the Water horse, but has similar amphibious and shape-shifting abilities. The Tarbh uisge is said to reproduce with standard cattle, the resulting progeny distinguishable by the small size of their ears. According to some myths, the calves of Water bulls and ordinary cows ought to be killed at birth by any method other than drowning – they cannot be killed by drowning – to avoid bringing disaster to the herd. Conversely, in the more northern areas of Scotland, the calves are considered to be of superior quality. However when the Manx Water bull mates with an ordinary cow, this usually results in the death of the cow after she produces a horrible dead lump of flesh and skin without bones. The Water bulls have no ears themselves and therefore produce calves with only half ears, described by folklorist John Gregorson Campbell as "knife-eared". Water bulls living at Leverburgh are said to produce offspring with disfigured crimson or purple-colored ears.

Belief in the existence of Water bulls persisted in Scotland until at least the last quarter of the 19th century. As with many mythological creatures, descriptions are imprecise. The Water bull is able to shape-shift into human form, and live on land or in water. A Tarbh uisge can be a monstrous, malevolent black beast, but not as nasty as the *Each uisge* or *Water-horse*. It can even be amiable and sometimes helpful. As a loch-creature the Water bull differs from the Manx *Tarroo ushtey*, which is more likely to be a resident of marshland. Accounts of snaring and destroying the beast are rare, as it is not generally considered to be a threat. In 1819 John MacCulloch, a noted geologist, described how inhabitants around the areas of Loch Awe and Loch Rannoch tried to capture a Water bull by shackling a sheep to an oak tree as an enticement, but the shackle was not strong enough. Another story describes a farmer and his two sons hunting a Water bull. The farmer's musket was filled with silver sixpence coins as the beast could only be killed with silver.

Tarrans

In Scottish folklore the *Tarrans* were believed to be the spirits of babies who had died without their baptism. They manifested as lights.

Tchico

In Jersey folklore, a black dog acting as an omen of death is called the *Tchico* or the *Black Dog of Bouley Bay*, but a related belief in the *Tchian d'Bouôlé* (Black Dog of Bouley) tells of a phantom dog whose appearance presages storms. The real reason for the superstition of the Black Dog of Bouley Bay is thought to be due to smugglers. If the superstition was fed and became 'real' to the locals, the bay would be deserted at night and the smuggling could continue in security. The pier at Bouley Bay made this an exceptionally easy task. A local pub retains the name "Black Dog".

Thevshi or Tash

Ghosts, in Ireland, are called *thevshi* or *tash* (*taidhbhse, tais*). They live in a state intermediary between this life and the next. They are held there by some earthly longing or affection, or some duty unfulfilled, or anger against the living. *"I will haunt you"*, is a common threat; and one hears such phrases as, *"She will haunt him, if she has any good in her"*. If one is sorrowing greatly after a dead friend, a neighbor will say, *"Be quiet now, you are keeping him from his rest"*; or, in the Western Isles, according to writer and poet Lady Wilde (1821-1896), they will tell you, *"You are waking the dog that watches to devour the souls of the dead"*. Those who die suddenly are believed to become haunting Ghosts. They go about moving the furniture, and in every way try to attract attention.

When the soul has left the body, it is drawn away, sometimes, by the *Fairies*. I have a story of a peasant who once saw, sitting in a Fairy rath, all who had died for years in his village. Such souls are considered lost. If a soul eludes the Fairies, it may be snapped up by the evil spirits. The vulnerable souls of young children are in especial danger. When a very young child dies, the western peasantry sprinkle the threshold with the blood of a chicken, so that the spirits may be drawn towards the blood. A Ghost is compelled to obey the commands of the living. Lady Wilde considers that it is only the spirits who are too bad for heaven, and too good for hell, who are thus plagued. They are compelled to obey someone they have wronged.

The souls of the dead sometimes take the shape of animals. There is a garden at Sligo where the gardener sees a previous owner in the shape of a rabbit. They will sometimes take the form of insects, especially butterflies. If you see one fluttering near a corpse, that is the soul, and is a sign of its having entered upon immortal happiness. The author of the *Parochial Survey of Ireland*, 1814, heard a woman say to a child who was chasing a butterfly, *"How do you know it is not the soul of your grandfather"*. On November eve the dead are abroad, and dance with the Fairies. As in Scotland, the *fetch* (the double) is commonly believed in. If you see the double, or fetch, of a friend in the morning, no ill follows; if at night, you are about to die.

Tom Dockin

Tom Dockin is mentioned by Elisabeth Mary Wright in her *Rustic Speech and Folk-Lore* (1913) as a terrifying Yorkshire *nursery-bogie* with iron teeth, who devours naughty children.

Tom-Poker

Tom-Poker is an East Anglian *nursery-bogie* and is mentioned by Elisabeth Mary Wright. Tom Poker hid in dark cupboards, holes under stairs, empty lofts and other places appropriate to bogies.

Tomten or Nisse

Tomten, Tomtegubben, Gårdstomten, Tomtrået, is a guardian of the farm in Nordic folklore. Tomten may also be called *Tomtevätte,* and in Skåne, Denmark and in Norway he is preferably called *Nisse* or *Goanisse.* In Sweden there is also *Puke* which is a small devil, *Pyske,* a small man, *Hempjäske* and *Pixy.* In Finnish there is *Tonttu,* which is borrowed from Swedish. Tomten are regarded as household-spirits like the Roman *Penates* and *Lares,* the Russian *Domovoy,* the *Hob* in England, the Scottish *Brownie* and the *Heinzelmännchen* in Germany. In Swedish folklore the Tomten is a kind of shadow farmer with supernatural powers who made sure that the farm attracted good luck. He was often assumed to be the first to raise that particular farm, and who does not come to rest after his death, but must constantly look after 'his' farm. He is described as an older man and smaller than an average human (exactly how small varies), often with a white beard, gray clothes and a hood. It was important to keep him friendly and not offend him in any way. Tomten had an angry temperament and could take revenge if, for example, one mistreated the animals or treated him disrespectfully. Above all, he watched over the animals in the stables and barn. In return for his good works, the farm owner gave Tomten a bowl of porridge. According to a later tradition, he was particularly fond of rice porridge (sweet porridge), which is why it is also called *Tomtens porridge.* Legends about Tomten include how he kills a cow in anger when he doesn't get a lump of butter in his porridge, or how he is rewarded with new clothes, which, however, make him think he is too good-looking to carry on with his work. The Tomten has a lot in common with the *Goblin.* Both belong to the ranks of the unruly dwarfish creatures and were said, for example, to dwell under the spring tree, and the Yard Washer is another name for Tomten. Tomten can be seen as part of the Old Norse religion that has survived syncretical with Christianity. St. Bridget warns in two places in her apparitions against honoring the "gods of the tomb" (*tompta gudhi, tompa gudhom*); similar warnings are issued in older sermon collections and biblical commentaries.

Tomtormar

In earlier times in Sweden, the *Tomtormar* fulfilled a role as household-spirits, while they were incarnated beings, usually represented by the *grass snake* (Natrix natrix) but also the *smooth snake* (Coronella austriaca – *hasselsnok* in Swedish). They lived near farm houses, barns and the stables where the cows were milked. Milk was often left as a sacrifice for the snakes. According to folklore, if the snakes were treated well, they would improve the happiness of livestock and protect the farm from accidents, such as lightning strokes. An Tomtormar was not to be killed; if it was, the farm could suffer great misfortune. Belief in Tomtormar has been widespread throughout Scandinavia, Finland and the Baltic States, which may be due to the snake's habit of seeking symbiosis with nearby humans. Particularly in coniferous forest areas, where leaf piles are lacking, the snipe needs manure piles to lay its eggs. Older researchers saw the provision of milk for the Tomtormar as a last vestige of an ancient pagan snake cult, which they also found hinted at in the dragon strings and animal ornamentation of rune stones. The snake cult was very strong in the Baltic region. Modern historians however, have not reached a consensus about snake worship in Sweden. During the Christianization of Scandinavia and the Baltic regions in the Middle Ages, the worship of snakes must have been an abomination to the Christians, who considered the snake to be the earthly representative of the devil himself.

Troll

A *Troll* is an unpredictable creature in Norse mythology, that embodies the forces of nature and the word is used as a generic term for such type of spirits. Especially in Sweden and Denmark, fairytales mixed the idea of dwarfs and other forest-, water- or mountain-spirits, sometimes also with that of human-friendly *Fairies* and Elves. Thus, "Troll" became a general term for any kind of more or less human-shaped mythical creature, similar to the Fairies of the Anglo-Celtic tradition.

Christianity demonized the Trolls, whose existence was still assumed in folk belief until the 19th century. The Trolls are often depicted as lonely, beastly or monstrously ugly beings, of 'giant' size, living in isolated mountains, dressed in rags or animal skins, or sometimes as dwarfish ugly fur-covered humanoids with a large nose and only four fingers on each hand. The Troll has remained an object of belief since the Middle Ages and Christianization, until the beginning of the 20th century when the numerous legends were collected by researchers.

Etymology

The Scandinavian terms Troll and also *droll* are borrowed from the Old Norse (Old Icelandic) *trǫll*, which appeared in medieval Norse literature to designate characters from mythology, with the meaning of "possessing magic or dark powers" according to Sveinsson (*Troll, an etymological note, Scandinavian Studies*, vol. 30, no 3, 1958). The term is also related to the Norse verb *trylla*, which means "to drive mad, to lead into a mighty rage, to fill with fury" or "to turn into a Troll, to enchant". In Norse texts, these terms are derived from *trollskapr* (witch) and *tryllskr* (of the nature of a Troll). Moreover, in modern Scandinavian languages, *Troll* and *trylla* are derived in numerous expressions, all related to (more or less harmful) magic: Danish: *troldom, trolderi, troldmand, trylle* (conjure), *tryllecraft* (magic power), *tryllemiddel, trylleri* (magic, enchantment), Swedish: *trolldom* (meaning witchcraft), *trolleri* (magic, enchantment), *trolla* (conjure), *trollsk* (magic), *trollkarl* (sorcerer)... Also found in medieval Middle High German are *Trolle* or *Trol* (ghost monster, witch), and *trüllen* (to play tricks, to deceive).

Evolution

The end of the Viking Age corresponds to the establishment of royal authority and the beginning of Christianization in Scandinavia, from the 10th century until the 13th century. As a result of the adoption of Christianity by the monarchy, and later by the whole country, traditional spiritual practices and beliefs were marginalized and their followers persecuted. The *völvas*, prophets of ancestral practices *(sejðr)*, were usually executed or exiled. The old gods and paganistic rites were replaced by beliefs in new pagan creatures: *Trolls, jötnars, Elves*. Symbolically the wild and uncivilized Troll, representing 'the forces of chaos, the enemies of God' became the most important opponent of Christianization. For example, the king and saint Olaf II of Norway, was depicted fighting the Trolls as a way of bringing his people into the new religion. It is difficult to determine with certainty the evolution of legends and folk beliefs between the Middle Ages and the modern era, in the absence of sufficient written evidence. Specialists, historians and folklorists base their assumptions on the philological study of Norse and later literary texts. There is no doubt that there are folk legends from the Middle Ages onwards about giant beings or 'Trolls' living in the mountains and rocks of Scandinavia or Iceland. These creatures were probably solitary. According to the Icelandic scholar Einar Ólafur Sveinsson *(The Folk-Stories of Iceland*, 1940*)*, the word 'Troll' took on a very vague meaning around 1200 (due to Christianization), but popular beliefs were not altered or diminished at that time. Belief in the existence of Trolls gradually diminished around 1600 in Iceland; the appearance of new Troll-legends is rare after the Protestant Reformation, and Icelandic Troll-stories from the 17th and 18th centuries seem to originate from before the Reformation. The Icelanders certainly believed that the Troll race had disappeared. The beliefs and characteristics of the Troll vary greatly, depending on the time and region of Scandinavia, making it difficult to attempt a general description of the Troll.

An important aspect of the legends is that, despite its today's cliche image, Troll's were rarely described physically in the old literature. Legendary accounts usually leave out the Troll's appearance and focus mainly on the Troll's actions and the explicit mention of his supernatural nature, i.e. his distinction from humans. The appearance of the Troll is sometimes even mentioned as being identical to humans, like the Trolls that inhabit the wild forests of central Sweden. The size of the Troll is rarely mentioned either; even when the Troll seems to inherit divine characteristics from the *Jötunn* of ancient mythology, its size is very rarely determined. The modern idea of the huge or 'giant' (or naive) Troll is mainly inherited from nineteenth-century fiction (fairytales, illustrations).

The legendary Troll is essentially defined by his connection to wild places and natural elements: the sea, certain forests, mountains or rocks, i.e. wild places, alien to human civilization. The Troll thus takes on its meaning as the symbol or embodiment of natural forces, regarded with respect and fear by man, because of their strangeness and danger. The Troll is also defined by its difference from man and the difficulty of peaceful cohabitation between the species. Legends repeatedly mention the problem of human encounters with Troll, the abduction of human women and children by Trolls, ways of avoiding, defeating or killing them; in particular, the Troll's weakness towards fire, lightning (storm) and light (sun). In some regions, the Troll's characteristics are identical to those of other supernatural creatures, or sometimes its powers are greatly diminished. This difference may be due to confusion between the Troll and other legendary creatures *(småfolk)* from Scandinavian or Germanic folklore. The characteristics of the Troll are sometimes confused with those of Elves, Huldra's, etc., especially in the southern regions (Denmark). When the Troll is assimilated to small (and not very dangerous) creatures, its characteristics are sometimes attributed to the Christian influence which fought against pagan beliefs and depreciated the influence of the Troll.

Trow

In the folklore of the Orkney and Shetland islands a *Trow*, also *Trowe*, *Drow* or *Dtrow*, figures as a malignant or mischievous *Fairy*. Speaking about Trows was taboo. It was also considered unlucky to catch sight of the creature. One exception on this rule however was made by a legendary witch, who married a so called *Kunal-Trow* or *King-Trow*, which is a type of Trow in the lore of Unst, Shetland, of a race without females, that consumes soil formed into shapes of fish and fowl, and even babies, which taste and smell like the real thing. They wander after dark and are sometimes found weeping, due to the lack of companionship. For this reason a Kunal-Trow sometimes takes a human wife, who however always dies after giving birth to a son. But according to one legend a witch once married a Kunal-Trow, extracted all the Trow's secrets, and gave birth to *Ganfer* (astral body) and *Finis* (an apparition who appears in the guise of someone whose death is imminent). She was believed to have cheated death with her arts.

Etymology derives the word "Trow" from "Troll". In Norwegian *Trold* (Troll) can signify not just a giant, but a *spøkelse* (specter, ghost) as well, and originally Troll used to be a blanket term for all kinds of supernatural creatures. As an alternate etymology, John Jamieson's Scottish dictionary conjectured that the word Trow may be a corruption of Scandinavian *Draug*, and indeed, Trow is also called *Drow* under its variant spelling in the Scots dialect; however, the term "drow" (mentioned by Walter Scott) could also be used in the sense of "the Devil" in Orkney. To make things even more complicated, the word Drow also occurs in the Shetland Norn language, where it – apart from *Troll-folk*, or *ghost* – means *Huldrefolk* (the hidden people).

Trows are shapeshifters who can take a human form, appear as giants – sometimes multi-headed, or quite the opposite, of short-statured dwarfs dressed in gray. One very peculiar trait of Trows is that they traditionally have a fondness for music and also play the fiddle themselves. Tales are also told of human fiddlers being abducted by Trows to their *Trowie knowes* (earthen mound dwellings), and although released after what seems a brief stay, many long years have elapsed in the outside world, and the victim turns to dust, or chooses to die. They are nocturnal creatures, like the Scandinavian Troll with which the Trow shares many similarities. They leave their Trowie knowes solely in the evening, and may enter households as the inhabitants sleep. Most mounds in Orkney are associated with "mound-dwellers" (*Hogboon*; Old Norse: *Haugbúinn*; Norwegian: *Haugbonde*) living inside them, and although local lore does not always specify, the dwellers are commonly considered to be the Trow. A reputedly Trow-haunted mound may not in fact be a burial mound. The Long Howe in Tankerness, a glacial mound, was believed to contain Trows, and thus was avoided after dark. A group of mounds around Trowie Glen in Hoy are also geological formations, but feared for its Trows throughout the valley, and therefore not visited after dark.

Sea-Trows
Apart from the *Hill-Trows*, or *Land-Trows*, there are also the *Sea-Trows*, and these two kinds were believed to be mortal enemies. The Sea-Trow of Orkney is *"the ugliest imaginable"* according to Orkney farmer and folklorist Walter Traill Dennison (1825-1894) in his *Orkney Folklore, Sea Myths*, 1891 – who furthermore says that it has been represented as a scaly creature with matted hair, a monkey-like face with a sloping forehead. It was said to be frail-bodied with disproportionately huge sets of limbs, disc-shaped feet *"round as a millstone"* with webbings on their hands and feet, causing them to move with a lumbering and "waddling" slow gait. An early account (1529) is that of the Sea-Trow of Stronsay, described in Joseph Ben's *Description of the Orkney Islands* as a creature with *Incubus*-features; *"...it was a maritime monster resembling a colt whose entire body was cloaked in seaweed, with a coiled or matted*

coat of hair, sexual organs like a horse's, and known to engage in sexual intercourse with the women of the island." However, in Shetland, *da Mokkl Sea-Trow*, was an evil spirit that dwelled in the depths, to take on the shape of a woman, at least in some instances. The Sea-Trow is blamed for stealing the fish caught on fishermen's lines, and were otherwise feared for causing storms, or causing ill luck to fishermen. In the form of a wailing woman, she portends misfortune. According to Samuel Hibbert-Ware (1782-1848) the Sea-Trow was a local version of the *Neckar*, and he specified that it was reputed to be lined with all kinds of stuff from the sea, especially seaweeds, of which its larger forms near the shore are known as *tang* in the Shetlands. And although Hibbert does not make the connection, Orkney folklorist Ernest Walker Marwick (1915-1977) equated the Sea-Trow with the *Tangy* or *Tangie*.

219
T

T'yeer-na-n-oge

There is a country called *T'yeer-na-n-oge* or *Tír-na-n-Og*, which means the Country of the Young, for age and death have not found it; neither tears nor loud laughter have gone near it. The shadiest boscage covers it perpetually. One man has gone there and returned; the bard, Oisin, who wandered away on a white horse, moving on the surface of the foam with his Fairy Niamh, lived there three hundred years, and then returned looking for his comrades. The moment his foot touched the ground his three hundred years fell on him, and he was bowed double, and his beard swept the ground. He described his sojourn in the Land of Youth to Patrick before he died. Since then many have seen it in many places; some in the depths of lakes, and have heard rising therefrom a vague sound of bells; more have seen it far off on the horizon, as they peered out from the western cliffs. Not three years ago a fisherman imagined that he saw it. It never appears unless to announce some national trouble.

There are many kindred beliefs. A Dutch pilot, settled in Dublin, told M. De La Boullage Le Cong, who traveled through Ireland in 1614, that around the poles were many islands; some hard to be approached because of the witches who inhabit them and destroy by storms those who seek to land. He had once, off the coast of Greenland, in sixty-one degrees of latitude, seen and approached such an island, only to see it vanish before his eyes. Sailing in an opposite direction, they met with the same island, and sailing near, were almost destroyed by a furious tempest.

According to many stories, T'yeer-na-n-oge is the favorite dwelling of the Fairies. Some say it is triple-the island of the living, the island of victories, and an underwater land.

Tylwyth Teg

The modern Welsh name for *Fairies* is *y Tylwyth Teg* (the fair folk or the fair family). This is sometimes lengthened into *y Tylwyth Teg yn y Coed* (the fair family in the woods) or *Tylwyth Teg y Mwn* (the fair folk of the mines). Other names for them include *Bendith y Mamau* (Blessing of the Mothers), named *Gwyllion* and *Ellyllon*. They are seen dancing in moonlit nights on the velvety grass, clad in airy and flowing robes of blue, green, white or scarlet – details as to color not often heard of, I think, in accounts of Fairies. They are spoken of as bestowing blessings on those mortals whom they select to be thus favored. To name these *Fairies* by a harsh epithet is to invoke their anger; to speak of them in flattering phrases is to propitiate their goodwill. Their usual king is *Gwyn ap Nudd*. Although in general y Tylwyth Teg are portrayed as benevolent, they are still capable of occasional mischief. Some of their later stories even profess improved behavior and good morals, such as promising rewards of silver to young women who keep tidy houses. They are more often associated with lakes than other Celtic Fairies, especially with Llyn y Fan Fach in South Wales. Another distinction is their fear of iron; unbaptized children should be guarded from y Tylwyth Teg by having an iron poker placed over the cradle. Like other Fairies, they are thought to possess magical cattle, the most famous of which is the *Speckled Cow of Hiraethog*. "Fairyland" in Welsh is often called *Gwlad y Tylwyth Teg*.

U

Uldra

The Norwegian *Uldra* – in contrast to the Lapland version (see *Spirit Beings in European Folklore*, compendium 2) – is described as a *water-sprite* (Harriet Martineau, *Feats on the Fiord*, 1856) or a "spirit of the vapor" (James Grant, *Bothwell: Or, The Days Of Mary Queen Of Scots*, vol. 1, 1851,). George Frederick Watts created a painting of the water-sprite in 1884 entitled *Uldra, The Scandinavian Spirit of the Rainbow in the Waterfall*. Derwent Conway, in *A Personal Narrative of a Journey Through Norway*, 1829, also described the Norwegian Uldras as river-spirits. He recounted a story of a peasant, going – as was customary – to leave a cake for one of these spirits. When he got there, he found the river frozen over. He was only able to hammer a small hole in the ice, but to his surprise, a tiny snow-white hand came through the hole and took the cake, which became small enough to pass through.

Uppvakningar

In Icelandic folklore the *Uppvakningar* (those who have been brought back from the dead) are dead people who are "spirited back" by black magic for various tasks, or they are *Fylgjur*, who can sometimes be ghosts or etherical discarnates. A characteristics of Icelandic ghosts, especially before the 20th century, is that the ghosts usually do not seem to be spirits but rather physical beings. Thus the Uppvakningar are the Icelandic equivalent of the many "undead-variations" we know from Eastern-European folklore.

Urchin

Urchin or *Hurgeon* is an English dialect name for a hedgehog, but it was also used for a small malicious *imp* or *Pixie*, as these spirits were believed to often take the form of a hedgehog. It is an old term, as Caliban, a figure in William Shakespeare's *The Tempest*, was tormented by Urchins at Prospero's command. Reginald Scot mentioned *Urchens* in his list of frightening spirits. Katherine Briggs pointed out that over time the name came into use for small, mischievous boys and fell into disuse to designate (a class of) *Fairies*.

Urdarköttur

In Icelandic folklore the *Urdarköttur* (Ghoul cat or fallen cat) or *Naköttur* (corpse cat) is a huge ghostly cat. Some folk-belief has it that any cat that goes feral in Iceland eventually becomes an Urdarköttur, just like all-white kittens born with their eyes open will sink into the ground and re-emerge after three years in this form. (See also the *Skoffin* and *Skuggabaldur.*) Shaggy, white or black furred, the creature grows up to the size of an ox, after which it kills indiscriminately and digs up corpses in graveyards.

Urdarmani

On Fróöa, Iceland, before an epidemic breaks out, an ominous sign is observed. There a half moon – the so-called *Urdarmani* (fallen moon) – moves against the course of the sun along the wall of the house. Urdarmani has variations in its appearance. At other places it may appear as a ball of reddish light.

Utburd

In Norse mythology the *Utburd*, like the Swedish *Myling*, was an evil spirit of an unwanted infant that was left to die. The Norwegians had the custom to get rid of a child that was sick or born with physical deformities by burying it in the snow. Infants who resulted from an extramarital relationship were often disposed of in the same way. Sometimes the baby's soul would come back as a ghost (Utburd) and take revenge on the living, and first of all on the mother. Often the victims of the Utburd received a warning in the form of a white owl, but it was almost impossible to escape its vengeance – the Utburds were extremely fast and strong. There is an analogue in the Icelandic *Útburdir* and in the mythology of the Nanai, Inuit, Chukchi and other northern peoples, specifically the *Angyak.*

Útburdir

Útburdir, like the Scandinavian *Utburd* and *Myling,* emerge from the spirits of abandoned infants (mostly girls) as a globe-shaped phantom, or the typical Icelandic Revenant-type of ghost. P.C.M. Sluijter (in *IJslandse Volksverhalen*) states that in pagan times, this habit of abandoning

children should probably be considered as a sacrifice to obtain fertility.
In the saga-era governmental law allowed this action in some cases. But
even prominent people – although there was no economic reason for it –
sometimes abandoned their child in the wilderness. Usually a shepherd,
taken into confidence by the mother, would take the child to relatives and
raise it there. But not all children were that lucky. In later times, it were
unbaptized, illegitimate children and children of the poor who – dead or
alive – were laid to rest soon after birth. And these Ütburdir then came
to remind the parents of their crime, or one had to assume that evil spirits
had taken possession of the unbaptized bodies. The sagas do not yet have
these representations; we are evidently facing a younger development here.

The Ütburdir are described as dark brown, round balls that move very
quickly on elbows and knees, keeping their hands and feet crossed. They
try to shoot between someone's feet and if they succeed, some person's life
is at stake. At night or in a fog they lead people astray; by circling around
them three times, they rob people of their reason. If one recites a certain
stanza or gives them a name – both the rhythmically bound word and
the name possess a strong magical potency – they become powerless.
However, it is wrong to respond randomly to their cries, which announce
disasters and special events. Sometimes they themselves reveal who their
father or mother is. When the body is brought to the mother, she suddenly
falls ill – in this latter case the Ütburdir were clearly animated corpses,
as is often understood by "a ghost" in Icelandic lore, in contrast to the
European continent interpretation of a ghost as a priori a discarnate being.

Utilegumenn

In later Icelandic folklore the *Utilegumenn* mostly took over the role
of the *Trölls* (Trolls) or the *giants* the Icelandic Trölls had fused with in
later times, like the *Bergbüar*, *Jötnar*, *Risar* or *Gýgjur*. Originally they
were banned criminals (or people who had committed something that
was regarded as a crime), of which some seemed to have survived the
Islandic wilderness somehow. Later they were regarded as some evil type
of *Alf* and when in the spring the sheep of the farmers were sent into
the mountains, it is to be understood that many of them got missing.
Especially when no bones were found, people thought the Utilegumenn
took them. Most notorious were the Utilegumenn however not for
robbing sheep, but for stealing girls.

V

Vættir

The *Vættir* (singular *Vættr*) are spirits of Norse mythology. The term can be used to refer to the full cosmos of supernatural beings, including the *Álfar* (Elves), *Dvergar* (dwarfs), *Jötnar* (giants) and gods (the *Æsir* and *Vanir*). Vættir can also refer more specifically to *Landvættir* (location bound nature-spirits), *Fjallvættir* (mountain-spirits), *Sjóvættir* (sea-spirits), *Skogvættir* (forest-spirits), *Vatnavættir* (guardians of the specific waters), or *Húsvættir* (house-spirits). The Old Norse term *véttr* / *vættr* and its English cognate *wight* have descended from the Proto-Germanic *wihtiz* (thing, creature), and from the Proto-Indo-European *wekti-* (object, thing). Vættr and wight normally refer to a supernatural being, especially Landvættr (land-spirit), but can actually refer to any creature. The Norwegian *Vette* is used much in the same way as the Old Norse Vættr, as are the corresponding Swedish cognate *Vätte* (dialect form *Vätter* – Old Swedish *Vætter*) and the Danish *Vætte*. A related form in the Slavic languages can be seen in Old Church Slavonic: вешть, *veštĭ*, meaning thing, matter, or subject.

Húsvættir

Húsvættir is a collective term for keepers of the household, like the Scottish *Brownie*, or the Nordic *Tomte* (also referred to as *Nisse*). The Tomte or Nisse is a solitary vätte, living on the farmstead. He is usually benevolent and helpful, which cannot be said about the innately mischievous *illvätte*. However, a Nisse can cause a lot of damage if he is displeased or angry, including the killing of livestock, or causing serious accidents.

Landvættir

In Icelandic and Norse folklore and Germanic neopaganism *Landvættir* (land wights; also: *Ármaðr*, and *Spámaðr*) are believed to be chthonic (related to the dead) or nature-spirits of the land. They protect and promote the flourishing of the specific places where they live, which can be as small as a rock or a corner of a field, or as large as a section of a country. With a rock as its dwelling place the spirit is called a *Bergbúi* (Rock dweller). There is one record of pre-Christian Icelanders

bringing offerings specifically to Landvættir in a section of Hauksbók.
A Christian bishop rails against "foolish women" who take food out to
rocks and hollows to feed the Landvættir in hopes of being blessed with a
prosperous household. The belief in local Landvættir lives on in Iceland,
with many farms having rocks around which mowing is not allowed and
on which children are not allowed to play. Sometimes the Landvættir are
the same spirit-class as the *Huldufólk*. When construction was about to
start on Keflavík air base, the Icelandic foreman dreamed that a woman
came to him asking to delay moving a boulder to give her family time to
move out. He did so for two weeks over American objections, until she
came to him in another dream telling him the Landvættir were all out. In
the coat of arms of Iceland four major Landvættir, traditionally regarded
as the protectors of the four quarters of Iceland, are depicted: *Dreki*, the
dragon in the East, *Gammur*, the eagle in the North, *Griðungur*, the bull
in the West, and *Bergrisi*, the giant in the South.

Landdísir

In Norse mythology and later Icelandic folklore, *Landdísir* (Old Norse:
dísir of the land) are beings who live in *Landdísasteinar*, specific stones
located in northwestern Iceland which were treated with reverence,
up into the 18th and 19th centuries. The Landdísir are not recorded
in Old Norse sources, but belief in them is assumed from the name
Landdísasteinar. Rudolf Simek (in *Dictionary of Northern Mythology*,
2007) says that the Landdísir *"are perhaps identical to the Dísir, female
protective guardian spirits, or else related in some way to the Landvætter"*.
According to Simek, since the Landdísir were believed to live in stones
and were venerated there, the practice could represent a form of ancestor
worship.

Vård

In Swedish folklore, a *vård* (pl.: *vårdar*) was the name given to a personal
guardian who accompanied the human soul from birth to the hour
of death. The word comes from the Old Swedish *varþer*, (guard or
protector), and it is also found in English as "warden". The vård could
at times manifest itself either as a *lyse* (little light) or as "the harbor of
man", that is to say, a semblance. The sense of another person's vård
could manifest itself as a physical phenomenon in the body, for example
a temporary itch in the hand or nostril, as a "hunch" which referred to

a dark sense of togetherness through which one could sense the fate of absent persons, or in various other forms of foreboding. If one thought one heard a person arriving a moment before he/she actually arrived, it is the person's Vård that gives this "premonition". (In the north-east Dutch region of Reiderland in the language of Lower Saxony this phenomena was known as *Veurloop*). The revelation of an absentee's vård as a visible harbor is called a *Vålnad* and the ghost of a departed person is called a *Genfärd*. Through Christianity the belief in two kinds of Vård, one good and one evil, developed as did the good and the evil conscience. *Fylgjor* and *Hamingjor* are guardian spirits in Norse mythology that are extremely similar to the belief in Vårdar. From *Vård* derives the term *Vårdträd* (vård tree), as these trees were thought to be the home of the guardian spirits of the household or farm. In Norwegian folklore, *Gardvord* is a synonym for the *Tomten*.

Vatnaormur

Vatnaormur are legendary Icelandic lake-serpents. The lakes of Iceland are home to a wide variety of these creatures. These serve as the Icelandic equivalent of *Lindorms, water-horses* and other malignant freshwater monsters. Most famous of these is the *Lagarfljótsormurinn* or *Lagarfljot serpent*. The story of the *Serpent of Skorradalsvatn* is identical to – and older than – that of the Lagarfljot serpent; it appears that its account was transposed to Lagarfljot over time. Other Icelandic *water-serpents* include the *Hvalvatn serpent* (striped with a cat-like head), the huge *Hvita River serpents* (gaudy in Arnessysla, striped in Borgarfjordur), the *Kleifarvatn serpent* (30 - 40 meters/32 - 43 yards long and black in color), the large *Skafta River serpent* (multi-colored) and the mysterious dry-land *Serpent of Surtshellir*. As with many mysterious Icelandic creatures these lake-serpents have both a cryptozoological and folkloric existence, the latter often attributing to them the typical qualities of nature-spirits.

Vitorm

In Swedish folklore the *Vitorm* (white snake) is a creature related to the *Lindworm* and the *Basilisk*. It appears in Nordic and also in German folk tales, represents the *King of Snakes* and is said in some tales to have a crown-like white head crest. The Vitorm radiates a lot of energy and its skin and body can give magical powers. In winter the Vitorm was believed to live under an oak tree, which then preserved its leaves and greenery. In Tyrol the Vitorm is called the *Haselwurm* and lives under an old hazel bush. By eating "white snake soup" or keeping a Vitorm in captivity, one could obtain several magical abilities, as understanding the language of the birds, retrieving food, moving one's body miraculously to another location and gain wealth.

W

Walküre

A *Walküre* or *Valkyrie*, also *battle maiden* or *shield maiden*, is in Norse and Germanic mythology a female spirit-being from the retinue of Odin (Wodan), the father of the gods. The *Walküren* or *Valkyries* (pl.) are related to the *Norns*, *Fylgia*, and the *Disen* through the possibility of fate. They choose the *Einherjer* (honorably fallen ones) who died on the battlefield to lead them to Valhalla. The name *Walküre* is a modern borrowing from Old Norse. The Old Norse word is *Valkyrja*, pl. *Valkyrjar*. It derives from the Old Norse words *valr* (corpses lying on the battlefield) and *kjósa* (to choose). The Old Norse *kjósa* is related to the German *kiesen* and the Dutch *(uit)kiezen*; *Valkyrja* is then translated as "gravedigger". The Old English term is *Wælcyrge*. The Valkyries were probably originally demons of the dead who guided the warriors who had fallen on the battlefield. In the company of Odin or his southern Germanic equivalent Wotan or Wodan, the Valkyries ride through the stormy skies as part of the northern version of the *Wild Hunt*, a huge procession of the dead. Gradually the idea of *Valhöll* (Valhalla) changed; at first Valhöll was the battlefield littered with corpses, from which the death demons (Valkyries) lead the fallen to a god of the dead. Later, Valhöll was imagined as Óðinn's festival hall. Parallel to this, the Valkyries also changed from death demons to earthly warriors with human features, who can also fall in love with warriors, such as the Valkyrie *Sigrdrífa* in the *Sigrdrífumál* or *Sváfa* in the *Helgakviða Hjörvarðssonar*.

The Vikings saw the aurora borealis as a sign of the presence of Valkyries on Earth and that a great battle had been fought somewhere on Midgard. In the belief of the people, it was the Valkyries who rode through the firmament after a successful battle and chose the most heroic fighters to be allowed to dine at Odin's table as Einherjer. In the imagination, the light of the moon was reflected in their shining armor and was the explanation for the play of colors in the night sky. In the *Helgakviða Hjörvarðssonar* the number of Valkyries is given as nine, in the *Darraðarljóð* as twelve. In fact, the number may have been unlimited in popular belief. In the song *Grímnismál* (stanza 36), thirteen names are given of Valkyries serving beer in Valhöll (Valhalla): *Hrist, Mist, Skeggjöld, Skögull, Hildr, Þrúðr, Hlökk, Herfjötur, Göll, Geirölul* (*Geirrömul, Geirahöd*), *Randgríðr, Radgríðr* and *Reginleifr*. The *Darraðarljóð* also names: *Göndul, Guðr* (*Gunnr*), *Hjörþrimul, Sanngríðr* and *Svipul*. The *Þulur* (Thulur) additionally name: *Herja, Geiravör, Skuld, Geirönul, Randgníð, Geirskögul, Hrund, Geirdriful, Randgríðr, Sveið, Þögn, Hjalmþrimul, Þrima, Skalmöld*. In heroic songs, the names *Sigrún, Kára, Sváfa*, and *Brynhildr* still occur.

In the 19th century, the German composer Richard Wagner adapted the legendary material in his four-part opera cycle *Der Ring des Nibelungen* (1848-1874), especially in the "First Day" of this tetralogy under the title *Die Walküre*. In Wagner's opera, the Valkyries are nine sisters, all daughters of the god Wotan, born from different wives. In addition to *Brünnhilde* (*Brynhildr*), the child of Wotan and Erda, eight other Valkyries appear here, whose names are freely invented by Wagner, except for *Siegrune* (from *Sigrún*). The others are called *Waltraute, Ortlinde, Roßweiße, Schwertleite, Gerhilde, Grimgerde* and *Helmwige*.

Water Wraiths

In Scottish folklore a *Wraith* is an apparition or specter. A *Water Wraith* is a female *water-spirit* who tries to lure unsuspecting travelers to their death by drowning them. They appear as old women with withered faces, lean and sullen, and dressed in green. Rev. J.M. McPherson in *Primitive Beliefs in the North-East of Scotland* (1929) hints that these water-spirits generally appeared when people were on their way home after a drinking binge.

Wee folk

Wee-folk is often used as a synonym for humanoid looking Elves, but the Scottish folklorist Donald A. Mackenzie writes of the Wee folk (*Elves and Heroes*, 1909):

> *"The Highland 'wee folk' are not so diminutive as the Fairies of England—at least that type of fairy, beloved of the poet, which hovers bee-like over flowers and feeds on honey-dew. They had the power to shrink in stature and to render themselves invisible, but they are invariably 'little people', from three to four feet high. It may be that the Gael's conception of humanized spirits may not have been uninfluenced by the traditions of that earlier diminutive race whose arrow-heads of flint were so long regarded as 'Elf-bolts'. The Fairies dwelt only in grassy knolls, on the summits of high hills, and inside cliffs. Although capable of living for several centuries, they were not immortal. They required food, and borrowed food and cooking utensils from human beings, and always returned what they received on loan. They could be heard within the knolls grinding corn and working at their anvils, and they were adepts at spinning and weaving and harvesting. When they went on long journeys they became invisible, and were carried through the air on eddies of western wind. At the seasonal changes of the year, 'the Wee folk' were for several days on end inspired – like all other supernatural furies – with enmity against mankind. Their evil influences could be nullified by spells and charms."*

WEREWOLF

– See *Spirit Beings in European Folklore*, Compendium 2

White Ladies

White Ladies is a generic term applied to apparitions of various nature, with the appearance of ghostly white ladies. They may be supernatural entities playing the roles of *Fairies*, witches, *Night washer-women* or harbingers of impending death, or they may be the ghosts of deceased women when they are specters haunting castles, or even ghostly hitchhikers. Legends of the White Ladies can be found throughout Europe and throughout the ages. In a popular medieval legend, a White Lady appears by day as well as by night in a house in which a family member is soon to die. In our modern times they sometimes appear within photos just before or after someone's death. There are many legends in which the Lady in White appears as the ghost of a woman who had lived a difficult or cruel life. For example, in Czech legends and oral traditions, the specter is dressed in white, yet she always wears a hennin (a female headdress in the shape of a cone, bell or truncated cone worn in the late Middle Ages by European noblewomen) on her head. Sometimes the White Lady, looking like a *Banshee*-like ghost of a woman, merges with a figure from German folk-mythology like Perchta, or a weather phenomenon like the ghostly looking low-hanging fog, as is often the case with the Dutch *Witte wieven* (White Women). In Welsh tradition, *Y Ladi Wen* (The White Lady) or *Dynes Mewn Gwyn* (Woman in White) is a common apparition in the Celtic Mythology of Wales. Dressed in white, and most common at *Calan Gaeaf* (the Welsh Halloween), she was often evoked to warn children about bad behavior. Y Ladi Wen is characterized in various ways, including being a terrifying ghost who may ask for help if you speak to her. Y Ladi Wen is also associated with restless spirits guarding hidden treasures. In England there are over a dozen tales which portray the White Lady as a victim of murder or suicide, who died before she could tell anyone the location of her murderer or some hidden treasure. In Switzerland for centuries a popular legend has been associated with the ruins of Rouelbeau Castle, in today's municipality of Meinier in the canton of Geneva. It centers around a woman without a name, supposedly the first wife of the knight Humbert de Choulex, under whose leadership the castle was constructed in a swampy area at the beginning of the 14th century. He reportedly repudiated her when she did not give birth to a son.

The ghost has been linked to the disappearance of people and deaths from unexplained causes. *The Maidens of Uley* is an East Siberian legend of the west Buryad people from the village of Ulei, Irkutsk, Russia. The legend tells about a young lady, Bulzhuuhai Duuhai, who did not want to marry but was forced to do so anyway. She kept running away from her husband, who treated her disrespectfully and locked her in a black yurt, instead of a traditional white one. Bulzhuuhai then hanged herself in a barn after singing and dancing at someone else's wedding for eight days and eight nights, feeling unwanted and unloved. After her death, she became a *zayan* (spirit). She joined other spirit maidens, who haunt fiancés on their wedding day, bewitching them with their beauty and dragging them to the netherworld.

Den Hvite Dame (The White Lady) at Utstein Kloster (Utstein Abbey)
in Stavanger, Norway, is a White Lady that haunts the former abbey.
She is the ghost of Cecilie Widding Garmann (1734-1759), who died
in childbirth. Her husband is said to have promised never to remarry,
but 20 years later he did. During the wedding in Stavanger Cathedral,
he claimed to see Cecilie, fell into a coma and died a week later. Today,
Cecilie is claimed to be the ghost of the monastery, called Den Hvite
Dame. In Hungarian mythology, a White Lady was the ghost of a girl
or young woman that usually had committed suicide, was murdered, or
died while imprisoned. The ghost is usually bound to a specific location
and is often identified as a specific person (i.e. Elizabeth Báthory). The
most famous White Lady of Estonia is said to reside in Haapsalu Castle.
According to the legend, she fell in love with a cannon, so she hid in the
castle disguised as a choir boy in order to be close to him, but she was
discovered when the Bishop of Ösel-Wiek visited Haapsalu and was
subsequently immured in the wall of the chapel for her crime. To this
day, she is said to look out of the baptistery's window and grieve for her
beloved man. According to legend, she can be seen on clear August full-
moon nights.

White Ladies attached to families

White Ladies related to important families and acting in a Banshee-like
way once were such a common phenomenon on the European mainland
that even the humanist philosopher Desiderius Erasmus wrote: *"One of
the most famous facts remains the appearance of the White Lady to the
princely families."* At the beginning of the sixteenth century, many great
European aristocratic families had their own White Lady. More stylish
than their ancestors, they did not scream and could even be protective,
such as the *White Lady of Krumlov*, attached to the powerful Rožmberk
(Rosenberg) family of Bohemia, who appeared several times in 1539
near the newborn heir. The White Lady attached to the Germanic house
of Neuhaus is ambivalent; if she wears black gloves she announces a
death, but when her gloves are white, it is seen as a good omen. We
find White Ladies attached to the Habsburgs, the Hohenzollerns, the
Brunswicks, the Brandenburgs, the Baden, the Pernsteins. A White Lady
also appeared to emperor Charles V in 1558, on the eve of his death,
in the monastery of Yuste where he had retired. This White Lady is the
origin of the character of "the Bloody Nun". The double appearance of
a White Lady to Prince Louis-Ferdinand of Prussia, on the day before

and on the day of his tragic death on the battlefield of Saalfeld, was also witnessed by Count Gregory Nortiz, who, Prussian by origin, entered to the service of Russia in 1813 and died in 1838 as aide-de-camp to Czar Nicholas. Count Nortiz wrote an account on October 9, 1806, around midnight, a few hours after the event at the castle of the Duke of Schwarzburg-Rudolstadt, which is preserved in the archives of the House of Hohenzollern. In July 1832, it is to Aiglon, son of Napoleon I, that she appeared the day before his death. In November 1835, while the Prince of Montfort was residing in Stuttgart with his uncle King William I of Württemberg, a white lady appeared in a gallery of the old castle, announcing by her presence the imminence of a death. The omen, reported by sentries, was taken seriously by the king, who was concerned for his sister, Princess Catherine of Wurtemberg, mother of the Prince of Montfort. She died in Lausanne on November 29, 1835. This same white lady, whom tradition presented as the specter of a mad infanticide, had already appeared in 1819 on the eve of the death of Catherine Pavlovna of Russia, the second wife of King William. In 1889, a servant reportedly saw a white lady prowling in the park of Mayerling on the night of the famous drama. During her stay in Caux, near Montreux, the empress Sissi claimed on August 30, 1898, to have seen the White Lady clearly, at night, 11 days before her assassination in Geneva.

Ghostly hitchhikers

A recent evolution of the myth of the White Lady is that of the ghost hitchhiker. These are almost exclusively apparitions of young women, although there are a few cases of hitchhikers. In the most common scenario, a young woman, dressed in white, hitchhiked at night and, after getting into a vehicle, suddenly disappeared, either when approaching a dangerous passage with a cry of alarm, or when arriving at the given address. This phenomenon is known all over the world and is generally considered as belonging to urban legends. Unlike White Lady "Fairies" or "messengers", who are entities, ghostly hitchhikers seem to be always the ghost of a contemporary person who died accidentally.

Will-o'-the-wisp or Ignis fatuus

In folklore, a *Will-o'-the-wisp*, *Will-o'-wisp* or *Ignis fatuus* (Latin for *giddy flame* or *foolish fire*, pl. *ignes fatui*) is an atmospheric ghost light seen by travelers at night, especially over bogs, swamps or marshes. In many

Will-o'-the-wisp that appeared as a huge flame on a French churchyard, July 2, 1750

European folklore tales this light is thought to be a ghost with a flickering lamp, that lures stray nighttime wanderers into a dangerous swamp. In eastern Europe, these ghostly lights are often associated with vampiric creatures roaming the countryside. Etymological research shows that the term *Jack-o'-lantern* (popularly known as the Halloween pumpkin) was originally used in English folklore to refer to the visual phenomenon Ignis fatuus/Will-o'-the-wisp. It was used mainly in eastern England, and the earliest known use dates from the 1660s. The term *Will-o'-the-wisp* consists of *wisp* (a bundle of sticks or paper sometimes used as a torch) and the proper name *Will*, thus: *Will-of-the-torch*. The term *Jack o'-lantern* is of the same construction: *Jack of [the] lantern*.

Other names

The phenomenon of Ignis fatuus is known in British and European folklore by a great variety of names. Apart from Will-o'-the-wisp and Jack-o'-lantern, other British names are for example: *Friar's Lantern* and *Hinkypunk*, but also over a dozen other regional names circulate, the following being a selection: *Hobby Lantern* (Hertfordshire), *Joan the Wad* (Cornwall and Somerset), *Jacky Lantern* (western provinces), *Spunkie* (Scotland) and *Will-o'-the-Wike* (Norfolk). On the European mainland, among many others we find the Spanish *Fuego fatuo*, the Portugese *Fogo-fátuo*, the French *Feu Follet* (Fire of Fools), the *Irrlicht* in Germany and the *Dwaallicht* in Holland and Flanders. Across the Atlantic we find the *St. Louis Light* in Saskatchewan, *Spooklight* in Southwestern Missouri, *Marfa lights* in Texas and *Paulding Light* in the upper Peninsula of Michigan. Other names used for the phenomenon are: *Corpse Candle, Brünnlig, Buchelmännle, Corpse Sans Âme, Dichepot, Draulicht, Dröglicht, Druckfackel, Dwallicht, Dwerlicht, Earthlights, Erlwischen, Flackerfür, Flämmstirn, Follet, Fuchtelmännlein, Füersteinmannli, Ghost Lights, Heerwisch, Huckepot, Irdflämmken, Irdlicht, Irreding, Irrlüchte, Irrwisch, Lichtkedräger, Lidércfény, Lüchtemannchen, Pützhüpfer, Quadlicht, Schäuble, Stäuble, Schwidnikes, Spoklecht, Spooky Lights, Stäuble, Stölten, Stöltenlicht, Tückebold, Tückebote, Tümmelding, Wipplötsche, Zunselwible. Gyl Burnt-tayl* is a jocular name for a female Will o' the wisp.

Hessdalen lights

The *Hessdalen Lights* of Norway are of unknown origin. They appear both by day and by night, and seem to float through and above the valleys. They are usually bright white, yellow or red and can appear above and below the horizon. The duration of the phenomenon may be a few seconds to well over an hour. Sometimes the lights move with enormous speed; at other times they seem to sway slowly back and forth. On still other occasions, they hover in mid-air. Unusual lights have been reported in the region since at least the 1930s. Activity was particularly high between December 1981 and mid-1984, when the lights were observed 15–20 times a week, attracting many night-time tourists. As of 2010, the number of observations had declined, with only 10 to 20 sightings per year. Today, however, the Hessdalen lights are associated more with UAP-phenomena (unidentified aerial phenomena) than with the classic marsh lights of folklore.

Folklore beliefs

In folklore, Wills-o'-the-wisps are typically attributed to ghosts, Fairies or elemental spirits. Modern science explains them as natural phenomena such as bioluminescence or chemiluminescence, caused by the oxidation of phosphine (PH_3), diphosphane (P_2H_4) and methane (CH_4) produced by organic decay. In literature, Will-o'-the-wisp metaphorically refers to a hope or goal that leads one on but is impossible to attain, or something one finds sinister or weird.

In Wales Will-o'-the-wisps are seen as spirits that have returned to seek out a dying relative, and the size of their light corresponds to the age of the person concerned; if the Will-o'-the-wisp is very small, it announces the death of a child. The malicious Imp *Pwcca* was also known to change into a small flame or light to mislead travelers. The Danes, Finns, Swedes, Estonians and Latvians – among others – believed that Will-o'-the-wisps indicated the location of treasures hidden in the ground or underwater, and that the treasure could only be found if it was dug up when the flame appeared. In Finland and other countries, midsummer was considered the best time of year to search for Will-o'-the-wisps and treasures.

Protection against Will-o'-the-wisps

Several protection rituals against Will-o'-the-wisps occur in different folklores, one was to stick a needle in the ground, to force the will-o'-the-wisps to pass through the eye and thus have enough time to be able to run away while they were doing so. Throwing a stone into the water was supposed to make the Will-o'-the-wisps go away, as they shone over the ponds, and they would rush into the water, giggling!

Wisht or Wish Hounds

The *Wisht* or *Wish Hounds* (*wisht* is a dialect word for "ghostly" or "haunted") are a related phenomenon and some folklorists regard them as identical to the *Yeth Hounds*. Wistman's Wood on Dartmoor in southern Devon is said to be the home of the Wisht Hounds as they make their hunting trips across the moor. The road known as the Abbot's Way and the valley of the Dewerstone are favored hunting grounds of the hounds. Their huntsman is presumably the Devil, and it is said that any dog that hears the howling of the hounds will die. According to one legend, the ghost of Sir Francis Drake sometimes rode at night in a black hearse on the road between Tavistock and Plymouth, drawn by headless horses and accompanied by demons and a mob of whining headless hounds.

Wulver

In the folklore of the Shetland Islands, the *Wulver* or *Wullver* is a kind of wolf-like humanoid creature. Jessia Saxby, in *Shetland Traditional Lore* (1932) reports of the Wulver, that it was a creature like a man with a wolf's head. He had short brown hair all over. His home was a cave, dug half way up into the side of a steep hill. He didn't bother people if people didn't bother him. He was fond of catching and eating fish, and had a small rock in the deep water which is known to this day as the "Wulver's Stane". There he would sit for hours, fishing for sillaks and piltaks. He was reported to frequently leave a few fish on the window-sill of someone poor.

Y

Yeth Hound

The *Yeth Hound* or *Yell Hound* is a kind of large black dog found in Devon folklore. According to Brewer's *Dictionary of Phrase and Fable* the Yeth Hound is a headless dog, said to be the spirit of an unbaptized child, that rambles through the woods at night making wailing noises. It is also mentioned in the *Denham Tracts*, a 19th century collection of folklore by Michael Denham. It may have been one of the inspirations for the ghost dog in Sir Arthur Conan Doyle's *The Hound of the Baskervilles* described as *"an enormous coal-black hound, but not such a hound as mortal eyes have ever seen – with fire in his eyes and in his breath"*.

LITERATURE AND DIGITAL SOURCES

- Abercromby, John – *The Pre- and Proto-historic Finns, both Eastern and Western with the Magic Songs of the West Finns – in two volumes*, published by David Nutt in the Strand, London, 1898
- Árnason, J.; Powell, G. E. J. and Magnússon, E. trans. – *Icelandic Legends* – Richard Bentley, London, 1864
- Arrowsmith, N. – *Field Guide to the Little People: A Curious Journey Into the Hidden Realm of Elves, Faeries, Hobgoblins & Other Not-so-mythical Creatures* – Llewellyn Worldwide., 1970/2009
- Barb, A.A. – *Antaura. The Mermaid and the Devil's Grandmother: A Lecture* – Journal of the Warburg and Courtauld Institutes, 1966
- Bardon, Franz – *Die Praxis der Magische Evokation* – Rüggeberg Verlag Wuppertal, 2003
- Bartsch, Karl – *Sagen, Märchen und Gebräuche aus Meklenburg*, vol. 1 – Vienna, Wilhelm Braumüller, 1879
- Beaumont, William Comyns – *Britain The Key To World History* – London, 1948
- Benwell, G. and Waugh, A. – *Sea Enchantress: The Tale of the Mermaid and her Kin* – Hutchinson, London, 1961
- Blau, Lajos (Ludwich) – *Das Altjüdische Zauberwesen* – 1897-98 Budapest / Graz, 1974
- Blécourt, W. de, – *"I Would Have Eaten You Too": Werewolf Legends in the Flemish, Dutch, and German Area* – 2007
- Bonnefoy, Yves, – *Asian Mythologies* – University of Chicago Press, 1993
- Bottiglioni, Gino – *Leggende e tradizioni di Sardegna (testi dialettali in grafia fonetica)* – 1922
- Briggs, Katharine – *An Encyclopedia of Fairies – Hobgoblins, Brownies, Bogies and Other Supernatural Creatures* – Pantheon Books, USA, 1976
- Calmet, Dom Augustine – *The Phantom World: The History and Philosophy of Spirits, Apparitions &c. Two Volumes in One* – Philadelphia: A Hart, Late Carey & Hart, 1850
- Campbell, J.G. – *Superstitions of the Highlands and Islands of Scotland* – James MacLehose and Sons, Glascow, 1900
- Conway, Moncure Daniel -*Demonology and Devil-Lore 1 & 2* – revised publication of the 1897 editions by VAMzzz Publishing, Amsterdam, 2015
- Conybeare, Frederick Cornwallis – *Testament of Solomon – Jewish Quaterly Review of October 1889* – revised edition VAMzzz Publishing, Amsterdam, 2015
- Corstorphine, Kevin & Kremmel, Laura R – *Horror in the Medieval North: The*

Troll, *The Palgrave Handbook to Horror Literature* – ed., 2018

- Courtney, M.A. – *Cornish Feasts and Folklore* – Beare and Son, Penzance, 1890
- Craigie, W.A. – *The Oldest Icelandic Folklore*, 1893
- Davidsson, O. *The Folk-lore of Icelandic Fishes,* 1900
- Dennison, W. Traill – *Orkney Folklore, Sea Myths* – Edinburgh University Press, 1891
- Dörler, Adolf Ferdinand (collected and edited by) – *Sagen aus Innsbruck's Umgebung, mit besonderer Berücksichtigung des Zillerthales* – Innsbruck, 1895
- Edmondston, Thomas – *An Etymological Glossary of the Shetland & Orkney Dialect* – Adam and Charles Black, 1866
- *Encyclopedia Brittanica online*
- Folkard, Richard – *Plant Lore Legends & Lyrics* – 1884, revised edition by VAMzzz Publishing, Amsterdam, 2021
- Frazer, Sir James George – *The Golden Bough: A Study in Magic and Religion* – edition 1906-15
- Genesin, Monica & Rizzo, Luana (Hrsg.) – *Magie, Tarantismus und Vampirismus; Eine interdisciplinäre Annäherung* – Verlag Dr. Kovač, Hamburg, 2013
- Gibbings W. W. – *Folk-lore and Legends* – *Germany,* London, 1892
- Gieysztor, Aleksander – *Mitologia Słowian* – Warszawa: Wydawnictwo Uniwersytetu Warszawskiego, 2006
- Gill, W. Walter – *A Second Manx Scrapbook* – Arrowsmith, London Bristol, 1932
- Grimm, Jacob – *Deutsche Mythologie* – Göttingen: Dieterich, 1835
- Hageland, A. van – *La Mer Magique* – Marabout, Paris, 1973
- Hall, Manly Palmer – *The Secret Teachings of All Ages: An Encyclopedic Outline of Masonic, Hermetic, Qabbalistic and Rosicrucian Symbolical Philosophy* – 1928
- Hanaur, J.E. – *Folk-Lore of the Holy Land – Moslim, Christian and Jewish* – Edited by Marmaduke Pickthall, London Duckworth & Co, 1907
- Henderson, William – *Notes on the folk-lore of the northern counties of England and the borders* – Longmans, Green, 1866
- Hlidberg, J. B. and Aegisson, S.; McQueen, F. J. M. and Kjartansson, R., trans. – *Meeting with Monsters* – JPV utgafa, Reykjavik, 2011 .
- Huizinga-Onnekes, E.J. – *Groninger Volksverhalen* – bewerkt door K. ter Laan, J.B.Wolters' Uitgevers Maatschappij N.V. Groningen – Den Haag, 1930
- *Jewish Encyclopedia online*
- Johnston, Sarah Iles – *Restless Dead: Encounters Between the Living and the Dead in Ancient Greece* – University of California Press, Berkeley-Los Angeles-London, 2013

- Karakurt, Deniz – *Türk Söylence Sözlüğü* (*Turkish Mythological Dictionary*) (OTRS: CC BY-SA 3.0), 2011
- Kivilson, Valerie A. & Worobec, Christine D. – *Witchcraft in Russia and Ukraine, 1000–1900: A Sourcebook* – Cornell University Press, Northern Illinois University Press, 2020
- Kreuter, Peter Mario – *Der Vampirglaube in Südosteuropa. Studien zur Genese, Bedeutung und Funktion. Rumänien und der Balkanraum* – Weidler, Berlin, 2001, (Dissertation Universität Bonn, 2001)
- Lachower, Fischel & Tishby, Isaiah; translations by David Goldstein – *Wisdom of the Zohar – An Anthology of Texts* – London, 1994
- Landt, George – *A description of the Faroe Islands, containing an account of their situation, climate, and productions, together with the manners and customs of the inhabitants, their trade etc.* – 1810
- Lawson, John Cuthbert, M.A. – *Modern Greek Folklore and Ancient Greek Religion – A Study in Survivals* – Cambridge: at the University Press, London: Fetter Lane, E.C., 1910
- Lecouteux, Claude:
  - *Witches, Werewolves and Fairies: Shapeshifters and Astral Doubles in the Middle Ages*, Inner Traditions (Rochester, Vermont) transl. Clare Frock, 2003
  - *The Return of the Dead: Ghosts, Ancestors and the Transparent Veil of the Pagan Mind*, Inner Traditions (Rochester, Vermont) transl. Jon E. Graham, 2009
  - *The Secret History of Vampires: Their Multiple Forms and Hidden Purposes*, Inner Traditions (Rochester, Vermont) transl. Jon E. Graham, 2010
  - *Phantom Armies of the Night: The Wild Hunt and Ghostly Processions of the Undead*, Inner Traditions (Rochester, Vermont) transl., Jon E. Graham, 2011
  - *The Tradition of Household Spirits. Ancestral Lore and Practice*, Inner Traditions (Rochester, Vermont) transl. Jon E. Graham, 2013
  - *Demons and Spirits of the Land: Ancestral Lore and Practices*, Inner Traditions (Rochester, Vermont) transl. Jon E. Graham, 2015
  - *The Hidden Historie of Elves and Dwarfs – Avatars of Invisible Realms*, Inner Traditions (Rochester, Vermont) transl. Jon E. Graham, 2018
- Libera, Roberto – *Storie di streghe, fantasmi e lupi mannari nei Castelli Romani, Genzano di Roma* – Consorzio SBCR editore, 2010
- Lindley, Charles, Viscount Halifax – *Lord Halifax Ghost Book* – first edition Glasgow, 1936
- Lomas, Adriano Garcia – *Mitología y supersticiones de Cantabria* – 1964
- Luzel, François-Marie – *Contes populaires de Basse-Bretagne* – 1881
- Mackenzie, Donald Alexander
  - *Wonder Tales from Scottish Myth and Legend* – Blackie and Son Limited,

London, Glasgow, Bombay, 1917

- *Scottish Folk-Lore and Folk Life. Studies in Race, Culture and Tradition* – 1935
- *Elves and Heroes* – 1909
- *Teutonic Myth and Legend* – 2nd Ed. 1934
• Mannhardt, Wilhelm:
- *Roggenwolf und Roggenhund* – *Beitrag zur Germanischen Sittenkunde* – Verlag von Constantin Ziemssen, Danzig, 1865
- *Die Korndämonen,* – *Beitrag zur Germanischen Sittenkunde* – Harrwitz und Gossmann, Berlin 1868
- *Wald- und Feldkulte. Band 1: Der Baumkultus der Germanen und ihrer Nachbarstämme: mythologische Untersuchungen* – Gebrüder Borntraeger, Berlin, 1875
- *Wald- und Feldkulte. Band 2: Antike Wald- und Feldkulte aus nordeuropäischer Überlieferung erläutert* – Gebrüder Borntraeger, Berlin, 1877
- *Mythologische Forschungen* – Karl J. Trüber, Strassburg – London 1884
• Marliave, Olivier de – *Trésor de la mythologie pyrénéenne* – Toulouse, Esper, 1987
• Marliave, Olivier de et Pertuzé, Jean-Claude – *Panthéon Pyrénéen* – Toulouse, Loubatières, 1990.
• Masani, R.P., M.A – *Folklore of Wells, being a study of Water Worship in East and West* – Bombay, D.B. Takapokevale Sons & Co, 1918
• Mathers, S.L. MacGregor / Knor von Rosenroth – *Kabbala Denudata / The Kabbalah Unveiled* – Samuel Weiser Inc. York Beach, Maine, 1989
• McAnally, David Russell – *Irish Wonders: The Ghosts, Giants, Pookas, Demons, Leprechawns, Banshees, Fairies, Witches, Widows, Old Maids, and other marvels of the Emerald Isle* – The Riverside Press Cambridge, 1888
• McIntosh, A – *Faerie Faith in Scotland* (2005) in *The Encyclopaedia of Religion and Nature* – edited by Bron Taylor, 2006
• McPherson, Rev. J. M. – *Primitive Beliefs in the North-East of Scotland* – London, New York and Toronto – Longmans, Green and Co., Ltd., 1929
• Meyer, Elard Hugo – *Mythologie der Germanen*, Straszburg, Verlag von Karl J. Trübner, 1930
• Nadmorski, Dr – *Kaszuby i Kociewie. Język, zwyczaje, przesądy, podania, zagadki i pieśni ludowe w północnej części Prus Zachodnich* – Poznań, 1892
• Paracelsus – *Four treatises of Theophrastus von Hohenheim, called Paracelsus* (1493-1541) – English translation of the German, Baltimore: Johns Hopkins Press, 1941
• Petiteau, Frantz-E. – *Contes, légendes et récits de la vallée d'Aure* – éditions Alan Sutton, 2007

241

- Plancy, Collin de, – *Dictionnaire Infernal* – 1818
- Podgórscy Barbara and Adam – *Wielka Księga Demonów Polskich. Leksykon i antologia demonologii ludowej* – Katowice: KOS, 2005
- Rajki, Andras – *Mongolian Ethymological Dictionary* 2006-2009 – via *academia.edu*
- Ralston, W. R. S., M.A.
  - *Russian Fairy Tales – A choice collection of Muscovite folk-lore* – New York: Hurst & Co., 1872
  - *The songs of the Russian people, as illustrative of Slavonic mythology and Russian social life* – London, Ellis, 1872
- Ritter, Johann Nepomuk von Alpenburg – *Deutsche Alpensagen* – Vienna, 1861
- Rose, C. – *Giants, Monsters, and Dragons* – W. W. Norton and Co., New York, 2000
- Rosenthal, Bernice Glatzer (editor) – *The Occult in Russian and Soviet Culture* – Cornell University, 1997
- Rhys, John – *Celtic Folklore Welsh and Manx* – Library of Alexandria, 2020
- Ryan, W.F. – *The Bathhouse at Midnight – An Historical Survey of Magic and Divination in Russia*, Pennsylvania State University Press, 1999
- Sacaze, Julien – *Le dieu Tantugou, légende du pays de Luchon* – (in Revue de Comminges, Tome III, 1887, p. 116-118), texte « patois » et traduction littérale
- Saxby, Jessie Margaret Edmondston – *Shetland Traditional Lore* – Edinburgh, Grant and Murray, 1932
- Sébillot, Paul – *Le Folk-Lore de France, Tome Premier: Le Ciel et la Terre* – 1904
- Sikes, Wirt – *British Goblins: Welsh Folk-Lore, Fairy Mythology, Legends and Traditions* – London, 1880
- Simpson, J. – *Icelandic Folktales and Legends* – University of California Press, Berkeley and Los Angeles, 1972
- Sinastrari of Ameno – transl. Liseux, Isidore 1876 – *Incubi and Succubi or Demoniality – A Historical Study of Sexual contacts with Demons* – Revised edition by VAMzzz Publishing, Amsterdam, 2017
- Sluijter, P.C.M. – *IJslands Volksgeloof* – H. D. Tjeenk Willink & Zoon N.V., Haarlem, 1936
- Spada, Dario – *Gnomi, Fate e Folletti e altri esseri fatati in Italia* – SugarCo, Milano, 2007
- Spiesberger, Karl – *Naturgeister wie Seher sie schauwen – wie Magier sie rufen* – Richard Schikowski Verlag, Berlin 1978
- Stefánsson, V. – *Icelandic Beast and Bird Lore* -1906
- Summers, Montague – *The Vampire in Lore and Legend* – Toronto 2001 (previously published as: *The Vampire in Europe*, London, 1929)

242

- Ter Laan, K. – *Groninger Overleveringen* – Erven B. van der Kamp, Groningen, 1930
- Thompson, Francis – *The Supernatural Highland* – Robert Hale, London, 1976
- Thorpe, Benjamin – *Northern mythology : comprising the principal popular traditions and superstitions of Scandinavia, North Germany, and the Netherlands* – 1852
- Veen, Abe J. van der – *Witte wieven, weerwolven en waternekkers – Een beschrijving van alle geesten, elfen en andere wondere wezens uit Nederland* – 2017
- Vries, A. de, – *Flanders: a cultural history* – Oxford University Press, Oxford, 2007
- Wippel I. – *Schabbock, Trud und Wilde Jagd* – Verlag für Sammler, Graz 1986
- Wikimedia Commons Licence folklore data via *Armenian, Austrian, Basque, Belarusian, Catalan, Dutch, Estonian, Danish, German, Finnish, Icelandic, Italian, French, Latvian, Lithuanian, Norwegian, Polish, Portuguese, Russian, Spanish, Swedish, Swiss, Turkish, and Ukrainian* Wikipedia-files
- Wlislocki, Dr Heinrich von – *Volksglaube und religiöser Brauch der Zigeuner* – Aschendorffsche Buchhandlung, Münster, 1891

244

Spirit Beings in European Folklore 2
Germany, Austria, Alpine regions,
Switzerland, Netherlands, Flanders,
Luxembourg, Lithuania, Latvia, Estonia,
Finland, Jewish influences
by Benjamin Adamah, 256 pages,
Paperback, ISBN 9789492355560
www.vamzzz.com

Compendium 2 of the *Spirit Beings in European Folklore*-series covers
the German-speaking parts of Central Europe, the Low Countries, the
Baltic region and Finland. Via the Ashkenazi Jews, spirit beings from the
Middle East entered Central European culture, which are also included.
This originally densely forested part of the continent is particularly rich
in nature-spirits and has a wide variety of beings that dwell in forests
and mountainous areas (*Berggeister*) or act as atmospheric forces.
Also dominant are the many field-spirits and variations of *Alp*-like
creatures (*Mare, Nightmare*). There is an overlap with the Nordic and
Eastern European *Revenant* and *Vampire*-types, and we find several
water- and sea-spirits. Among the German-speaking and Baltic peoples,
invoking field-spirits was an integrated part of agriculture, with
rites continuing into the early 20th century. The Alpine regions have
spirits who watch over cattle. In general, forest-spirits are prominent.
Germany has its *Moosweiblein* and *Wilder Mann* (*Woodwose*), the
Baltic region has its *Mātes*, and Finland its *Metsän Väki*. Then there are
ghostly animals, and earth- and house-spirits such as the many kinds
of *Kobolds*, the Dutch *Kabouter,* and the *Kaukas* of Prussia and Latvia.

Compendium 2 discusses 228 spirit beings in detail, including their
alternative names, with additional references to related or subordinate
beings and a unique selection of illustrations.

CONTENTS:

245

Spirit Beings in European Folklore 3
Russia, Belarus, Ukraine, Poland,
Romania, Hungary, Bulgaria, Czechia,
Slovenia, Serbia, Croatia, Albania,
Georgia, Turkish regions, Roma-culture
by Benjamin Adamah, 246 pages,
Paperback, ISBN 9789492355577
www.vamzzz.com

Compendium 3 of the *Spirit Beings in European Folklore*-series offers an overview of the mysterious, sometimes beautiful and often shadowy entities of the Slavic countries, the Balkans, the Carpathians, Albania, Georgia, and the Turkish and Romani peoples. Many types of *Vampires* and vampiric *Revenants* are included – in their original state and purged of later applied disinformation. The undead are prominent in the folklore of Eastern Europe and Albania. Also typical are farm- and household-spirits such as the *Domovoy*, water-spirits and forest demons like the Russian *Leshy*, the *Chuhaister,* or the evil Polish *Bełt*, who like the Ukrainian *Blud*, leads travelers off their path until they are lost in the deepest part of the forest. Unique is the Russian *Bannik* or spirit of the bathhouse. Amongst the Slavs, some 'demons', like the *Boginka* for example, originally belonged to the pre-Christian pantheon. Eastern Europe, in contrast to its returning dead, is rich in seductive female spirits such as the Romanian *Iele*, the Russian *Russalka*, the *Vila* of the Eastern and Southern Slavs and the Bulgarian *Samodiva*. Via the Balkans, Greek influences entered Slavic culture, while there are also spirits that intersect Germanic and Nordic folklore.

Compendium 3 discusses 255 spirit beings in detail, including their alternative names, with additional references to related or subordinate beings and a unique selection of illustrations.

CONTENTS:

247

FROM THE SAME SERIES

248

Spirit Beings in European Folklore 4
*France, Brittany, Wallonia, Portugal,
Italy, South Tyrol, Malta, Greece,
Spain – Basque Country, Asturias,
Catalonia, Cantabria, Galicia, Valencia*
by Benjamin Adamah, 250 pages,
Paperback, ISBN 9789492355584
www.vamzzz.com

Compendium 4 of the *Spirit Beings in European Folklore*-series covers an area that starts with Wallonia and continues via France and the Pyrenees, through the Iberian Peninsula, to Italy and Greece. This results in a very diverse and colourful collection of spirit beings, due to the many included Basque nature-spirits or *Ireluak*, the Spanish *Duendes*, the Celtic spirits of Brittany, the prankster Italian *Folletti* and the creatures from Greece. Some creatures from Breton folklore are particularly gruesome, such as the hollow-eyed *Ankou*, the *Werewolf*-like *Bugul-nôz*, or the ghostly and *Will-o'-the-wisp*-like *Yan-gant-y-tan*, who roams the night roads with his five lit candles. Most Italian ghosts are less gloomy, while the Iberian Peninsula is home to everything ranging from the 'Beauty' to the 'Beast'. Compendium 4 contains – amongst other things – many kinds of dwarf-spirits or *Goblins* (*Lutins, Nutons, Folletti, Farfadettes, Korrigans, Minairons*) various seductive and feminine spring creatures, *Wild Man*-varieties (*Basajaunak, Jentilak*) and an extensive section on the *Incubus-Succubus*. It is fascinating to discover how many types of European spirit beings (from *Kobold* to many female spring-spirits), described in the other Compendiums, can be traced back to creatures from Ancient Greece.

Compendium 4 discusses 270 spirit beings in detail, includes their alternative names, additional references to subordinate beings and a unique selection of illustrations.

CONTENTS: